I enjoy sharing
my books as
I do my
friends, asking
only that you treat
them well and see
them safely home

Books by Jay Monaghan

Bibliography of Lincolniana, 1839-1939
Diplomat in Carpet Slippers:
Lincoln Deals with Foreign Affairs
Last of the Bad Men: *The Legend of Tom Horn*
The Overland Trail
This Is Illinois
The Great Rascal:
The Life and Adventures of Ned Buntline
Civil War on the Western Border: 1854-1865
The Man Who Elected Lincoln

From an original in the Huntington Library

THE MAN WHO ELECTED LINCOLN

Dr. Charles H. Ray

The Man Who Elected Lincoln

By **JAY MONAGHAN**

THE BOBBS-MERRILL COMPANY, INC.
PUBLISHERS
INDIANAPOLIS · NEW YORK

Printed in the United States of America

Library of Congress Catalog Card Number: 56-6781

First Edition

Dedicated to

MRS. JAMES P. ANDREWS,

daughter of the North's
Fighter for Freedom:

DR. CHARLES HENRY RAY

Preface

AMONG the many giants in the American Civil War, Dr. Charles Henry Ray seems to have been overlooked. He receives no recognition in the general histories of his time and only brief mention in a few of the more specialized works. Yet Ray, as editor-in-chief of the *Chicago Tribune* during the savage years following the passage of the Kansas-Nebraska Act, had an important role in helping to arouse people of the North against slavery and incite them into a war for its abolition.

The reasons for Ray's obscurity can easily be explained. He cared more for the excitement of aggressive attack than he did for resting on the laurels of accomplishment. Moreover, he died while comparatively young—almost two decades before the other men who had known Lincoln were being urged to write their memoirs. Thus Charles Ray had no opportunity to perpetuate himself as one of the pillars of the Civil War period, even if he had been so inclined. He was a man intensely interested in the future, not in the past, despite the fact that he helped to found the Chicago Historical Society. His temperament drove him always into new battles for human freedom.

The influence of the *Chicago Tribune* on Western opinion prior to the war is generally conceded. Lincoln himself admitted that it was tremendous. But many historians associate the *Tribune* with Joseph Medill rather than with Charles Ray, who sold his stock and resigned shortly after the signing of the Emancipation Proclamation, his great goal. Since Medill was a powerful editor in his own right, the earlier, policy-making days when Charles Ray was editor-in-chief have been generally overlooked.

This book is based on the personal papers of Dr. Ray, the

memoirs of a few men who knew him, the Lincoln Papers in the Library of Congress, and contemporary issues of the *Chicago Tribune*. Granting that any biographical study tends to enhance the importance of its subject in every situation, one must admit that the unadorned facts indicate that Charles Ray had more influence on the rise of Abraham Lincoln than is generally acknowledged. Of course no one man made the Martyr President. However, Ray and Lincoln were closely associated. They co-authored the original Republican Party platform. Ray helped plan the Lincoln-Douglas debates, gave them national publicity, and presumed to coach Lincoln privately on both his argument and platform manner.

Charles Ray distrusted Stephen A. Douglas long before the Little Giant became notorious as a sponsor of the Kansas-Nebraska Bill. The origin of Ray's suspicion may interest some readers. Certainly the culmination of his distrust had a powerful influence on American history. Ray's newspaper, more than any other, prevented the Little Giant from joining the Republican Party. Had Douglas been admitted, Lincoln might well have been sidetracked, and the slavery issue, as Ray feared, might have slipped back into the Democratic Party groove. Perhaps it is no exaggeration to say that this blocking of Douglas may have given a momentous, even a key, turn to the development of the last hundred years of American history. If the Republican Party had been quashed in 1858, the United States would have had a vastly different future.

In recent years there has been a tendency to defend Douglas and malign the antislavery radicals for precipitating a needless war. It is notable that this revision in history has come in an age more concerned with the prevention of war than with the abolition of human slavery. This book is not written as a part of this argument. Its purpose is to present the personality, public utterances, and political activity of a powerful and neglected champion of the antislavery crusade.

Douglas' defenders have gone to some length to show the injustice done him by the first generation of Civil War historians. They point out that Douglas had a solution for the slavery controversy in the territories—a solution, it must be added, that did not work and was therefore no solution at all. Charles Ray was quick to see the faults in the Douglas plan. He voiced the sentiments of Douglas' opponents, and present-day devotees of the Little Giant who read this book will probably censure Ray as much as his political opponents did in 1856.

The author of this book does not intend to be a special pleader for Charles Ray and his fellows in their fight for human freedom. The facts must speak for themselves. It is only fair to admit, however, that a steeping in the personal papers of a conscientious crusader is likely to engender a sympathy and admiration for him. The author hopes that his enthusiasm has not prompted him unduly to overplay Dr. Ray's importance to Lincoln's career. Obviously the importance of Ray's contribution to the prairie lawyer's Freeport Doctrine can be only conjectural. Perhaps the note which Ray sent to Lincoln preceding the debate at Freeport was mere coincidence, although it must be remembered that Lincoln preserved the missive in his personal files.

Ray's prominence at the nominating convention in Chicago is well attested by the fact that Governor Andrew, head of the Massachusetts delegation, considered him to be the key man among the Illinoisans-for-Lincoln. It is notable too that the ruthless prosecution of the war which the *Chicago Tribune* urged eventually became the accepted war policy. Lincoln, as has been said, acknowledged the power of the *Tribune*. "You and your *Tribune*," he told Joe Medill, "had more influence than any paper in the Northwest in making this war. You can influence greater masses."

The same authority also quotes Lincoln as saying, "You called for war until we had it. You called for emancipation and I have given it to you. Whatever you have asked for you have had." These remarks were made after Dr. Ray left the paper, but Lincoln was of course including him, for he well knew that Charles Ray had been editor-in-chief during the years when the *Tribune* was crusading for war and for emancipation.

J. M.

CONTENTS

THE MAN WHO ELECTED LINCOLN

1 The Decision

WHAT would be the best way to spend an unexpected inheritance? This problem confronted Dr. Charles Henry Ray in the winter of 1851-1852. On March 12 he would celebrate his thirty-first birthday, and a rasping New England conscience goaded him constantly for his lack of outstanding success in life. He was tall, well-built, and handsome, with sparkling blue eyes, a clear rosy complexion, and curly hair which any girl would envy. He had a wife, a baby daughter, and two part-time jobs which earned him barely enough to keep bill collectors from the door. This inheritance, if spent wisely, might assuage his haunting desire to be a prominent, prosperous, and truly useful citizen.

Charles Ray had experimented with several kinds of work and had always been reasonably successful, but he had never made enough money to live as he wanted to or even to pay off the debts he had incurred in getting his education. The urge to do more than just live well, like a prize animal, always nagged at him. Perhaps he would have been better satisfied with his present employment if he had failed more often in other undertakings. His job as editorial writer for the Galena, Illinois, *Jeffersonian*, a four-page paper devoted mostly to advertisements of groceries, dry goods, and medicines, took little of his time. Only two-thirds of one page was devoted to news and "leaders," as editorials were called. To make extra money, Dr. Ray practiced medicine in partnership with George E. Robinson, but neither of them was getting rich.

Charles Ray had been in Galena less than a year. He liked this town in the extreme northwestern corner of Illinois better than any other place where he had worked. Certainly Galena had a brighter future than that pestilential shantytown across the state known as Chicago. In the first place, Galena stood on a hill high enough to be above the deadly miasmas which people believed responsible for fever and ague, their name for malaria. Fine brick houses stood in tiers, one above the other, on the steep slope north of the docks on Fever River, a short tributary of the Mississippi. Ten or fifteen river boats often unloaded there at the same time. In territorial days the Illinois boundary had been extended northward to include Galena in order that the population might be sufficient for statehood. Galena had the prestige of age and respectability. Businesses were well-established, and the citizens conservative. Democratic Congressman Thompson Campbell and prominent Whig politician Elihu B. Washburne both lived in Galena. Washburne, a graduate of Harvard Law School, had been delegate to two Whig national conventions.

Galena had a variety of small but moderately prosperous businesses. For example, Grant and Collins operated a leather-goods store. Jesse Grant spent most of his time in Ohio, but his son Simpson worked in the Galena store under Collins. Another of Grant's sons was a lieutenant in the Army, making insufficient money to support his family properly. However, the Galena business did not tempt him at this time.

Charles Ray's legacy was small, but it was more than he had ever had in one sum. His father, Levi Ray, had died at his home in Norwich, Chenango County, New York, bequeathing one-third of his estate to each of his sons, Charles and George, and the other third to his wife. Levi, a skilled mechanic, had been born in Massachusetts in 1796. Proud of his industry and his New England heritage, he had instilled this pride into his sons, making them dissatisfied to lead little lives. Levi's ambition, like his son Charles's, had prompted him constantly to borrow money for the expansion of his business—a warranted indebtedness, for he owned a "shop of three fires" and also had a third interest in one of four fires at the time of his death. His wife had helped build the estate by cooking for the "help," usually eight or ten "hearty men."

With the ascendancy of Andrew Jackson, Levi Ray had become a devoted Democrat. He admired Old Hickory's fight against the national bank and his championship of the common man. Young Charles had been reared in the Jacksonian philosophy that one man's rights were as good as another's. He remembered the Democratic contest of 1835 in New York, when workingmen in Tammany Hall took control of the city caucus by striking loco-foco matches, preventing their opponents from terminating the meeting by turning off the gas. The event caused great political excitement, and Charles's father had sympathized with the Loco-foco, or working man's, faction.

Although always an employer, Levi Ray believed in a political system which would permit ambitious laborers to become capitalists. Charles had heard this preached as long as he could remember. He also knew that his grandmother traced her ancestry back to Miles Standish. To be a fighter for the rights of man was in Charles's blood. Justice to his father's memory demanded that his inheritance be spent in such a cause. But how?

Dr. Ray pondered this question in the office of the *Jeffersonian.* In his thirty years of life he had had many experiences and had made mistakes which he did not care to repeat. As a youth in his teens in Norwich, he had wanted to be a doctor. He "read" in the office of a local practitioner until a juvenile escapade terminated the relationship. Young Ray determined to continue his studies in New York. His father wanted him to remain in Norwich, saying that a boy who lacked energy and imagination to get into mischief was not apt to amount to much, but Charles was sensitive and went anyway, leaving a sweetheart named Jane PerLee behind in Norwich. For more than two years he served without a diploma as a surgeon's mate and then as surgeon in the 105th New York Infantry. Though urged by his friends to return home and finish his education, he decided instead to embark on a two-year whaling expedition to the Indian Ocean.

On June 19, 1841, he set sail from New Bedford on the brig *Newton*, taking with him a library of books on surgery as well as several volumes by Goldsmith and Shakespeare. Always he had enjoyed reading the best literature. In his sea chest he packed six quires of paper, quills, and four dozen tobacco pipes. He half planned to write about his experiences—a conventional thing for adventurous young men to do at that time. Richard Henry Dana had just made a name for himself by publishing *Two Years Before the Mast*, and another young man, J. Ross Browne, signed on a New Bedford whaler the year after Ray did. Browne planned to study sailors' working conditions and write a book in the hope of ameliorating them. Herman Melville had sailed on a similar trip in 1841.

On the day the *Newton* hoisted anchor, Charles Ray lost overboard his hat and an unopened letter from Jane PerLee. For two years he wondered what she had written. The voyage failed to supply the inspiration Charles had hoped for. He read the books he had taken along, helped in the pursuit of whales, talked politics to the crew, and called himself "the crack Loco Foco in the ship's Company." Back in New Bedford at the age of twenty-two, he had little to show for the cruise except repugnance for the undemocratic one-man rule of a sailing ship and a strong dislike for the first mate, a native of Charleston, South Carolina, whom Ray described as a combination of "all the fiery and vindictive qualities of Southerners in general without any of their noble feelings of generosity." Charles Ray spent his scant accumulation of wages for landsman's togs—a silk cravat, six collars, four shirt bosoms, some new underwear, and a linen coat. At Norwich he found Jane waiting for him. That winter he lived at home, renewing his medical studies, and in the spring of 1844 he received a diploma to practice in New York. The opportunity for making a living, however, seemed exceptionally meager, so he looked around for a new location.

Jane's brother had married and moved to Michigan. Letters from his wife, Zadie PerLee, to Jane were full of hope and hardships. The pioneer newlyweds in the backwoods had no money, ate monotonous food, and were reduced to making moccasins like the Indians' for shoes. Once when guests called they had been mortified by having to serve cold water in tin cups. Charles told Jane that he did not intend to submit her to such privations, but he did believe the West to be a land of opportunity. He would go alone, establish himself, and send for her. Mutual friends put him in touch with an elderly physician in Bloomington, Iowa, and Charles Ray set off in high hope of making his fortune.

The expense of the trip added to the money he had already borrowed left him badly in debt. At Bloomington he had to pay cash for board and room, while his patients paid him in produce or livestock or not at all. The purchase of a horse and saddle for country calls increased his already insurmountable indebtedness. In this predicament, a serious illness confined him to bed. When his strength returned he went back to Norwich, more in debt than ever. During the winter Charles Ray, a burden to his father and financially unable to marry Jane, decided to return to the West.

At Buffalo he stopped to see Millard Fillmore, former New York congressman, who said that there was a good opportunity for a young man in the new capital of Illinois at Springfield. Fillmore gave Ray a letter of introduction to a Whig colleague out there, one John T. Stuart, who was, or had been, a partner in the law business with a man named Abraham Lincoln—or was it Abram Lincoln? No matter. Fillmore's letter stated that Ray had come to him "highly recommended for his scientific and professional attainments. . . . I therefore take great pleasure in introducing him to your acquaintance. . . . His appearance certainly indicates that he may be a desirable acquisition for any place or State."

Springfield was a difficult town for Ray to reach from the East in 1845. A passenger boat sailed from Buffalo to Chicago, on the mud flats of Lake Michigan. From there Ray boarded the four-horse stage which for $12.00 carried passengers some two hundred miles across the prairies to Springfield in three days' time. The capital had only three or four thousand inhabitants, but the new two-story stone statehouse, with its Doric columns front and back, was an imposing edifice. A railroad had connected Springfield with steamboats on the Illinois River thirty-five miles to the west, but was now discontinued as dangerous and impracticable. People said there was no future in railroads except as playthings.

Ray, with his strong Democratic principles, found Stuart and Lincoln interested in Whig activities which he disapproved. They both associated with the town's aristocracy. Lincoln's wife was the sister-in-law of a well-known state senator whose father had been a United States Senator and territorial governor of Illinois. The family were lineage-proud and socially prominent.

Springfield's cultural standard was high. Ray made friends with Tench S. Fairchild, who suggested that the two of them might publish a temperance tract. The idea appealed to Ray. He had heard much of the moral crusade which was sweeping the country, and there seemed to be a good opportunity to extend it in central Illinois. Its activities were very different from those of the moribund temperance societies of previous decades. The new approach called on reformed drunkards to tell audiences about their debauches and describe their resurrection from the depths. Men with histrionic ability held audiences spellbound for hours describing drunken experiences.

The performances of an old actor, John B. Gough, were making him a national figure. With professional manner and magnetic voice, Gough alternately pictured the pleasures of the primrose path and the serpentine horrors at the bottom of the pit. The drama he enacted was vivid and appealing. All America became excited about him. Lawyer Lincoln was addressing meetings in Illinois—not as a reformed drunkard but as an advocate of temperance. Surely Fairchild and Ray could build a good subscription list.

Fairchild's plan was for Ray to stay in Springfield and edit the paper while he traveled across the state selling subscriptions at temperance meetings. Ray undertook the job with enthusiasm, but Fairchild never sent in as much money as he had promised in the beginning. Once again Ray found himself hard pressed to pay his board. Next the whole crusade was discredited. John Gough cracked and went on drinking sprees. Fairchild, equally insecure, confided to Ray in a letter that on his lecture tour he had met another itinerant crusader who had known him in Ohio "under circumstances not so favorable to my present employment." Fairchild added, "But I knew he had to run away so we both agreed to say nothing."

In the spring of 1846 the little paper was discontinued. Ray had made $250 from his year's work and spent all of it for board and room. He could have done as well practicing medicine for carrots and potatoes. He quit and moved sixty miles north to Mackinaw, a village fifteen miles east of the Illinois River. Here he began practicing medicine again. Jane came from New York to marry him, and they lived in the village for six years. Here baby Maria Cuyler was born, and the Rays reached middle age, as thirty years was then considered. At this time of life many men became reconciled to mediocrity, gave up youthful dreams, and adjusted themselves to inconspicuous happiness.

The Rays seemed to be drifting with this current. They bought a lot in town and built a one-room house of unburned bricks. A fireplace served for cooking. When they could afford it, a second room was added, then a porch along the back of both rooms. They used this as a kitchen in summer until a third room was added in an ell. Then the first rooms were papered and the ceilings whitewashed. Behind the house they put in a large garden and built a stable for the horse and a calf shed. Charles enjoyed working with little pigs, chicks, and puppies. Animals responded more rapidly to doctoring than humans. When he was called to the country on a case, a neighbor boy cut wood for Jane and fetched water from the well. Finally Charles bought a buggy, and Jane, for the first time, drove outside the village.

The Rays wrote home that they were really comfortable. They had fared better than Jane's brother up in Michigan and were able to send him boxes of clothes and food. Zadie PerLee suggested that her sister-in-law take one of their children for a year or two. Charles's brother, George, came to stay with them. He wanted to "read" for a doctor's diploma or become a druggist. Tench Fairchild learned about his former partner's prosperity and asked to come and stay, too. He wrote that his luck had turned from bad to worse: "My jig is up in the temperance line." The letter then explained how the writer had been expelled from the American Temperance Union. He had got drunk, he said, and was almost killed. Then he concluded, "I never shall attempt to gull the dear public in that way hereafter."

With all his apparent prosperity, Charles Ray had difficulty making both ends meet. For a time he served as postmaster of Mackinaw. In addition, the young doctor peddled clocks and hammers as he made the rounds of his patients. His father had sent these articles from New York. Once Ray drove a herd of horses to Chicago to sell—an unsuccessful venture that he did not repeat. He even considered running for Congress but decided that he could not afford it. A neighbor, Mathias Mount, told him that he remembered splitting rails with the present congressman, Abraham Lincoln. So Lincoln had started as a rail splitter! The Lincoln Ray remembered from Springfield was a member of the top social set, not a rail splitter. Certainly the fellow had gone up in the world.

Being isolated from the active world hurt Charles Ray. The

Mexican War had come and gone with little effect on Mackinaw. Returning soldiers brought back Santa Anna's wooden leg, allegedly left by the Mexican general in his carriage after the battle at Buena Vista. Charles had strapped the leg to his bended knee and stumped into the room where Jane lay ill with ague. He pronounced her merry laughter better medicine than the quinine he had been prescribing.

From the Mexican War also came rumors of a great argument in Washington over the extension of slavery into the newly captured territories. Charles Ray had never been much concerned about Negroes. Back in Norwich colored visitors had been disliked on account of their strange crudeness. Here in Mackinaw, so near the Illinois River with its New Orleans steamboats, Negroes were more common. People took them for granted and accepted slavery in the South without thinking much about it. Laborers were treated badly in every society. Look at the millworkers in New England. But the arguments in Congress caused Charles Ray to see things differently. The idea of extending the archaic slave code for regulating labor in new national territories aroused his indignation. A new serial story called *Uncle Tom's Cabin* had become immensely popular in the North. The villain, Simon Legree, seemed to be the counterpart of the mate on the whaler. The author evidently knew Southerners. In spite of the fact that she was a woman, she seemed to understand the slave system. Her descriptions of Southern ways seemed convincingly lifelike to Charles.

As Ray pondered the iniquities of slavery, he noticed that the South seemed to be constantly plotting against the interests of the Northwest. Not only did the South want to keep out free laborers by importing slaves into the territories, but the slave-power opposed homesteads for settlers and voted consistently against tariffs which would provide money to improve western canals. Southern orators and editors actually urged the reopening of the African slave trade. Certainly the time had come to stop that tide of reaction.

In order to get into this impending fight for freedom, Charles

Ray had given up his successful but uninspiring life at Mackinaw and had moved to Galena, where he could work part-time on the *Jeffersonian* while he built up a new medical practice. He was working in this dual capacity when the inheritance from his father's estate became available to him. His first impulse was to buy a newspaper and enter the political fray. The written word had always been his strongest weapon, and the nation needed every idealist it could muster. With a journal of his own, he could strike telling blows against Southerners who had forgotten the lesson of the Revolution and the principle that all men are entitled to life, liberty, and the pursuit of happiness.

With only a small sum to invest, Ray had to decide where to buy his journal. He did not want to spend his money traveling around hunting for a location. Galena and Chicago seemed to be the outstanding cities of the future. Of the two, he had already decided that Galena, because of its direct water connection with St. Louis, Cincinnati, and New Orleans was the more promising. The Illinois and Michigan Canal permitted small boats from the Great Lakes to dock at Galena. The route was circuitous, it was true, but better than the muddy prairie roads. The canal promised to be the chief artery of the state. Already a hundred and seventy thousand people lived along it. Chicago, at the lake end of the canal, would always be a loading and unloading point, but the swamps along the Chicago River could never support a city. The miry streets between the shanties over there were bottomless. For miles around, roads would have to be planked before wagons could be driven into town. Taxes for such construction would bankrupt any municipality.

In late years there had been much talk about replacing water transportation with railroads. Charles Ray was dubious. He remembered that a railroad had failed near Springfield. Experiments with iron rails had been talked about for fifteen years, all to no purpose—and fifteen years seemed a long time to a thirty-year-old man. However, since the Mexican War better engines and rails had been tried. But even if the new Iron Horse did prove successful, Galena could still hold its own with Chicago. Since 1848 a railroad, the Galena & Chicago Union, had been operating out of Chicago, though four years' profits had not been sufficient to allow its extension to its Galena terminus. Whenever that was accomplished, Galena would be the nearest unloading point on the Mississippi for Great Lakes traffic. And this was not all! Another railroad, the Illinois Central, was to connect the southern tip of the state with Galena. If railways ever proved as efficient as canals, Galena stood an excellent chance of becoming the leading commercial city of Illinois.

The *Jeffersonian* was admirably situated to grow with Galena. The paper was Democratic in politics and needed only a more progressive management to succeed. As an employee, Ray envisioned many desirable changes, especially in format. He would put news instead of advertising on the front page. That would be an innovation, but Ray would like to try it. He went to the two owners and made an offer, and one of them agreed to sell his interest—more than half the stock. Thus Charles Ray gained control of the paper at a time when the Northwest was beginning to feel its strength, to throb with the life of uncounted millions. What better use could be made of Levi Ray's inheritance?

II The *Jeffersonian*

IN FEBRUARY 1852, as proprietor of the *Jeffersonian*, Charles Ray sat in the editor's chair smoking, writing, and looking out the frosted window at glittering snow draped on house gables and drifted behind board fences. Horses' hoofs crunched on the white streets. Sleigh bells jingled defiance at the numbing cold. Since the river was frozen, no steamboats brought news from the South. A packet of newspapers came on the stage line which connected with unfinished sections of the Galena & Chicago Union Railroad. Dr. Ray's editorial eye noticed a "leader"—exciting news! A railroad had reached Chicago from the East.

This was provoking information for a newspaperman who had just invested his all in the little town which was still hoping to be the western terminus of the Galena & Chicago Union. Furthermore, the news came as a climax to a distressing revelation which had disturbed northwestern Illinois all summer. Senator Stephen A. Douglas had betrayed Galena and thwarted her railroad ambitions. Ray had known before he purchased the *Jeffersonian* that the route for the proposed Illinois Central had been altered, but he had not realized the magnitude of the change nor Douglas' part in the shifty manipulations.

Sidney Breese, a little, near-sighted, plodding Illinois senator, had urged Congress for years to grant blocks of government land for the financing of a road direct from Cairo to Galena. Having difficulty mustering sufficient votes, he had combined his followers with Douglas', agreeing to change the road's route to a new terminal in Illinois which, according to accepted gossip, was about halfway between Galena and Chicago. This route had seemed sure of acceptance by the next Congress, but United States Senators were then elected by state legislatures, and Illinois gave Breese's seat to another man.

Without Breese, a revised bill passed—one of those involved Douglas compromises which Charles Ray was learning to suspect. Under this act the central route was retained with a terminal track curving west to Galena and a branch from Springfield, down in central Illinois, running straight to Chicago. Thus on paper Douglas had given everybody everything he wanted, but gossips repeated the ugly story that Douglas' Illinois henchmen had defeated Breese to get rid of northwest Illinois's champion, shift the railroad to Chicago and make the Galena line a mere stub.

Dr. Ray's first reaction to this political trickery was to strike back through the columns of the *Jeffersonian*. During the summer of 1852 he made his little paper a power in northwestern Illinois and established himself as a man of importance. For the first time in his life he felt that he had become truly useful. Readers delighted in his short, vigorous comments on the news —especially his thrusts at the sleepy, aristocratic Whigs. Ray used a printer's device, a little pointing hand, to call attention to his best shots. One editorial announced:

> We belong to no clique, no faction, no sect, no man or party of men. There is no question that we dare not examine, when examination is necessary, no man whom we dare not censure when censure is deserved. We shall beg no man's patronage, nor shall we change an opinion, alter a line or erase a word to secure it.

Readers liked this independence—at first. Congressman Thompson Campbell sent his speeches from Washington, and Ray printed them with his blessing. Politicians appreciated this method of reaching their constituents. Ray also praised President Franklin Pierce as the West's best hope, a man who would improve rivers and harbors at Federal expense, making Galena a shipping point for farmers' grain. He assured readers that Pierce "never had opposed and never will oppose needed improvements that are within the nation's means and against which well founded constitutional objections do not hold good." Apparently he was sure that the Fever River would be kept open for vessels from the Mississippi.

Ray also turned his attention to sound banking practices. Seeking information on this subject, he corresponded with John Locke Scripps, a young man from Cape Girardeau, Missouri, who was now employed by a Chicago newspaper. This was the beginning of an important friendship for Ray.

The circulation of the *Jeffersonian* began to increase, but Ray soon learned that readers who applauded his independence stormed against him when he opposed their personal interests. Powerful groups of elderly citizens did not want the railroad, did not welcome new industries, new faces, new houses. They were satisfied with things as they were and feared that new conditions might upset their fixed and comfortable lives. Let Chicago grow, they would continue to import goods from New Orleans and tell the preachers what to say on the Sabbath.

Ray began to wish that he had invested his heritage in Chicago, but it was too late now. His money was planted here, and he had already assumed new debts to improve the paper. He was unwilling to stoop to the level of these unimaginative yokels, but he must conserve what he could of his patrimony.

His editorship had introduced him to the leading politicians of the area. He turned now to them. He would continue with the paper, but would supplement his work with outside activities which paid better than the practice of medicine. Certainly only a small part of his time was required for writing the squibs on two-thirds of one editorial page. Ray wrote first to Elihu B. Washburne, the congressman who had succeeded Campbell, to solicit a job as Federal census taker in Illinois. He could easily do that work and keep the newspaper going.

Then startling news came from Washington, and Charles Ray forgot his worries in the new excitement. On January 4, 1854, Stephen A. Douglas presented a bill in the Senate to open Nebraska Territory, including Kansas, to settlement. That was all right, but Douglas had incorporated in the bill a provision that slavery might be introduced into the area—a direct violation of the Compromise of 1820. Northern Illinoisans promptly accused Douglas of being a traitor to his constituents.

Dr. Ray had been duped by Douglas' manipulations of the Illinois Central Railroad bill, so he was already prejudiced against the man. In the newspapers that came to his office from Eastern cities he read that Douglas had sold out the North to get Southern support for his own ambition to be President of the United States. Whole columns were devoted to denunciations of the Little Giant. Church congregations complained vociferously. Antislavery societies urged voters to write their congressmen. Quaker meetings joined the censure—and Charles Ray had always been an admirer of William Penn. In New England 3050 ministers signed a monster petition, and in New York mass meetings protested the legislation. Congress was swamped with letters and memorials. President Pierce ignored the protests and insisted that the bill was an administrative measure and a vote on it a test of party regularity.

A second bombshell exploded on January 24, 1854, when an article entitled "Appeal of the Independent Democrats" appeared in the *National Era*. Ray read it eagerly. The writers urged congressmen of all parties to fight the administration's surrender to the slave-power. Some of the most prominent senators in Washington had signed the appeal. At the head of the list Ray read the name of Salmon P. Chase, Democrat from Ohio. Here was a fellow Democrat after Ray's own heart, a man who would fight a party member when he was wrong rather than truckle to him for the sake of unity. Northern legislatures debated the controversial bill, and five of them passed resolutions condemning it. In Illinois a special session was called for February 9, 1854. Charles Ray decided that he must attend and report proceedings for the *Jeffersonian.* He believed that he could make extra money while in the state capital by writing dispatches for Horace Greeley's *New York Tribune.*

The trip to Chicago by stagecoach and train, then on to Springfield by train opened Charles Ray's eyes. The Lake City's 20,000 population had multiplied miraculously with the coming of railroads and now numbered over 60,000. The streets were still mudholes, half-frozen at this time, but new houses were rising thick as mushrooms among the shanties. Sidewalks were still wooden platforms in front of the buildings, and pedestrians tripped up and down steps to the different levels. Horses, mules, and oxen slipped and sloshed through the slush in the streets, but Ray felt a constant breeze of feverish activity—men running, shouting, whipping, hammering, and sawing. Everybody was doing something and doing it fast, eager to finish and begin something else. Galena was nothing like this, and Charles Ray, at thirty-two, felt his own blood surge to the city's rhythm. Here was the life for him. With people like these he could express himself and put his own shoulder to the wheel of progress.

When Ray stepped off the cars at Springfield, he saw the same amazing growth that he had noticed in Chicago. A solid block of buildings two and three stories high stood in a rectangle around the pillared capitol's buff stone walls. The old whipping post in the yard was gone. Both the front and rear porticoes of the capitol, as well as the surrounding streets, were black with frock-coated lawmakers, lobbying farmers, townsmen, beggars. On street corners groups of women in hoop skirts and shawls resembled a village of Indian tepees. A sign swinging from a staircase entrance indicated the law office of Lincoln and Herndon upstairs over a store. So the aristocratic Mr. Lincoln had a new partner now!

The sight of Springfield's familiar square recalled many half-forgotten experiences to Ray's mind. He remembered how bored he had been writing about temperance in this town. Constantly he had sandwiched political news into the reform tract. Time and again he had reminded readers of the advantages of good old Democratic doctrine. It may or may not have helped his paper's circulation and was all forgotten history now.

Charles Ray was a distinguished figure in any group of men. He was tall, stood erect, and weighed more than two hundred pounds. Some legislators, recognizing him as editor of the *Jeffersonian*—leading paper in northwest Illinois—spoke to him cordially. Others passed him sullenly. Illinois had been settled by people from both North and South, and they did not mingle on friendly terms. The Southerners had come first, crossing the Ohio River. Their settlements were thickest in the counties below Springfield. Most of northern Illinois's population had arrived more recently. They had come first by way of the Great Lakes and were now streaming in by thousands on the new railroads. These newcomers were building cities and staking out farms on prairies which had been considered unsuitable for cultivation. Southerners still clung to the streams, where wood and water were "handy." Ray knew both kinds of people—the conservative steamboat, river-bottom folk and the Yankees experimenting on the bleak prairies. The former seemed sympathetic to Douglas, but the latter, although also Democrats, violently opposed his latest action. Representatives of both groups now took their seats in the capitol.

At the first recess members of both houses crowded out the doors into the cold February air. They scampered briskly down the steps below the Doric columns and hurried, with coattails wagging, along the snow-bordered walks toward Fifth Street. At dinner in the boardinghouses, the desultory discussion of Douglas' perfidy continued. Ray learned that Douglas had disguised his breach of trust as a trade with the slavery interests for votes in favor of starting the first transcontinental railroad from Chicago. Politicians pointed out that the Little Giant had already deflected the Illinois Central for personal reasons. Now if he could draw the terminus of the transcontinental railroad to Chicago, that city would become the railroad center of the West, and Douglas' land there would be worth millions. So a fortune in land and Southern support for the presidency were Douglas' motives! Ray helped himself from the brimming bowl of boiled meat and potatoes which a buxom waitress plumped on the table and mentally chalked up another score against Senator Douglas. Horace Greeley would surely like an article on this for the *Tribune*.

On the streets outside and in the hotels, where people congregated around roaring stoves after stamping the snow from their boots onto the sawdust-covered floors, Ray heard nothing but complaints about the manner in which the Little Giant had betrayed the North. The whole state—really only its northern part—seemed to have gone mad over this surrender to slaverydom. But later, when a vote was called on a resolution commending the Nebraska Bill, the legislature voted for it. Ray believed that this sudden switch in sentiment was in response to orders from Senator Douglas in Washington. The Douglas machine had cracked its whip, and the Illinois assemblymen had fallen into line. Ray was outraged at this evidence of subservience to a political boss.

Ray remembered that his fellow townsman, the Whig Congressman Washburne, had actively supported construction of a railroad to Galena. The Whigs, not the Democrats, seemed to be the party of progress, and Ray wrote Washburne that he was done with Douglas, President Pierce, and their "infamous act." "I have but just begun to hate them, and to fight it," he wrote. With blue eyes flashing in anticipation of the looming battle against slavery, he walked to the Springfield station and boarded one of the little flat-topped railroad coaches for home. At Chicago he climbed up in a hack to drive across town to the westbound train. Jolting over the half-frozen ruts, he noticed changes in the city even in the few days he had been in Springfield. He was told that rails would soon be laid all the way to Galena, making that city much closer to Lake Michigan—not Lake Michigan closer to Galena.

Rattling west on the "train of cars," as it was called, he noticed thousands of acres of fertile prairie on both sides of the track, limitless wheatlands. Fellow passengers said that the crop this coming summer would be twice the size of last year's. Illinois was destined to be the breadbasket of the nation. Handling this enormous amount of wheat would make Chicago one of the great cities of the future.

Galena looked old-fashioned and run-down to Charles Ray when he reached the little city. Melting March snow lay in dirty drifts around the market house. The winter's accumulation of corncobs, rags, broken crockery, and funiture stood in high piles behind many houses. Untidy boats lay bottoms up among the dead weeds along Fever River. The brick houses on the hill looked shabbier than usual. People had neglected to paint the shutters or repair their sagging hinges. Even the horses jogged listlessly in front of rattling buggies. In the stores men still sat around the stoves. In low tones they gossiped about the price of hogs, noted over and over that the south hillsides could already be plowed, that Aunt Patience's hens had begun to lay—a sure sign of an early spring. These men were not excited about the Kansas-Nebraska Bill nor the danger of appeasing the slavery interests. They showed none of the alertness of the people of Springfield and Chicago. Oh, for a home where things really happened!

Dr. Ray greeted his partner in the *Jeffersonian* office and talked for a few minutes about the great excitement sweeping the country. He explained his own eagerness to enlist the paper's readers in the new crusade against the administration and to wean them from Douglas' ambition, even at the cost of spreading slavery into the free states, to become President. Formerly a staunch Democrat, Ray had grown to detest his party's senior senator.

Ray opened his carpetbag and took out packets of papers he had brought from Chicago. Here were newspaper clippings from the latest dispatches, pages and pages of his own notes, and letters from senators and congressmen in Washington. From these pieces of paper he planned to write a dozen editorials exposing Douglas' perfidy. By all accounts the Little Giant seemed unperturbed and confident of his ultimate success. He had been a fighter all his life and had always come out victor. Now he blamed radicals of his own party for stirring up needless trouble over a bill which he had introduced to assuage rising Southern resentment. The Kansas-Nebraska Bill, he maintained, was fair to both sections. It proposed to leave the question of slavery to the settlers themselves. This popular sovereignty, as he called it, promised to mollify the South and prevent a civil war.

"Prevent a civil war, indeed," Ray scoffed. "Give the South everything it asks and establish slavery in the North because Southerners threaten to make trouble. Has the Senator no feeling about the wrong of slavery?" Some of the newspapers Ray had brought home quoted Douglas at length. The little bulldog talked like a frontier riverman. A clipping from the *New York Courier* said that his language was "more becoming a pothouse than the Senate." Charles Ray, too, had learned some "pothouse language" on the local river front, and if that was what the people needed to jar them out of their complacency, he would fling words into the next *Jeffersonian* equal to Douglas' worst. Let the "Little Whelp"—he liked the phrase—show his constituents whether he represented Illinois or the Southern slavocracy.

Ray wrote with the fury of conviction. He scoffed at stubborn party men "who worshipped Douglas as the Democratic Christ." His phrases cut into readers' minds. The words drew blood. Men repeated them around the stove and stopped one another on the street to discuss the editor's latest articles. Conservative citizens who wanted to maintain the old Galena without change begged him to be more cautious, to hold his tongue;

oppose the bill if he must, but spare Douglas and the administration.

Charles Ray had no intention of sparing anybody who trucked with wrong. Party men called on him in his office, threatening to start an opposition paper and put him out of business. He told them to go ahead. He maintained that he was a good Democrat and would keep on writing the truth. If the *Jeffersonian* failed he could go back and practice medicine in Mackinaw. At least he would have the satisfaction of knowing that he had been true to his principles.

Then a friendly letter from Elihu Washburne confirmed Ray's determination to fight slavery regardless of party. The Whig congressman sent his antislavery speeches, and Ray published them in his paper. Washburne also reported on the bitter congressional debates over the Kansas-Nebraska Bill.

Ray, reading Washburne's letters and all the newspaper dispatches, visualized what was happening in the gaudy Senate Chamber amid the ornate frescoes and bronzes. Knowing Douglas, he could imagine hearing him scorch the bigotry of "Black abolitionists" who willfully endangered national harmony by unjustly prohibiting slave property in territories rightfully belonging to the South as much as the North. The Little Giant had a point there, but Senator Seward's reply reassured Ray.

The New York Whig was almost as small a man as Douglas, almost as powerful in the Senate, fully as pugnacious, and considerably more witty. His sharp eyes twinkled above a sharp nose. His tight-lipped mouth appeared to be held together with a pucker string. Skillfully he exposed the sophistry in Douglas' argument about the injustice to slaveholders. They had been given their share of the territories by the Missouri Compromise. Now to allow slavery in territories north of the line drawn at that time was tantamount to prohibiting free laborers from going there, for free workers would not go voluntarily and compete with slaves.

This rebuttal appealed to Charles Ray. He would broadcast it to his readers in the Northwest. He learned with delight that Seward had lost his temper in the heat of the argument, had unloosed the pucker string, and had spilled invectives fully as galling as anything Douglas had said. Bully for the free-soil Whig! Charles Ray was more convinced than ever that he was in the wrong party, unless the free-soil Democrats could get control. The habit of a lifetime still held him in the fold, but he read with interest that an anti-Nebraska party had been founded across the state line in Wisconsin, at a place called Ripon. The organization named itself "Republican."

Administration newspapers reported the excitement in Washington very differently from the free-soil sheets. Editor Ray watched the leading editions from both factions. They arrived in Galena a day after publication in Chicago, sometimes two days after. From all reports the tension was increasing in Congress. Senator Andrew Pickens Butler of South Carolina had replied to Seward vehemently. Butler was known as a Calhoun man. He even brushed his gray hair as the great slavery defender did. Negro slaves, Butler shouted, were far better for the territories than the "Hessians" sent out by the North—a reference to the large number of German Americans who had recently swelled the population in Illinois and were becoming politically important in Chicago and around Alton, Belleville, and other towns across the river from St. Louis. So the South was playing on antiforeign prejudices nursed since Revolutionary days! Ray drew his pencil around the words. He knew both the Illinois legislature and Congress to be full of men who owed their seats to these foreigners. These lawmakers would be obliged to fight for the honor of their constituents. Ray decided to write an editorial on this subject. Let all Germans in Illinois know that the South was against them.

A bundle of *Jeffersonians* was dispatched to Congressman Washburne. Ray wanted him to see for himself that one Democratic editor was unintimidated by the Douglas machine. A fortnight later a letter came from Washington with a congressional frank. Ray tore open the envelope. It was from Washburne, saying that the final decision on the Kansas-Nebraska Bill would be made in about two weeks. The vote, the congressman said, would determine the political future of every man in the Senate and House. Ray marked the day on his calendar and met all trains to get the latest dispatches from the East. After hurrying back to the office, he devoured every political item and scribbled off his editorials. Always he wrote twice as much as he had space to fill. He wished for more room to express himself, but dared not crowd out the advertisements. The political drama of the century was opening in Washington—the prelude to a test which would determine whether the Declaration of Independence was to be a mockery or an ideal. Charles Ray laid everything aside to watch the battle royal.

III The Kansas-Nebraska Act

As the alternating winds and sunshine of March 1854, smacked, then kissed, the sodden hills around Galena, Illinois, Charles Ray followed the progress of the Kansas-Nebraska Bill in faraway Washington. Spring came early on the sheltered south slope where the town nestled. For the first time since last fall, a fire was unnecessary in the *Jeffersonian* office. From an open window, when the sun shone, Ray could see cotton-white clouds sailing grandly in from the shores of a distant world. The daily train puffing over the eastern horizon brought a dozen newspapers from which the editor could reconstruct the political scene in the national capital. What was the chance of the bill's passage? How would the solons vote on it? Ray took two pages of foolscap. On one he listed the senators who might vote against the measure. On the other he wrote the names of those sure to vote for it. Usually Whigs could be expected to vote against any Democratic bill as a matter of party principle, but the slavery clause in Douglas' proposal had split both parties, and a completely new alignment in the normally Democratic Congress might be expected.

At the head of the list of Whigs opposed to the bill, Charles Ray wrote the name of William H. Seward, a little up-state New Yorker who habitually wore mussed clothes. Seward wielded great power and was outspoken on the slavery issue. Another party titan certain to oppose the bill was Charles Sumner, a lion-maned senator from Massachusetts who always roared against anything favoring slavery. But his colleague, Edward Everett, was one of those New Englanders who could not be relied upon. An intellectual prodigy who could speak Latin and think in Greek, he was essentially a man of ideas rather than of decision. Would he value peace between the sections more than the principle of freedom and compromise when the time came to fight? Perhaps he would say both "Yes" and "No," with scholarly reservations. His brother-in-law, Charles Francis Adams, maintained that Everett was made of "stuff not good enough to wear in rainy weather, though bright enough in sunshine." Ray could not know then that nine years later Everett would admit that Abraham Lincoln had said more in three minutes at Gettysburg than he himself had said in two hours. He wondered only how Everett would vote now. Many other Whigs seemed to have aligned themselves with the proslavery interests.

Charles Ray headed his list of Democrats who were sure to favor the bill with David Rice Atchison, a florid giant who had helped roll the Kansas-Nebraska pill which Douglas was forcing down the Senate's throat. His Missouri constituents hoped to acquire plantations in the new territory. James Murray Mason's name followed Atchison's. Grandson of George Mason, an originator of the Bill of Rights, this Virginian was sure to vote for the extension of slavery. How the liberals of one generation beget the reactionaries of the next!

The other senator from Virginia, R. M. T. Hunter, could also be depended on to vote for the perpetuation of the slaveholders' way of life. Hunter was a quiet, unobtrusive fellow, but he had been a disciple of John C. Calhoun in his defense of the slavery interests. Another loyal Democrat was ancient Lewis Cass, whose once rugged features now sagged with age. The seventy-two-year-old veteran was sure to vote with his party, since he was the man who had originated Douglas' plan of squatter sovereignty.

Also safe for the measure was John Slidell of Louisiana, an ex-New York adventurer with a bad name for political corruption and a reputation for getting his own way. Slidell appeared mellow and benevolent, with thinning white hair combed over a lobster-red scalp. He had married into an old Creole family, owned a fine plantation on the banks of the Mississippi, and raised his charming daughters to speak French as well as English. Slidell's questionable past was well-veneered with an aristocratic bearing. His vote on some issues might be uncertain, but not on one concerning slavery.

Ray checked over his list of other Democrats sure to vote for the Kansas-Nebraska Bill. There was no question about Senator Archibald Dixon of Kentucky. This second-rater from a border state had consistently toadied to the slave-power. He was responsible for adding the clause which specifically wiped out the Missouri Compromise and enraged all right-minded Northerners. A Northern Democrat who would probably favor the bill was Augustus Caesar Dodge of Iowa. Ray had lived long enough in that state to understand what ailed Dodge. An uneducated man, he represented the frontiersmen and the ignorant river element who troubled Ray so much in Galena. Dodge was too stubbornly local-minded to sense the magnitude of the antislavery issue or to adjust himself to it. He had been elected on his record as an Indian fighter. He wanted the transcontinental railroad for his constituents and would vote to extend slavery to get it. The *Jeffersonian* circulated across the Mississippi in Iowa, and Ray determined to see Dodge defeated when next he ran for election.

Other Democrats, so far as Ray knew, had not expressed themselves. Uncertainly he poised his pencil over the name of William M. Gwin, senator from California. Gwin was an enigma. He had favored the admission of California as a slave state, yet the free-state victors had elected him their first Senator. His aggressive, prognathous jaw and the peculiar slant of his eyes warranted watching. The man behind that face could not be fathomed, but in all probability he would vote for whichever side promised a railroad to the Pacific. He would probably support Douglas' bill.

Another Democrat was more perplexing. Although a Southerner, the extravagantly dressed Texan Sam Houston often acted independently of his colleagues. Adventurer, duelist, slaveholder, former Governor of Tennessee, former president of the Republic of Texas, former husband of an Indian woman, Houston could be counted on to vote fearlessly and without subservience to party.

Still another unpredictable Democrat was James Shields from Illinois, former Governor of Oregon Territory. Ray remembered that Shields had been a popular politician before he had gone to the Pacific. His open, engaging face won friends. His mouth, with its broad Irish upper lip covered with a gray mustache, smiled easily. His pleasant eyes attracted strangers. Shields had a flair for politics, and his wit was enhanced by a rich brogue. People still chuckled over a duel he had almost fought with lawyer Lincoln. Shields had advanced brilliantly since then, while Lincoln had retrograded politically and few people, if any, outside Illinois knew him. In 1850 Shields had taken a stand against the proslavery interests when he voted for the admission of California as a free state, but he was a politician still. Would he risk his future by voting contrary to his party's will again?

The New England Democrats might be expected to vote against the extension of slavery, but Charles Ray knew that party discipline was second nature to a seasoned politician. Hannibal Hamlin of Maine was one of the uncertain regulars. A man's man, with a swarthy face almost as dark as a mulatto's, Hamlin worked hard, spoke seldom during sessions, and kept his own counsel. Intimate companions knew him as a poker-faced card player, an inveterate smoker, and an excellent shot and expert fly fisherman, but admitted that they were never posted on his political opinions. Hamlin's reticence had paid political dividends. He had sat successively in the Maine assembly, in the House, and now in the Senate. He had supported Pierce for President, as Ray had done, and was considered a party wheel horse. His conservatism showed even in the old-fashioned rusty black swallow-tailed coat and linen stock he insisted upon wearing. His silence was suspicious and his vote would be revealing. However he was a law partner of young William Pitt Fessenden's father, and Fessenden, now serving his first term in the Senate, had expressed his opposition to the bill. Hamlin might vote for it in order to appeal to all clients' politics. These lawyers had devious ways.

A few Democrats on Ray's list had already registered their opposition to the bill. Foremost among these was Salmon P. Chase of Ohio. Ray admired him for his forthrightness and wished that more Northern Democrats might be like him. Chase's giant form, with its domed, slightly balding head, was a rallying beacon for antislavery ranks. One of his eyelids drooped with a sinister appearance which Douglas' turncoats had better watch. Whereas Douglas called the slavery issue unimportant and party unity the great issue, Chase put slavery above party—even hinted that a new party might be organized for abolition. Chase's name had headed the list of signers of the "Appeal of the Independent Democrats," and Ray thought his idea splendid. Certainly the Whigs, with all their promises of railroads and river improvements, were much too tolerant of slavery. Only a new party could combine all the progressive measures necessary for the nation's development.

When the day of the vote on the Kansas-Nebraska Bill finally arrived, Ray had to wait some hours after the battle before he learned whether it was lost or won. In fact he was unable to reconstruct the entire scene until several days had passed, but the final picture that came through the press stayed with him always. In his mind's eye he saw the ornate Senate Chamber with its rows of desks that fanned in concentric semicircles from the rostrum. On the right sat the Democrats, on the left the Whigs. But the voting on this bill did not follow regular party lines. First to seek the floor was John Bell, Whig from Tennessee. He was a handsome, smooth-shaven man with whisker tabs before his ears and thinning hair brushed smartly back. John Bell's personal appearance connoted wealth and social position. He spoke with assurance and fearlessness. A large slaveholder himself, he decried this bill as a slaveholders' measure which would effect nothing except the possible destruction of the Union.

Another Whig, George E. Badger of North Carolina, replied in favor of the bill. Douglas, with a twinkle in his knowing eye, watched his Whig opposition split in two. Badger extolled the virtues of slavery and the feeling of loyalty between master and slave. He explained that he had been reared from babyhood by a Negro "mammy" who was respected as much as any other member of the family. "Now," he concluded, "unless this bill is passed I shall be denied the right to take my dear old 'mammy' to Kansas."

Bluff Ben Wade, Whig from Ohio, snarled that the act would not prevent him from taking her—it would only prevent him from selling her after he arrived.

The Whigs seemed to have lost all unity, giving Douglas a great chance to win. William Pitt Fessenden, the new Whig Senator from Maine, asked permission to deliver his maiden speech in the Senate. Curious members turned their heads to see a proud, thin man with circles beneath his eyes and hollow cheeks framed with a beard. Senators whispered that he had been born out of wedlock. But when Fessenden began to talk, they forgot everything but his eloquence as he poured out impassioned arguments against the bill.

Senator Douglas took the floor to defend the measure. Leader of the majority party, he stepped out cockily, with fists clenched and head thrown back, his satin vest pulling on the buttons across his enlarging stomach. He had been in many a tight political squeeze before this, and he began to speak with apparent confidence. Party men would be brave indeed to defy Douglas' and President Pierce's order in this crisis.

Senator Seward sat insultingly inattentive. He seemed to

enjoy discomfiting a political opponent by turning his upholstered chair sideways to his desk during an oration. He liked to tip back his head and scan the cut glass chandelier or domed ceiling above it. Yet he was always sufficiently attentive to thrust a witty remark into an opponent's oration and puncture the decorum of the Chamber with a gale of laughter that brought down the president's gavel. Another crusty joker who might break the spell which Douglas hoped to weave over the assembly was frowzy, farmerish Ben Wade. Wade had been scoffed at by chivalric Southerners for refusing to accept challenges to fight duels until he finally laid a squirrel rifle across his desk when he rose to speak.

As the debate on the Nebraska Bill continued, many senators hid their hostility behind impassive faces, but Douglas had counted his votes and trusted that none would betray him. An old parliamentarian, he knew that no votes were assured before they were cast, but he had taken every precaution to build his wall against defeat. With his usual aplomb, knowing that his words would be printed in important journals across the country, Douglas deplored the furor over this innocent measure. He stated that the purpose of his bill was to restore peace between the North and South, to obviate the ugly scenes which had agitated Congress in recent years, and to turn the perplexing issue of slavery in the territories "to the arbitrament of those [the settlers] who were immediately interested in and alone responsible for its existence." He summed up the arguments for the bill, now familiar to all his colleagues. The Missouri Compromise, he said, was not a compact between the North and South which had been respected for thirty years, as the bill's opponents claimed. The Compromise was only an act of Congress, like the present one. It had originally been passed by a bare majority after much bickering and could, of course, be changed whenever a majority wished to do so. Several previous attempts had been made to repeal it, and no cry of bad faith had been raised. In 1837 part of the free territory had been sold to the slave state of Missouri as the Platte Purchase, and again there was no question of infidelity. The vast areas recently acquired from Mexico and adjoining the Nebraska Territory had been legally opened to slavery, so it was only consistent and equitable to allow the same status in Kansas. Ray had an answer to that argument which he would use in his next editorial.

Douglas concluded his speech and waited for the deciding vote. Edward Everett stood up, seeking recognition from the chair. His tall stock accentuated the schoolteacherish rigidity of his slender form. He had listened to all the debate with attention. He had also heard the rumbling of distant resolutions passed by mass meetings in New England and the protests in the nation's press. In spite of his timidity, he could at times show unusual resolve. As president of Harvard he had insisted that a Negro be allowed to take the entrance examinations. "If the white students choose to withdraw," he said, "all the income of the College will be devoted to his education." But the Senate Chamber was not Harvard, and Everett seemed uncertain. With long words and involved sentences he beclouded his position on the bill behind a beautiful cumulus of scholarly language. Cautiously he qualified his opinion and piled up reservations on his conclusions—exactly as Charles Ray had expected. Much upset after he concluded, Everett slunk from the room, and his chair stood vacant when the roll was called for voting.

Edward Everett stumbled out into the night, leaving the senators bickering in their ornate chamber. Sam Houston consulted his elaborate watch. He pushed back his chair on its casters and rose to his full resplendent height. Morning was approaching, he said, and the debate had been unseemly long. Why not settle the matter at once and go home? Houston always spoke fearlessly. As a large slave owner himself, he gave the lie to the contention that slavery would die naturally in the West. Like Bell and other wealthy slaveholders in the South, he also despised the Calhoun secessionist wing of his party. He wanted none of this bill and said so. He wanted to go home.

Dawn of March 4, 1854, glowed through the stained glass windows of the Senate Chamber as the final roll was called. At 5:00 A.M., a teller announced the result—thirty-seven to fourteen in favor of the bill. The only hope of killing it now rested with the House. Among those Senators approving the bill were Atchison, Badger, Cass, Dixon, Dodge, Douglas, Gwin, Hunter, Mason, Slidell, and Shields. It was by no means a sectional vote but one that split both parties. Charles Ray checked the final tally against his list and noted that he had guessed correctly in most instances. He reported the vote in his *Jeffersonian.* Some of these senators were coming up for re-election in the fall, and Ray would remind his readers how they had voted.

The *Jeffersonian* joined the chorus of press protests raging across the North. Stephen Arnold Douglas was denominated the "Benedict Arnold of 1854." Horace Greeley denounced the bill as "the first great effort of slavery to take American freedom directly by the throat." In Cincinnati a mass meeting warned the state's congressmen that they were being watched and declared that no member who dared vote for the bill would be re-elected.

The entire nation was alert when frail little Alexander Hamilton Stephens of Georgia offered to sponsor the Kansas-Nebraska Bill in the House of Representatives. His state had passed a resolution in favor of the act. Antislavery congressmen counted possible votes and believed themselves outnumbered. Charles Ray checked over the list of members, as he had for the Senate, and watched with interest to see whether a skilled minority might kill the measure. He had seen this happen when he reported the legislature's session in Springfield, and he longed for more of those exciting days.

In the House the bill's opponents tried to put off balloting with endless debate. All of May ninth and most of the tenth were consumed by monotonous speeches totaling thirty-six hours. Finally leaders on both sides agreed to adjourn over the week end. The solons crowded out to lobby in boardinghouses, while their horsehair chairs stood empty. Congressman Gerrit Smith, wealthy idealist from New York, watched the political bickering with disgust. He was working with a man named John Brown to establish a colony for freed Negroes in the Adirondacks. He believed in open-faced reform, not logrolling. If what he saw here was democracy, Gerrit Smith determined to achieve progress by more direct and "honest" methods. Out in Michigan, grim, goateed Zach Chandler, still smarting under an unsuccessful campaign for the governorship, decided to promote a new political party in the state—like the one in Ripon, Wisconsin—if this bill could not be killed.

Ray wondered how the bill would emerge from the muddle. He had full confidence in the two congressmen from northern Illinois. Elihu Washburne saw eye to eye with him on this bill, as he had on building a railroad to Galena, in spite of many citizens' opposition. Congressman Wentworth, or Long John, as the six-foot-six, three hundred-pound representative from Cook County was called, had also blurted out his opposition to the bill. Wentworth was an eccentric character, as Houston was in the Senate. He had trudged into the village of Chicago in 1836 when it was a fur-trading post. Growing up with the city, he had worked indefatigably for railroads and had finally induced several to center in Chicago. Thus he was, in a way, responsible for the city's booming prosperity. He probably realized that the Kansas-Nebraska Bill was part of a bargain to make Chicago the terminus of the Pacific Railroad—a thing he wanted—but Long John knew the temper of his constituents better than Douglas did. He would vote always for freedom as opposed to slavery. What was more, he would speak his mind with the crushing finality of a meat cleaver.

Knowing Wentworth, Ray wasn't surprised three years

later when, in a campaign for mayor of Chicago, Wentworth said, "You damned fools . . .You can either vote for me for mayor or you can go to hell." What a man! Why was it that the strongest characters hailed from Chicago? Charles Ray wanted to fight on the side of men of Wentworth's pattern, be they Whig or Democrat. Issues were more important to him than party. Also sure to fight the bill in Congress was Richard Yates, hard-drinking and hard-slugging Whig from Illinois, who had an eye on the governorship.

Of all the members of the House, the most important and certainly the most interesting was Thomas Hart Benton of Missouri. He represented everything Dr. Ray believed in. A lifelong Democrat, he had fought for hard money and freedom of the slave. After thirty years in the Senate he was defeated on the slavery issue by his Democratic colleague David Rice Atchison—a row between two party stalwarts. Taking a seat in the House, Benton waited a chance to settle old scores with Atchison in the next election, if God and the cancer gnawing at his massive frame let him live that long. Charles Ray marked Benton as another man with whom he wanted to work. Let the free state of Illinois and the free-staters of Missouri pull together.

This Kansas-Nebraska Bill put Benton in a corner. Most of his constituents wanted Kansas opened to settlement, slavery or no slavery, and might defeat him in the next election if he voted against the bill. On the other hand, freedom-loving Germans around St. Louis constituted a strong element of his support. These voters objected to the bill's proslavery clause. In addition the bill carried a clause known as the Clayton Amendment, denying full rights to foreign settlers in the new territory. If Benton voted for such a measure, he would lose his German following. On the other hand, if he voted against it, he would lose the Americans who had supported him for a generation.

Charles Ray had watched the Missouri papers for months.

He pictured old war horse Benton fuming at the barrier ahead. Why had the Senate let such a bill come down to embarrass him in the House? Ray would have chuckled over an alleged interview in which Benton was quoted as saying: "The Senate is emasculated, sir. Yes, sir, it is emasculated. A majority do not belong to the masculine gender." Benton was also alleged to have declared, "The bill will be sent to h—, sir, and its authors will be sent there with it, sir."

Ray agreed with these sentiments and looked with satisfaction on his own editorials in the *Jeffersonian*, but down in Washington, Alexander H. Stephens, with the backing of Senator Douglas and President Pierce, marshaled the party forces. To placate Democratic Germans, the Clayton amendment was lopped off. Benton watched Stephens' strategy with vociferous contempt. "Sir," he said, referring to the Little Giant, "the meanest man in our country is a poor white man who marries a woman with niggers"—a slur at the plantation slaves inherited by Douglas' late wife. Charles Ray, fearing the power of Douglas' brilliant oratory, could say, "Amen."

On May 22, 1854, the bill was brought up for the last time. Stephens, with furious energy and political tricks that outwitted the opposition, succeeded in driving the bill through final readings amid alternate applause and hissing from the galleries. Interrupted by continual cries of "Order, order," the final vote was taken and reported to be one hundred against the measure, one hundred and thirteen for it. The bill, lacking the Clayton Amendment, was rushed back to the Senate and passed. President Pierce signed it on May 30, 1854, and Zachary Chandler called on all free-state Michiganders to rally at Jackson and organize the antislavery party he had been contemplating. Other states across the North followed suit. Charles Ray determined that he must establish himself in a larger metropolis and take part in the political revolution now sure to break across the nation.

IV "I Have Bought The *Chicago Tribune*"

SENATOR DOUGLAS returned triumphantly to Chicago after Congress adjourned in the summer of 1854. To his amazement, crowds hooted at him from all the way stations. Flags hung at half-mast, bells tolled as for a funeral, and at more than one place he saw his own effigy burning beside the track. In Chicago he called a mass meeting in order to explain the advantages of the Kansas-Nebraska Act. A mob came, not to listen but to boo him off the platform. At Galena Charles Ray filled all available space in the *Jeffersonian* with pungent thrusts at the Little Giant. He noticed that other states were forming anti-Nebraska parties, and in September he called on Illinois Democrats to consider "formally excommunicating the adherents of Douglas' Nebraska scheme from the great Democratic brotherhood." His editorials were read in St. Louis by young Frank Blair, powerful old-line Democrat, who wrote to Ray commending the *Jeffersonian's* stand and urging cooperation in the formation of a national party of protest. He suggested his mentor, Thomas Hart Benton, as a leader for the movement.

During the first week in October hundreds of farmers assembled in Springfield to attend the State Fair. A minister from Princeton, Illinois, begged them to leave the display booths for an hour or two and help organize the Republican Party, as other states were doing. Preacher Owen Lovejoy was an eloquent and popular speaker. His brother, Elijah, had been killed by a proslavery mob for daring to print diatribes against slavery, and Owen had sworn to dedicate his life to avenge the murder. If he could not fire the popular heart, who could?

Ray watched for a report of this laudable program, but he learned when Lovejoy came north that the politicians had shunned the meeting. Only twenty-six men had attended. Lincoln had left town—purposely, men thought, in order not to commit himself. In his absence the would-be Republicans had appointed him to their proposed central committee, but Lincoln, when he returned, refused to serve. Ray saw that the people must be converted to the new party before the politicians would dare to join it. In leader after leader he continued to pound away at slavery. Conservative readers warned him to desist. Some canceled their subscriptions. Ray realized the danger of losing the money he needed to pay his debts, but people had tried to intimidate him before, and he was never one to compromise principles for business considerations.

In November Charles Ray enjoyed the satisfaction of seeing Northern voters repudiate the Kansas-Nebraska Act by refusing to return to office many of the congressmen who had supported it. There would be great excitement in Springfield when the legislature met in January 1855. Another exciting event, the birth of a new baby to the Rays, was scheduled for about the same date. Charles decided to send Jane to New York, where she could be confined at her mother's home. Then he would go to Springfield in time to report legislative proceedings for his readers. Before leaving Galena Ray sold his interest in the *Jeffersonian* but retained the editorship until the close of the legislative session—an important consideration, for the prestige of that position might win him a good job with the politicians. The office of clerk of the Senate paid $6.00 per day, a magnificent sum in an age when a good meal cost twenty-five cents. The clerkship was one of the much-sought plums which someone would receive when the assemblymen convened in Springfield. After the legislature adjourned, Ray hoped to find permanent employment in a city larger than Galena.

Highly elated with the sale of his Galena newspaper, Charles Ray wrote to Washburne:

> I am tired almost to death of the unceasing and constant worry of duns and debts, and if God will help me in my resolution, I will never have to do again with a one horse paper in a one horse town, particularly if that paper depends for its support upon a horde of damn unlikked Irish whelps and Dutch ignoramuses.

Concluding the sale, Ray joined his wife in New York. Before he arrived, the baby was born, sooner than expected. From North Norwich, Dr. Ray wrote Washburne: "He is an anti-Nebraska man already." The doting father could spare only a few days before he boarded the cars for the Illinois capital. Ray was starting west early so that he might lay plans of his own before the legislators convened. Two objectives were uppermost in his mind: to become clerk of the Senate and to use all his persuasive powers in urging the lawmakers to elect a strong antislavery man for the United States Senate.

In Chicago Ray stopped to sample the political weather and marvel at the booming city. Whole blocks of houses had risen since he had passed through on his way to New York. Ray called at the office of the *Tribune*, an antiforeign prohibition paper, and also at Long John Wentworth's *Democrat*. He asked everyone, "Who is the best man for the Senate?" The politicos disparaged Lincoln—too weak on slavery, too strong on aristocratic Whiggery for the common herd, unacceptable to the Know-Nothings because he failed to come out definitely against allowing immigrants to vote. These issues were important for any candidate. The Know-Nothing group constituted a new and powerful party in the West. It was supported by American laborers who hoped to protect themselves from competition with the thousands of foreigners who had migrated recently from Europe. The Know-Nothing Party was considered to be stronger than the Republican. It refused to commit itself on slavery—the all-important issue to Ray. Like other Americans, he had found foreigners to be "pig-headed" and bigoted, apt to vote in blocs under orders from political bosses. He did not blame native-born Americans for resenting immigrants who worked cheaper and took their jobs. However he realized that all Americans had been immigrants at one time and that the German vote might be necessary for an anti-Nebraska victory and the ultimate freedom of the slaves.

The selection of a winner for the United States Senate was not easy. The longer Ray talked with informed men, the more uncertain he became regarding the best candidate. He knew that many legislators in Springfield would come to him begging the support of the *Jeffersonian* for their particular aspirants, and he did not intend to commit himself until he had studied the field. Before boarding the train for Springfield he wrote another letter to Washburne. "You, of course, as much as any one," Ray said, "know that the battle with the slave-power is now to be fought out to the end." Ray stopped, then began writing a new paragraph:

I must confess I am afraid of "Abe." He is Southern by birth, Southern in his associations and Southern, if I mistake not, in his sympathies. I have thought that he would not come squarely up to the mark in a hand to hand fight with Southern influence and dictation. His wife, you know, is a Todd, of a proslavery family, and so are all his kin. My candidate must be like Caesar's wife—not only not suspected, but above suspicion. But give us a Salmon Chase in Illinois, and in his senatorial term we would effectually lay out any Douglas man in the State. After all, Abe may be the man. At all events I will take your advice and see him as soon as I get to Springfield.

Ray found the capital city very different from last year. New gas lamps on iron posts illuminated the square—a truly magnificent spectacle when falling snow created a halo over each light. Springfield was more crowded than usual with lawmakers, lobbyists, carefree young blades, and careful matrons who had brought eligible daughters to town for the social whirl. The congressional housecleaning after the Kansas-Nebraska excitement had reacted on the state assembly. The big issues were slavery and the election of a new United States Senator by the legislature.

Charles Ray engaged a room at the hotel, sharing it with three other men at a cost of a dollar a week each—reasonable, but not cheap. Ray would have preferred more privacy, but he realized that was impossible while the legislature was in session. He put his carpetbag on the bed assigned him and looked casually at the baggage on the other beds. What kind of men had he drawn for roommates? Before the day was over he found out. One was a state senator. The other was a correspondent from the *Chicago Tribune*—a fellow named Stuart who, like Ray, had come to report the session, but not to get a political job besides, Ray hoped.

In the hotel lobby Ray greeted friends he had met last year and chatted with them about the session's problems. State Senator Norman B. Judd asked to speak privately with him, and the two went into a room together. Judd was a medium-sized man with colorless hair and quiet mien, but his mind worked smoothly and fast. He was an attorney for the Rock Island Railroad and a power in the Senate. He believed most victories were won by quietly preparing to act ahead of the other fellow. Now he wanted to organize the legislature. With it in hand, a caucus could determine who would be United States Senator. Ray, with his *Jeffersonian*, might be of great help. Would the editor serve as clerk of the Senate if nominated and elected?

Dr. Ray was delighted and, with this settled, the two men

discussed possible senatorial candidates. Ray suggested Congressman William H. Bissell, who had proved to be a vote-getter on the slavery issue. He had achieved great popularity with his antislavery constituents by accepting a challenge to a duel from Jeff Davis. True a paralytic stroke had put Bissell on crutches, and he could speak only from a chair, but he had campaigned for office on an independent ticket—neither Whig nor Democrat—and had been elected to Congress. Judd wanted to keep Bissell where he was and elect either Lincoln or Lyman Trumbull to the Senate. Of the two, Trumbull was the better known. An eminent Belleville lawyer, he had been a justice in the state supreme court and also secretary of state. As a Democrat, he might be more successful in defeating the Douglas machine than a former Whig. Ray and Judd parted without coming to any agreement, but each understood the other's point of view.

On the opening day of the session Judd nominated Charles Ray for clerk of the Senate, as planned. He was elected so quickly that the surprised Old Guard suspected a prearrangement. They had not yet completed their own alignments and saw that the anti-Nebraskans had beaten them to the gun. Charles Ray took the official chair behind the desk under the president's rostrum. From this vantage post he could observe the political maneuvering and report details to the readers of the *Jeffersonian*. In addition he planned to write again for Horace Greeley's *New York Tribune*. With surplus funds, Charles Ray felt rich. Never one to be cautious with money, he invested in a real estate project down at Cairo, Illinois, where the Ohio joins the Mississippi. The town was inundated by spring floods nearly every year. Only six miles up the Ohio a knoll stood above high water. Ray's associates planned to build a rival city on this mound. Undoubtedly businessmen would move to such a propitious location—but they didn't and his investment later proved to be a failure.

Charles Ray pondered his new lesson about the fickleness of

human nature as he sat in the clerk's chair looking into the circle of senators' faces. He noticed, as he had at the last session, that men from the northern part of the state had a different appearance from the slavery sympathizers of southern Illinois. Slavery seemed to mark men who came in contact with it. They looked more slouchy and easygoing. They reminded Ray of the people in the old river villages like Galena and a half-dozen others. The new villages built by the incoming Northerners seemed more progressive. Ray preferred the new "go-ahead" Yankees. The future of Illinois, of the West, and even the nation, lay with them, he was sure. No more Bloomington, Iowa, or Mackinaw or Cairo, Illinois, for him. He was glad to be leaving Galena, too.

During a recess Ray walked across the square and climbed the dark stairs to Lincoln's office. He found the lanky lawyer seated behind a shabby table cluttered with papers, pens, and a spattered earthenware inkwell. Pigeonholes bulging with documents, an untidy bookcase, and a rickety sofa leaning against the wall added to the disorderly appearance of the room. The grimy windows showed no sign of ever having been washed. Certainly the office did not appear suitable for the society man Ray remembered. Had Lincoln changed, or had Ray's new position in the world altered his perceptions?

Lincoln had aged in the ten years since Ray had first met him here in Springfield. Over forty-five years old now—twelve years Ray's senior—he had evidently lost some teeth, for his cheeks appeared more sunken. His eyes, however, twinkled with animation when he spoke. Lincoln asked Ray to sit down. The editor lighted a cigar. The tobacco habit had grown steadily on him since his whaling days, and smoking eased the formality prescribed for opening an interview.

Through a swirling curtain of fragrant smoke, the two men discussed the senatorial post. Ray had risen far above the editorship of an unsuccessful temperance sheet in Springfield. Knowing his power, he said frankly that Lincoln could not get enough support unless he made a definite commitment against slavery. Ray was disappointed when Lincoln procrastinated, refused to declare himself, and was reminded of a funny story. Laughing graciously, Ray picked up his high hat and placed it on his curly head, then walked down the narrow stairs and crossed the plaza to the capitol. The editor had decided that Lincoln was not the best man. Abe's rival, Lyman Trumbull the Belleville lawyer, had a more positive personality. Already Trumbull had taken a stand against slavery extension and had been elected to Congress on the anti-Nebraska ticket. He was not so simon-pure an abolitionist as Ray wished but he seemed a stronger, safer man than Lincoln. A week later, however, Ray changed his mind and decided that Lincoln was best for the post. Abe had been campaigning all week, shaking hands with legislators, stalking up and down the halls telling funny stories, proving himself to be a popular vote-getter.

At last the day came for the legislature to elect a senator. On the first ballot Lincoln polled the most votes, as Ray had prophesied, but did not have a majority. As the voting continued, Lincoln's closest rivals were Lyman Trumbull and Joel Matteson. The latter, a Democrat, might well win if Trumbull and Lincoln continued to split the anti-Nebraska vote. To forestall this possibility, Lincoln released his supporters to vote for Trumbull and keep a proslavery man out of the United States Senate. The Trumbull partisans, on their part, agreed to vote for Lincoln when Douglas' seat became vacant three years hence.

Trumbull's election to the Senate was the most important event of the session, and the promise for Lincoln votes in 1858 was cherished by the political-minded. Ray, writing dispatches for Greeley, asked the great editor's advice about employment after the legislature adjourned. He was disgusted with Galena, he said, and wanted to live in a growing city. Greeley replied that there was a great opportunity to serve the cause of freedom by starting a penny paper in Chicago. Make it cheap enough for immigrants and working people. They had the votes which must be won if the new Republican Party survived. The New York editor suggested that Ray get in touch with Joseph Medill, an Ohio newspaperman, who was also looking for a new location.

Ray considered Greeley's advice seriously. He wrote Jane that his "heart was in the cause." If he could only raise sufficient funds he would start a paper dedicated to freedom for all men. He would expose the corruption of the present proslavery administration. Then he added, a little belatedly, "Don't name the baby Frankie. It is not manly, a name for some squirt like Frank Pierce."

To help finance his newspaper venture, Ray wrote to Congressman Washburne, asking for a loan. Before he received a reply he boarded the cars for Chicago to look around. He learned that the *Chicago Tribune* was for sale—buying it would surely be a much safer investment than starting a new paper. The *Tribune* was properly antislavery and anti-Douglas, but some of the paper's policies would have to be changed, for it was also antiforeign, anti-Catholic, and antiliquor—a natural trinity, since all foreigners were supposed to be Papists and winebibbers. Ray agreed with Greeley that the antislavery crusade must enlist the foreign vote. With control of the *Tribune*, Ray believed that he could write editorials that would accomplish this. But where could he raise enough capital for the purchase? Why had he invested so much in that proposed Mound City above Cairo? He did have some money left from the sale of the *Jeffersonian*, and a letter from Washburne promised him a loan. Everything might be arranged if that man Medill, about whom Greeley had written, could furnish the necessary balance. Ray urged Medill to come to Chicago. Waiting for the conference, he remembered his wife's birthday and wrote to her in New York. He addressed her "My dear old Jane." She was thirty-four—old for that day.

Then, with mid-nineteenth-century sentiment, he wrote: "We may, hand in hand, jog down the hill, the summit of which at our thirty-four years, is fully in view—loving and trusting to the last." Love was never more blind, for Charles and Jane were far from starting on the downgrade of life. Instead they were just coming in sight of the peak of a career more exhilarating than either of them could ever have imagined.

When Joe Medill arrived in Chicago, Charles Ray found him to be a serious, handsome man two years younger than himself. Smooth-shaven, steady-eyed, with a determined chin, Medill was dedicated to the antislavery cause and had behind him much practical newspaper experience. Formerly a Whig in politics, he believed the Whigs dead as Lazarus. He had worked to organize an antislavery party in Ohio even before the Kansas-Nebraska Act had agitated the entire nation. In Cleveland he had consolidated his last newspaper with another edited by a South Carolina abolitionist named John C. Vaughan. The two had worked earnestly to defeat Franklin Pierce in the last election, but had lost. They were closely associated with Senator Salmon P. Chase in his fight for freedom and thought that the cause could best be served by starting a stronger paper in the growing metropolis of Chicago. Ray suggested that Medill visit the *Tribune* offices with him. He believed the paper worth the price asked by its owners.

Medill and Ray walked over to the Ashland Block on Clark Street and talked with the newspaper's proprietors. Ray wanted to know about the readers. Who were they? What were their politics? Medill was most interested in the plant's equipment. He inspected the building, tallied the stock of paper, checked the subscription lists, and looked critically at the presses. Ray, determined to buy, puffed nervously on a cigar while waiting for Medill's decision. Irritable when delayed, Ray watched the crowds clumping along the city's wooden sidewalks. How could he best appeal to those people in a crusade for the new party? He felt sure that many *Tribune* readers were probably Know-Nothings—people who hated the Germans and Irish whom Greeley said must be enlisted for the new party. Ray believed that he could solve this problem in time. In 1854 the Know-Nothings had put their antiforeign plank above slavery, but now, in 1855, they were splitting on the slavery issue. Here was an opportunity for the right editor. Ray was already famous in his small world for fathoming popular reactions ahead of other editors. Now he saw, or thought he saw, that many Know-Nothings could be led into an antislavery camp and eventually persuaded to abandon their hatred of foreigners in a crusade against slaveholders.

Medill finished his inspection. With his usual business exactness, he came to Ray with many figures jotted on a piece of paper. The price asked seemed reasonable, but the two men could not raise sufficient money for the purchase. They did have enough, however, for Ray to buy a quarter and Medill a third. This gave them control of the paper, and, on this basis, the owners agreed to sell. In high spirits Ray wrote Jane in New York to be ready to come west at once. "With others," he said, "I have bought the *Chicago Tribune*." The *Democratic Press* was the only other paper in Chicago of comparable size. The *Missouri Republican*, a Democratic sheet in St. Louis, was the only journal larger in the entire Northwest. What a chance to convert a vast area to freedom for all men! Ray told his wife that he was to receive the handsome salary of $1200 a year as editor and would also receive his share of the paper's profits.

The practical-minded Medill insisted that new presses be purchased and John Vaughan, who had come on from Cleveland, went east to buy them. Medill and Ray took their places at desks in a long, bare room on the third floor. From the windows they could look down on Clark Street where wagons sank almost hub deep in the April mud. Some wag had once erected a sign near by, reading: NO BOTTOM HERE. The city's population now numbered 85,000. Ten trunk lines centered in the booming metropolis, and every train brought hundreds of prospective citizens. Flies swarmed into the *Tribune* office from near-by livery stables, and the stench from garbage thrown into the streets during the winter permeated the building. The Chicago River was being dredged to admit larger vessels, and the excavated sand was used to build up the streets. Eventually this should fill the mudholes and make dry land on which a city could be built. Now, however, the smell and the noise were terrific. Ray wanted to fetch his family, but feared for their health in this steaming inferno. The city's death rate was reported to be the highest in America—another Chicago superlative perhaps but enough to make a father worry.

At first Ray planned to have Jane and the babies board in the city—expensive, yes, but house rents were enormous, and a nurse could be boarded with other servants at half-rates. In case cholera broke out during the summer, the family would move to the north shore. The Chicago & Milwaukee Railroad ran trains out to Waukegan, thirty miles away, where pure air blew in from the lake all summer. If no cholera developed, Ray hoped to buy a house close enough to the office for him to walk down town, but he realized that the city was growing so fast that this might be impossible. He wrote Jane that his *sine qua non* would be a "parlour and bed room."

Planning, inspecting available houses, and working furiously on editorials, Charles Ray slept in the office and ate his meals at the Tremont House, which was already becoming the headquarters for Republicans visiting Chicago. Medill, a sharp businessman, bustled in and out of the office, watching all details of purchases and expenses. He eliminated duplication of work in the counting room and cut $80 a week from the $700 budget. Ray drew his salary and watched profits grow. In every letter east he enclosed money, telling Jane to buy the best of clothes in order that she would make a good appearance in the city when she arrived. Profits from the business, he said, promised to exceed his salary. He invested in another $1000 insurance policy, payable to his wife, for the second baby. Now, at last, he felt able to support a family adequately. "A thousand for my successive young'uns," he wrote Jane. "How many thousand in all, before we get through—eh?"

The *Tribune's* first problem with its readers came after the spring election. Ray and Medill did not change the paper's policy immediately and, true to tradition, backed the anti-foreign, antiliquor candidates—and lost. Next morning the Germans, Scandinavians, and Irish, all workers whom Ray hoped to bring under the *Tribune's* antislavery standard, paraded past the office with a giant banner draped in black lamenting the death of the *Chicago Tribune*. A brass band played the "Dead March." Ray watched from the window, then returned to his desk. Next day Chicagoans read in the paper:

The *Chicago Tribune* is not dead. If not now, the principles which it supports will by and by be triumphant. We may endure the mortification of a hundred other defeats. The crepe may be borne by our door ninety and nine times, but sooner or later the victory will perch on the banner we carry aloft. The Almighty has ordained it.

Charles Ray made it a point never to back down, once the paper had taken a stand. However, it was noticeable that in the issues which followed this incident less space and prominence were given to temperance and anti-Catholic editorials. Instead, Ray served his readers dispatches from Washington and national news comments. His vigorous language attracted attention, and readers forgot old controversies as they read Ray's vituperative editorials. He referred to President Pierce as "a poor, weak, vacillating proslavery tool." "Let the heroic band of Republicans in Washington stand as firm as the slave-power," he cried. "There is a power above the law, the spirit of the people. Let them manifest a national bravery, as firm as the eternal hills."

The old *Tribune's* cold-water editors had never written with such positiveness. Chicagoans understood Ray's language, and the paper's circulation increased. One day the tall figure of Abraham Lincoln climbed the long flight of stairs and asked to "see Doctor Ray." Medill remembered him later as a figure with "absurdly long" legs and enormous hands and feet, who carried in one hand a carpet bag three or four feet long and so deep that, tall as he was, it barely cleared the floor. The lanky Springfield lawyer took a leather purse from his pocket, untied the strap, counted out four dollars, and asked to have his name added to the paper's list of subscribers. "I like your paper," he said. "I didn't like it before you boys took hold of it; it was too much of a know-nothing sheet."

This was exactly what Ray had thought and had hoped to correct. He had admired the magnaminity of this slab-sided lawyer from Springfield when he had withdrawn from the Senate race in favor of Lyman Trumbull. Now Lincoln was showing rare understanding of the political forces in the streets—a trait which Charles Ray possessed to a marked degree.

The hot summer weather in Chicago was almost stifling in the third-floor office. Occasional cool breezes from the lake refreshed the entire city but failed to reach inside the buildings. This was not a pleasant prospect for Jane, but the Rays had known hot weather in upper New York and also at Mackinaw in central Illinois. Surely Jane would know how to keep reasonably comfortable in a home across the river.

Houses were hard to find, however, and it was August 19, 1855, when he wrote her that he had finally leased a two-story frame building for $350 a year—dear, but worth it, as the house had running water and gaslights. The parlor and dining room were smaller than he liked, but there were enough sleeping rooms for the family and two servant girls. Located a quarter-mile from the lake, north of the river, and only half-a-mile from the office, it was close enough for Charles to come home for meals. Busy as he was with his editorial writing, he found time to buy furnishings, hair mattresses, pillows, and curtains. Every morning after his copy was delivered to the printers, he walked out to the new home, arranged furniture, and tacked down carpets on the floors.

In each letter to Jane he said that he hoped to be able to come for her and the family any day now. But always fresh news broke and he dared not desert his post. He warned Jane to be ready to travel the moment he arrived as he would be able to stay in the East only a day. August slipped by, but he could not leave until after the Illinois State Fair was held in Springfield on September 10-12. To this gathering of farmers politicians came from all over the state, and Ray wanted to give a firsthand account to *Tribune* readers. Immediately after the Fair closed he hoped that he would be able to go for Jane, but again business delayed him. A newspaperman's time was no more his own than a doctor's.

Autumn was tinting the leaves on the upper Delaware when Charles Ray rushed into Norwich and rushed out with Jane and the children. He had brought along a packet of *Tribunes*, and he pointed with pride to his name, which now appeared for the first time as editor, although he had been employed in that capacity all summer. Below the announcement was heartening news, something to make Jane very proud:

> We have the pleasure of informing the numerous friends and readers of the Tribune that its present income is highly satisfactory; that its circulation is rapidly increasing; that its advertising was never so large as during the last quarter. The number of dailies now issued and sold is rising 3000; tri-weeklies 5000, and weeklies 4500.

v Kansas, 1856: The Beginning of Great Events

EARLY in February 1856, three men stopped far out on the frozen Mississippi River west of Quincy, Illinois. They were Martin F. Conway, George W. Smith, and James S. Emery, all fugitives from injustice in Kansas. One of them carried a jug of the type usually used by Missourians for whisky. Having crossed the ice into the jurisdiction of Illinois, they broke the jug, distributed the papers they had hidden in it and trudged into Quincy with the precious documents in their pockets.

They had come to Illinois to publicize the tyranny imposed by the slave-power on free-soil settlers in Kansas. Charles Ray had prophesied that Douglas' popular sovereignty would lead to tyranny, and these men brought the stories that he wanted for readers of the *Tribune*. The Kansas-Nebraska Act, promulgated by Douglas as a solution to the slavery problem, had succeeded only in aggravating it. Although the Little Giant had promised unrestricted immigration of both slaveholding and free settlers, the slave-power, headed by Senator David Rice Atchison, had organized to keep out free-soil men. Popular sovereignty had degenerated into the sovereignty of a few squatters who took the law into their own hands. Slavery advocates in Missouri had harried free-state immigrants who traveled the roads. Ferrymen were said to have staked cows at their docks and refused passage to travelers who called the animals "keows," Northern pronunciation.

In November 1854, when the time had come for the first

territorial election, proslavery Missourians had crossed into Kansas by hundreds to vote into office a proslavery legislature. According to reports which reached Chicago, the ballot-box stuffing had been disgraceful. In the seventh district 604 votes were cast, but three months later the place had only fifty-three resident voters. In the eleventh district 245 votes were counted, but in February 1855, this district had only twenty-four voters. In Leavenworth, with only three or four houses erected, seventy-five or a hundred Missourians had surrounded the polls and let none except proslavery men vote. Thus by giving lip service to democracy, dictators were taking charge. The *Chicago Tribune's* editor determined to print the facts—or what reached his office as facts. The time had come to educate the masses to the threatening menace.

The outrages had not stopped with ballot-box stuffing. The fraudulently elected legislature had refused to seat legally elected members who were known to be antislavery. This had disgusted Conway, a South Carolina-born member. He resigned and, with two companions, hid the incriminating documents in the jug and came to Illinois. Known as Young Man Eloquent, he decided to devote his talents to exposing the dictators' plot. Charles Ray could be counted on to help him fight, in the pages of the *Tribune*, for honest government in the territory.

George W. Smith, one of the men who arrived in Illinois with Conway, was a close associate of the editor of the Kansas *Herald of Freedom*—a newspaper published in Ohio before its editor left his old home. Smith had taken an active part in the free-state cause, had been chairman of the great protest meeting at Big Springs, and had, therefore, been singled out by slaveholders as a dangerous man. The slave-power had no intention of permitting freedom of the press in Kansas, and this man brought more ammunition for Charles Ray's *Tribune*.

The third man, J. S. Emery, had gone to Kansas with the

first organized party of free-soilers and had been a delegate to the Big Springs Convention. The proslavery legislature had ignored this demonstration of popular will and had proceeded to pass a slave code for Kansas which abridged freedom of speech and the press. The death penalty was imposed for helping a slave insurrection by either printed or spoken encouragement. A fine of $500 might be imposed on anyone who refused to help apprehend a fugitive slave. Persons convicted of violating the Fugitive Slave Act or refusing to take an oath to uphold it were disfranchised, and the sheriff was empowered to exclude certain people from jury duty in cases that involved slavery. Since no period of residence was specified as necessary for voters, outsiders could always come to Kansas and swing any election.

Democracy had come to this plight in order that slavery might be fixed on Kansas, and the slaveholders obviously planned to use this pattern to extend slavery to the Pacific. Atchison had admitted as much in a letter to that other sponsor of the Kansas-Nebraska Act, Robert M. T. Hunter. There might be no freedom of the press in Kansas, but Charles Ray, through his *Tribune*, could assure his readers that it still existed in Chicago and that he dared exercise it to stop the encroaching despotism of slavery from being imposed on the entire nation.

In Kansas the free-state settlers had not submitted without protest to the abridgment of their constitutional rights. While statutes limiting freedom of the press and of speech were being passed against them, they had built a concrete fort in their largest town, Lawrence, and had armed themselves with Sharps rifles. In meeting after meeting they repudiated the "Bogus" Legislature and its oppressive laws. Some resolved on open rebellion. Others, more modest, suggested solving the situation by the more peaceable means of a state convention at which a free-state constitution might be drawn up and submitted to Congress, by-passing the proslavery legislature. Emery had been accredited to this assembly as well as to the Big Springs Convention.

Ray had seen the trouble coming. Already he had prepared his readers for this situation. Before the three Kansas envoys arrived, the *Tribune*, on January 7, 1856, had summoned a mass meeting in South Market Hall in Chicago. To get workingmen behind this crusade, Ray captioned the call with: "Laborers of Chicago, it is your turn now to be felt. The hand which seeks to enslave Kansas would fetter you."

At this meeting the whole ugly history of Kansas was recounted. The audience was told how free-state settlers had assembled last September to form a government of the majority of settlers. Shortly thereafter a proslavery man had killed a free-stater in a quarrel over a claim boundary, and then had fled to the protection of the proslavery government. Proslavery sheriff Samuel J. Jones had arrested the murdered man's friend, Jacob Branson, witness to the quarrel. The free-state mob had released Branson, and the sheriff had appealed to the governor for militia to enforce the laws. The governor had issued the call, but only a handful had responded, since the majority of the militia sympathized with the free-state cause. Then the slave-power had sent the Missouri militia, an army with cannon and troops of horses, led by David Rice Atchison, ex-senator and powerful politician in Washington. This proslavery tycoon had arrived with his column to override popular will. Yet he had done so with the innocent declaration that he was only coming to enforce the laws—the old dictator's hypocrisy! His term of office had expired, but he continued to be known as "Senator Atchison."

The free-state settlers, claiming that they were not responsible for the action of the little mob that had released Branson, had congregated in Lawrence to defend themselves. This was in December 1855, just a month before the three refugees had left Kansas with the incriminating papers in the jug. Among those embattled settlers had been a tall, gaunt man named John Brown, associate of Gerrit Smith in the Adirondack Negro colony. Now he was accompanied by his stalwart sons. Each wore a pistol in his belt and a cutlass at his side. In his hand each carried a pole surmounted by a bayonet. No patriots at Bunker Hill had stood with more determination.

Senator Atchison's Missouri invaders had stopped four miles from Lawrence and encamped, hoping to starve the patriots. During the siege a proslavery Missouri patrol had killed a free-state settler who was riding from Lawrence to his claim. The man's two companions had escaped. An appeal for intervention had been made to Governor Shannon, who came unwillingly to the scene of action, inspected the free-state line and ordered the Missourians to return to their own state. He, like his predecessor, Governor Andrew H. Reeder, saw that the majority of the Kansas settlers were free-state men, and he refused to be a party to dominating them by force of arms. Then the Missouri proslavery machine threatened the governor himself, and Shannon was forced to take refuge in the free-state lines.

Shortly after this so-called Wakarusa War, a vote had been taken on the free-state settlers' constitution, which was ratified by a substantial majority. Conway, Smith, and Emery had decided to take a record of all the facts east to get aid for freedom in Kansas. They knew that they could not cross Missouri in a buggy without being spied upon and that they would be roughly treated if the nature of their errand were known. Smith had solved the problem of smuggling out the documents.

"Boys, I've hit it," he said. "In Missouri everybody carries a *jug*. There a jug never excites suspicion. Put the papers in jugs with corncob stoppers and they'll be safe." With this precaution they had made the trip to Illinois successfully and now, with Ray's aid, began organizing a national committee to send relief—and more freedom-loving settlers—to Kansas.

The *Tribune* entered eagerly into the campaign. The editor soon announced that $2000 had been raised to help make Kansas free. He sent a letter to George Washington Brown's *Herald of Freedom* stating:

> We will send more and when spring comes you may look for a large number of emigrants who will handle an axe or a Sharpe's rifle as the occasion may require. Though the heavens fall or the Union be rent in twain, Kansas shall not be cursed with slavery, is the voice of the North.

Ray printed a copy of his letter in the *Tribune* and stated in an article:

> Whenever the people of the North can be educated up to the point of resolutely saying to the slaveholders, and backing up what they say, "thus far shall your accursed system go but no farther, dissolve the Union if you dare," then and never until then will the aggressions and the outrages of slavery cease.

Along with this bold language, accounts appeared in the paper about slaves escaping across the Ohio River on the ice—the Uncle Tom incident in real life. In another news note a mother was reported to have cut the throat of her child to save it from being dragged back into slavery. Ray also reprinted a platform of principles adopted by the Chicago Republicans—there was as yet no state organization. Undoubtedly Ray authored it, for the style is his. Note the following:

> United by a common resolve to maintain Right against Wrong [Ray admitted no trimming on the institution of slavery], and believing in the determination of a virtuous and intelligent people to sustain justice, we declare:
>
> 1. That governments are instituted among men to secure the inalienable rights of Life, Liberty and the Pursuit of Happiness.

2. That the mission of the Republican Party is to maintain the Liberties of the People, the Sovereignty of the States, and the Perpetuity of the Union.

3. That the Federal Government being one of limited powers derived wholly from the Constitution, its agents should construe those powers strictly and never exercise a doubtful authority—always inexpedient and dangerous.

4. That if the plain Jeffersonian policy [Ray was obviously still a Democrat] were carried out, the Federal Government would relieve itself of all responsibility for the existence of Slavery, which Republicanism insists it should, and means it *shall do*.

Charles Ray maintained, as Lincoln would do later, that the South had revived the slavery controversy after it was presumably put to rest by the Compromise of 1820 and the later one of 1850 which applied to the territory acquired from Mexico. It had now become the paramount national issue. Ray urged that a committee be appointed with members from all parts of the state to organize the Republican Party and to hold a state convention, as was being done this year in Ohio, Indiana, Wisconsin, and Vermont.

The *Chicago Times*, a Democratic sheet claiming the foreign vote, tried to offset the enthusiasm being aroused by the *Tribune* with a story claiming that the *Tribune* editor was a member of the Know-Nothing lodge. Ray's *Tribune* had been Know-Nothing, true enough, but from the beginning Ray had determined to get the foreign vote for the Republicans. He was still sure that he could do this by hammering at the slave-power's usurpation of democratic government—certainly a more serious menace to the country than the Irish and German immigrants. Reckoning Kansas as the epitome of the proslavery cabal's tactics, he wrote:

If we disappoint any of our readers, by the space we devote to the affairs of Kansas, we beg them to remember, that just now we are at the beginning of great events of which that Territory is to be the theatre; and that a CIVIL WAR for the extension of Slavery and the subjugation of a free people, is a danger most imminent and pressing. . . . We wish the people to be fully informed of the purposes of the Slave Power, and the means it is using to make its purposes effective,—to the end, that, when the hour comes in which they must act, they may act intelligently and as becomes men who have a righteous cause to serve.

Charles Ray realized that the American people—any busy people—might be negligent in protecting their inheritance of freedom. Constantly they must be warned of the threat ahead, taught to see the danger and to organize against it. Yet all his efforts to form a new party outside Chicago had elicited only a slight response. He had seen Owen Lovejoy fail too. That preacher-politician had been unable to fire the hearts of assembled farmers and politicians into forming the new party at the Illinois State Fair in Springfield last fall, and Lovejoy was as eloquent a speaker as the state possessed.

An ordinary newspaper editor interested only in his job might have given up hope and devoted his energies to improving the paper along other lines. Ray, however, believed that there must be a better way to start the much-needed political party. Then one day he read an editorial in the downstate *Morgan Journal* which appealed to him. The editor, Paul Selby, suggested that instead of rallying politicians and independent voters as had been done in the past, all interested newspaper editors should meet at Decatur to decide on the best united action against the slave-power. This seemed a capital idea, and Charles Ray decided to attend.

The date was set for February 22, 1856, Washington's Birthday—suitable, Ray thought, for a new protest against tyranny. The day of departure was cold and stormy, with water from Lake Michigan freezing on the pilings along the beaches. Cab horses slopped through the snow in the streets, and it was good to get on the cars and huddle near a stove. Among the passengers Ray recognized a man he knew, George Schneider, editor of the *Staats Zeitung*, who was also going to the convention. The two talked over the problems ahead as the train lurched out of town, left the lake shore, and trundled south across the yellow and white prairies. Schneider was a bookish man who peered uncertainly through little gold-rimmed spectacles. His hair was receding and his beard was aggressive. His main interest in the present break-up of political parties was to protect the rights of his readers, the Chicago Germans. He was sure that they were antislavery at heart and that they would join the Republicans if assured that the organization had no connection with the antiforeign Know-Nothing Party. Ray agreed with him, but he knew that many of the dissatisfied people who had split from the Whigs and Democrats were Know-Nothings and that their vote was large. How far would the assembled editors dare go with this precarious conflict of interests?

Ray and Schneider got off the train at Decatur. A cold wind made them turn up their coat collars. They climbed into a hack bound for the Cassell House. People everywhere were talking about the storm; no one seemed to sense that a meeting great in the history of the nation was about to open. Farmers slipped past the hack in wagon boxes on sled runners. Stylish cutters darted through the streets with a jingle of merry bells and a sparkle of feminine smiles under fur bonnets and paisley shawls. In the lobby of the Cassell House Ray met a few editors sitting around the stove. The men all shook hands, looked through the frosted windows, and complained that the weather had prevented many ardent editors from coming. Paul Selby, a tall, studious man, suggested that the few who were present had better meet and form an organization. Selby was promptly elected chairman, and he appointed a committee to draft a suitable platform for the editorial campaign. He named Dr. Ray, Mr. Schneider, and four others. The six men withdrew to a separate room. Ray was elected chairman and the group set to work. All agreed that they must not be labeled abolitionists. On the other hand, the slave-power must not be allowed to rule the United States by setting aside the country's democratic principles. George Schneider reminded the committee that the Germans' rights must be respected if they were to join the cause. In the midst of the discussion there was a knock at the door, and the tall figure of Abraham Lincoln appeared. The lawyer had driven over from Springfield with friends. Indeed several more people had joined the convention out in the main room. Lincoln said that he, as a Whig politician, was very much interested in the convention's platform, as upon it might depend the entire plan to organize a new party.

Charles Ray watched Lincoln closely. The man's shrewd deference to Lyman Trumbull's ambition for a seat in the Senate in 1855 had impressed him mightily. Ray could not forget, however, that Lincoln had refused to take part in the Springfield meeting in 1854, although his law partner, William H. Herndon, had attended. Since then the development of the new party had progressed in state after state. The slave-power's lawless effort to take over Kansas had stimulated its growth amazingly. Now if Lincoln, the cautious Whig, had come to join the movement it must be succeeding.

The exact authorship of the platform finally drawn cannot be determined. Paul Selby said later that it was written by Lincoln and Ray, with George Schneider adding the provision for religious tolerance and maintenance of the naturalization laws. On the slavery issue the platform protested the Kansas-Nebraska Act (a direct slam at the Democratic Party's champion, Stephen A. Douglas), insisted that the Missouri Compromise prohibiting slavery above the 36°-30′ parallel be maintained, and reassured all slaveholders that their property right would not be disturbed where it now existed.

The assembled editors accepted this platform and agreed to promote it in their columns. The meeting then resolved to call a state convention in Bloomington on May 29, 1856, to organize an Anti-Nebraska Party. They were not yet ready to accept the name "Republican" being adopted by the new party in other states. The editors agreed that their first move was to test their readers' reactions to the platform for two months and, if it should be acceptable to them, to organize the party around it.

In the evening the little group sat down to dine together in the Cassell House. Charles Ray and several other editors delivered speeches. Lincoln was called upon. Dr. Ray had not heard him speak since the old temperance days. Lincoln began by apologizing for being present among the editors, saying that the situation reminded him of a story about a coarse-featured horseman who met a fair lady on a bridle path. The man reined his horse to one side to let the fair creature pass. To his surprise, the handsome lady reined up her mount also. She looked at him and said, "Well, for land sake, you are the homeliest man I ever saw."

"Yes, madam," he replied, "but I can't help it."

"No, I suppose not," she replied, "but you might stay at home." That, Lincoln concluded, was the way he felt in this group of editors. He might have stayed home.

Ray, still undecided about Lincoln's political stature, admitted to himself that the fellow had a knack for catching an audience's attention. The tall lawyer followed his joke by outlining the purpose of the new party as he understood it. Success, he reiterated, depended on enlisting the dissatisfied members in both the Whig and Democratic parties. Lincoln said further that he had been approached as the new party's possible candidate for governor. He wished to thank his sponsors for the compliment, but he believed that his nomination would be a great mistake. He said:

If I should be chosen, the Democrats would say it was nothing more than an attempt to resurrect the dead body of the old Whig Party. I would secure the vote of that party and no more and our defeat would follow as a matter of course. But I can suggest a name that will secure not only the old Whig vote, but enough Anti-Nebraska Democrats to give us the victory. That name is Col. William H. Bissell.

Again Lincoln had shown canny foresight in deferring to others.

Applauding with the other editors, Ray watched as he clapped. Yes, this man Lincoln had the making of a real politician. But Bissell was much better known. He had proved his popularity in the antislavery cause and would be an excellent man to launch the new party.

Dr. Ray returned to Chicago confident that history was being made. He cleaned up the accumulated mail on his desk at the *Tribune* office, then turned his attention to organizing the Chicago Historical Society and was elected its corresponding secretary.

On March 1, 1856, the *Tribune* admonished readers: "To your posts, men of Illinois! Organize and prepare for action. ACT in '56 as the Fathers acted in '76, and so help save the Republic and its liberties."

Out in Kansas, on March 4, the free-state government met and approved a memorial addressed to Congress asking for admission as a state. Here was a solution to the Kansas trouble if President Pierce had the courage to act against the slave-power. He and Douglas had both professed to believe in popular sovereignty. The people had expressed their approval of the free-state constitution. Did Pierce and Douglas dare refuse the free-staters' request and ally themselves with the slave-power? Charles Ray watched the Washington dispatches for a report on their action and counted the days until the Bloomington Convention on May 29. As he waited rumors came to him of a plot to ruin Bissell and the germinating Republican organization in Illinois. Scheming Douglas Democrats—"Nebraskals," Ray called them—had arranged with delegates to the Know-

Nothing Convention to nominate Bissell as their candidate for governor, thus putting the antiforeign taint on him and preventing his nomination by the Republicans—a sly intrigue. Ray had learned about the plot through a German at Belleville named Engelmann.

Ray contemplated what next to do. Finally he decided to attend the Know-Nothing Convention himself and mingle with the delegates, explaining to them that the nomination of Bissell was a scheme concocted by their worst enemies, the Democrats, merely to ruin the Republicans and the Know-Nothings too. The only result the Know-Nothings could hope to achieve by nominating Bissell was a victory for the Democrats.

The Know-Nothing delegates saw the logic in Ray's words and dropped Bissell, leaving the way clear for the impending Bloomington Convention.

VI Lincoln's Lost Speech

As the time for the Bloomington Convention approached, Charles Ray insisted that the Kansas atrocities must be the battle cry for the Republican Party. Nothing could be more important than stopping the slow encroachment of the slave dictatorship! On May 20, 1856, he wrote:

> Does the reader say, the strife rages only in the small Territory of Kansas—that it is afar off—that the combatants are a handful of men? Let him turn to our own history, and answer his own statements. Who stood at Thermopylae? Who caused the Reformation? . . . Who made Bunker Hill sacred? The "handful"—the few, have done earth's greatest deeds.

The properly approved free-state constitution for Kansas was taken to Washington by James Henry Lane and Charles Robinson, the senator and governor elected by the extralegal free-state settlers. The whole nation watched to see what the President would do now. Would he recommend that the squatters' will be accepted, or would he bow again to the slave-power? Joe Medill went from the *Chicago Tribune* to report. Ray employed James Redpath, a young Scotsman in Kansas, to send dispatches from the front.

Redpath, a boy wonder, was skilled in shorthand and was able to record details faster than most reporters. He was dedicated to the abolition cause, and if he overstated the Kansas atrocities to spice his dispatches no one in the East was the wiser. Redpath reported also for Horace Greeley's *New York Tribune* and was credited with inventing the name "Border Ruffian" which Greeley used to such good advantage as a description of the Missouri slavemen. According to Redpath's accounts, which had been coming in since January, the civil war had continued since the Wakarusa War. Redpath described as a common occurrence the finding of free-state settlers' bodies along the road or beside their burning cabins. Although his stories were exaggerated, they held some truth, and no stretch of the imagination could excuse the slavocracy's usurpation of the Kansas government. Both sides might be guilty of lawlessness, but of the two the slavocrats were certainly the worse offenders.

The South's case was blackened further by the reception of Robinson and Lane in Washington. Senator Douglas and President Pierce had evinced a belief in squatter sovereignty as the cure for the slavery problem, but when the squatters came with a free-state constitution both of them hedged. The proslavery interests must not be alienated.

Charles Ray had watched Stephen A. Douglas in action before. The Little Giant always had an indirect and convincing answer. Now in Medill's dispatches Ray read that Douglas was running true to form. First he complained that Kansas had insufficient population for statehood. Many more settlers were known to be on the road from the South. Wait until they arrived and cast their votes, he suggested, then admit the state according to the majority's desire. Next Douglas noticed that some alterations had been made in the constitution presented to Congress, and he declared the entire document a possible forgery. Thus the Little Giant showed himself to be a *little* giant indeed, and the disappointed squatters' representatives returned to Kansas.

The report of Southern immigration interested Ray more than Douglas' devious performance. A steamboatload of settlers commanded by "Colonel" Jefferson Buford was said to be steaming up the Mississippi. Ray sent a correspondent down on the Illinois Central to intercept them at Cairo and report their appearance and character. A dispatch from this correspondent described them as a motley crew of 400 "despicable ruffians and cut-throats." Most of them were from Alabama and South Carolina. They carried state banners instead of plowshares and, altogether, seemed more military than agricultural. A fine state of affairs this, with Southern states augmenting the Missouri army to subjugate Kansas!

The arrival of the Southern reinforcements was greeted by the Missouri slave-power with a renewed display of excesses. Congress had sent out a committee to investigate the alleged civil war, and it arrived in time to see many of the chief witnesses indicted or subpoenaed for a hearing on charges of treason to be held before a proslavery grand jury. Redpath reported the hearing to be a scheme to frighten the principal free-state leaders away from the country and prevent them from testifying before the congressional committee. One of the committeemen, John Sherman, talked the ugly situation over with the free-state's governor, Charles Robinson, and urged him to leave before he was served or arrested. Sherman gave him a report of the committee's findings, which, though incomplete, were already incriminating enough. He told Robinson to deliver them to Nathaniel Banks, speaker of the United States House of Representatives. Assassins, he said, might prevent a completed report from being issued.

Robinson and his wife drove to the Missouri River and engaged steamboat passage to the East. At Lexington, Missouri, the ship was boarded by a Missouri sheriff and Robinson was taken off and charged with escaping from an indictment for treason. Mrs. Robinson stayed in the stateroom and arrived in Illinois with the partly finished testimony. She planned to lay her case before Dr. Charles Ray and then to go on to see Salmon P. Chase.

Former Governor Reeder, who had been removed by

Pierce because he insisted on having the majority in Kansas rule, braved the threat of conviction for treason and appeared before the investigating committee. While he was testifying, a deputy marshal of the proslavery machine tried to arrest him. Reeder grasped the butt of his pistol and claimed immunity from arrest on the ground that he was under subpoena for the congressional hearing. The baffled officer left for further instructions. Before he could return, the ex-governor had fled to Kansas City, shaved his beard, dyed his hair, disguised himself as a workman, and escaped to a steamboat bound for Illinois, eager to bear witness against the highhanded methods of the slave-power. If the Bloomington Convention or any other anti-Democratic convention wanted to hear his story, he would be glad to speak.

Robinson's and Reeder's stories were not the only ones that would inflame all believers in democratic government. Defiance of slavocracy's dictatorship in Kansas had not ended with their flight. Redpath sent accounts of new outrages which were occurring constantly. The proslavery sheriff, Samuel J. Jones, emboldened by the arrival of the 400 settlers from Alabama and South Carolina, decided to demonstrate his authority over the free-state settlers. He attempted to arrest the participants in the Branson rescue, was repeatedly stopped by free-state mobs, and finally wounded with a pistol ball. Redpath likened the Kansans to patriots and redcoats on Boston Common. The free-state government claimed rightly that it did not sanction these acts of resistance, but the border slave-power refused to accept this claim and called the militia in central and western Missouri to enforce proslavery laws in Kansas. Once more Senator Atchison rode across the border at the head of a column. The recently arrived companies from Alabama and South Carolina marched with the militia. The congressional investigating committee, on its way back to the East, watched this new army streaming into Kansas to uphold the slaveowners' laws and added this last bit of evidence to their report. James Redpath sent all the details to the *Chicago Tribune* with this conclusion: "There will in all probability be a battle in a day or two between the men of the North and the minions of the Slave Power in Kansas."

The whole nation waited in suspense, and down in Washington Charles Sumner announced that he planned to address the Senate on the "Crime against Kansas." On May 19, 1856, he rose to speak. Joe Medill, in the crowded gallery, took notes. The day was stiflingly hot. With bitter language, Sumner reviewed the many violations of democracy perpetrated by the slave-power in Kansas. He recited in detail all the murders committed for political ascendancy. He was particularly bitter against Senators Douglas and Atchison, who had sponsored the Kansas-Nebraska Bill. Then he turned on Senator Andrew Pickens Butler from South Carolina and boldly accused him of loving the hideous institution of slavery—saying that "though ugly to others [it] is always lovely to him; though polluted in the sight of the world, is chaste in his sight."

Congressman Preston S. Brooks, from South Carolina, a cousin of the senator's, determined to flog Sumner for his insolence. With a companion he skulked around the Capitol for two days. Finally he walked into the Senate Chamber, where Sumner was writing at his desk. Raising a gutta-percha cane, he beat the senator over the head until Sumner fell to the floor. The congressman's Southern constituents cheered his act and sent him dozens of new canes. The Northern newspapers could not have asked for a better example of the temper of the slavocrats.

With the news of this incident came word from Kansas that the Missouri army, with the Alabama and South Carolina contingents, had marched into Lawrence. Meeting no resistance, they had destroyed the hotel—the best in Kansas—pillaged the stores, and marched back to Missouri. Redpath sent Ray details of the destruction lurid enough to satisfy the most sensation-minded reader. Then, to crown accounts of the cumulating abuses, the Kansas refugees promised to appear in person and tell their own stories at Bloomington.

Stories of the Kansas outrages were printed in the newspapers which members of the Republican Convention stuffed into their pockets as they boarded trains and stagecoaches for Bloomington. Dr. Ray had been elected one of the seventeen delegates, Whig and Democrat, from Chicago. On the train with him rode former Congressman Long John Wentworth, occupying two seats. Owner of the *Democrat*, this giant was now one of the wealthy men of Chicago. In another seat was Assemblyman Isaac N. Arnold, perhaps the best of the city's attorneys. Also there were Charlie Wilson, boisterous *Journal* reporter, and George Schneider, the German editor. Ray had been working for over a month with the elected delegates, persuading them that the new party must denounce Know-Nothingism and seek the foreign vote. He was sure that a strong plank on this subject would win votes from the Germans, English, Protestant Irish, Scotch, and Scandinavians.

Joseph Medill, recently back from Washington, went to Bloomington to report for the *Tribune*, while Ray attended to his official duties as delegate. The *Daily Democratic Press* had sent John Locke Scripps. Excitement over the effort of the administration to take Kansas with armed force keyed everybody to emotional tenseness. All the reporters knew that they were about to witness the story of the decade.

The train arrived at Bloomington at 8:00 A. M. on May 29, 1856, a fine spring morning with the smell of fresh-plowed soil in the air. The railroad platform was crowded with bearded men in tall hats and frock coats. Women in shawls and bonnets waved handkerchiefs to the new arrivals as they descended from the cars. Along the street leading to the Pike House, convention headquarters, politicians greeted friends, arranged for future conferences, and speculated on the political consequences of the Sumner caning in Washington. A crowd filled the street around the Pike House, and vociferous orators spoke almost continually from one of the three galleries across the front of the hotel. A grand stairway, now packed with people, led from the street to the lobby on the second floor.

Dr. Ray pressed his way through the crowd. Over broadcloth shoulders he saw the face of Richard Oglesby, a former Kentuckian from Decatur, Illinois, who had come back from the Mexican War with a commission and back from California without having found gold. Almost out of sight in the press of men stood Richard Yates, the political gamecock with a comb of curly hair. As Whig congressman he had voted against the Kansas-Nebraska Bill and was eager to repudiate it and the party which sponsored it. Then there was young John G. Nicolay with his Hungarian accent. He had already worked himself into ownership of the *Pittsfield Free Press*. These country editors would be the backbone of the new movement.

Orville H. Browning, defeated state senator, was there too. He had seemed reluctant to bolt the Whig Party but evidently had made up his mind at last. Pugnacious little Billy Herndon appeared with his tall, smiling law partner, Abraham Lincoln. Ray also saw elderly Stephen T. Logan, an ex-partner of Lincoln's. The wizened little man's long scrawny neck was devoid of either stock or tie, yet he was one of the best-paid lawyers in the state. His voice was shrill and querulous, but his gigantic intellect made him a leader of the bar. His mop of frowzy white hair above deep-set contemplative eyes and sour, turned-down mouth were noticeable in any crowd.

Charles Ray missed the long, studious face of Paul Selby, who had originally suggested calling this convention and, of all others, should be here. Ray asked about him and learned that the poor fellow had been waylaid by political opponents in Jacksonville and pommeled so that he was unable to attend. Too bad, for this assembly included the state's most talented politicians. Many more of them had come than were expected, and all were apparently eager to form a new party opposed to the proslavery wing of the Democrats.

Elbowing through the crowd and greeting old friends, Ray heard that Governor Reeder, the fugitive from Kansas, had arrived safely and would tell his experiences with the Border Ruffians. As a Democratic appointee of President Pierce's, his remarks would carry great weight with the Democrats. James S. Emery, one of the three who had escaped from Kansas last January with the incriminating documents in the whisky jug, was scheduled to speak. He had been present when Senator Atchison supervised the sack of Lawrence, and he could be counted on to tell a harrowing story. Also in town was Mrs. Charles Robinson, a small, sweet-faced young woman with a lace collar around her sloping shoulders. Mrs. Robinson did not yet know her husband's fate after he had been taken from her on the Missouri River steamboat.

At 10:00 A. M. the convention assembled in Major's Hall. The room was packed almost to the point of suffocation. The temporary chairman appointed a committee to nominate permanent officers. These men retired to deliberate, and Emery was called upon to relate his Kansas experiences. The events were still fresh in his mind. He told how the Border Ruffians had formed in military ranks outside of Lawrence, their banners inscribed with the names of the Southern states from which they came. Like an army, with rumbling cannon, they marched into town, demanded the citizens' guns, looted the stores, and wrecked two newspaper offices, throwing the presses into the street and the type into the Kaw River. The Free State Hotel had been blown up, and the proslavery minions had marched away with books fluttering on their bayonets—flagrant usurpation beyond a doubt.

At the end of Emery's narration, the committee on nominations returned to the convention and offered the name of John M. Palmer as permanent chairman. Palmer was a recent candidate for the state senate on a non-party ticket—as William H.

Bissell had been in the congressional election—and he, too, had won. Such a nonpartisan was just the man to preside over this assembly, and the members elected him with a roar of approval. He was also delegated to attend the national Republican Convention to be held in Philadelphia.

The purpose of the Bloomington Convention was outlined by Orville H. Browning, Isaac N. Arnold, and other attorneys. Senator Douglas was denounced by all for betraying his trust and initiating the nefarious Kansas-Nebraska Bill. Then Mr. Leander Munsell of Edgar County nominated Congressman Bissell, Lincoln's choice, as the new party's candidate for governor of Illinois. This nomination was seconded. Finally George T. Brown, a fellow townsman of the nominee, asked permission to read a communication before the delegates voted on the nomination. Waving a folded sheet of paper for silence, Brown began. The letter was from Bissell himself. The candidate described his health as bad, though improving constantly. If he were nominated, Bissell wrote, he could not campaign actively. But "if, in view of these facts, the convention deem it proper to nominate me, I shall not decline the honor, though I say, in all candor, I prefer that the nomination should fall on another individual; and should that happen, you can rely upon my most zealous and cheerful efforts in his behalf."

After these words the entire convention rose to its feet and with nine long cheers approved Bissell's nomination. Chairman Palmer pronounced the vote unanimous. Next Richard Yates asked for the floor. In his Kentucky accents, he told the assembly of his voting against Douglas' measure in the House on that hectic dawn two years ago. The demonstration before him now vindicated his decision at that time, and he felt that the selection of Bissell as candidate for governor augured well for the new party's success. The convention then recessed until two o'clock in the afternoon.

At the appointed time, the delegates reassembled to hear other impassioned orations. Nominations were made for the state ticket, and Orville Browning read the report of the resolutions committee. In a stirring speech he urged all Clay-Whigs to concur in the resolutions, pronounced to be basically the same as those written by Charles Ray and Abraham Lincoln three months earlier. These resolutions accused the Democratic administration of devoting all its energies to the propagation and extension of slavery and the suppression of freedom of speech and the press and of planning ultimately to change the form of government. The new party pledged itself to uphold the principles of Washington and Jefferson and to restore to Congress its constitutional right to prohibit slavery in the territories.

A motion for unanimous approval of these resolutions passed with a cheer, and Dr. Charles Ray saw his earlier work approved. Chairman Palmer immediately announced that former Governor Reeder would tell his outrageous Kansas experiences that evening in the courthouse square. Next Owen Lovejoy spoke for half an hour, disappointing some who hoped for a more vindictive discourse. Finally Lincoln was called on for a speech. It was getting late, but no one in the packed house stirred. Dr. Ray watched the tall, angular man stalk to the rostrum. His face seemed to reflect the full significance of the day. This assembly was forming a new political party on the premise that slavery must be restricted until it would eventually die out in the United States. Such a premise might precipitate a civil war. If it did, many of the men here assembled would die in uniform. Ray noticed Lincoln's high falsetto voice as he began to speak. Soon the audience forgot everything but the magic of his ideas. Reporters dropped their pencils, failing to record his words, and sat entranced until Lincoln stopped.

This oration has been called Lincoln's Lost Speech—perhaps his most inspired. No effort to reconstruct it has been successful. The emotional memories of those who heard it retained only fragments. George Schneider remembered that Lincoln warned the people against thoughtless violence. "I'll tell you what we'll do," he quoted Lincoln as saying, "We'll wait until November and then shoot paper ballots at them." Thomas Henderson, a delegate, recalled that Lincoln had raised his long arms toward the ceiling, electrifying the audience by shouting: "We do not intend to dissolve the Union, nor do we intend to let you dissolve it."

John Locke Scripps, of the *Chicago Democratic Press*, reported:

> Never has it been our fortune to listen to a more eloquent and masterly presentation of a subject. I shall not mar any of its fine proportions or brilliant passages by attempting even a synopsis of it. Mr. Lincoln must write it out and let it go before all the people. For an hour and a half he held the assemblage spellbound by the power of his argument, the intense irony of his invective, and the deep earnestness and fervid brilliancy of his eloquence. When he concluded, the audience sprang to their feet and cheer after cheer told how deeply their hearts had been touched, and their souls warmed up to a generous enthusiasm.

A vice-president of the convention, John H. Bryant of Princeton, Illinois, wrote his brother, William Cullen Bryant, that this impassioned meeting, with its firsthand reports of the Kansas outrages, had goaded the people to frenzy. Members of all parties, he said, have united "to save our heritage of liberty from destruction, and to drive back the all-grasping power of slavery to its acknowledged bounds."

Charles Ray had also been deeply moved. As Lincoln stopped speaking, he watched the assembled politicians. Darkness fell and they still seemed reluctant to leave. Finally Burton C. Cook of Chicago broke the spell by giving a humorous speech. With a laugh and final cheer, the audience filed out into the evening twilight, into the cool breath of the prairie springtime with tree frogs chirping in the darkness. Ray was sure that the party had found in Abraham Lincoln a matchless standard-bearer who would be invaluable in rallying voters to the party.

After supper six or eight hundred people assembled in the courthouse square to hear Reeder relate his Kansas experiences. For three hours he described the slavocrat atrocities. He told how he had been abused for refusing to recognize illegal election returns until he had had to flee for his life dressed as a laborer, with a shovel and a clay pipe. His hair was still stained from the silver nitrate used in his disguise. Friends had rowed him out into the Missouri where he had boarded a down-river steamboat bound for the free state of Illinois. He had previously visited President Pierce in Washington, he said, and had told him the whole story but got no sympathy. The administration and the Democratic Party were hopelessly shackled to the proslavery chariot. This despotism must be overthrown or democracy would disappear in the United States.

Dr. Ray felt that the seed planted and cultivated by the *Tribune* was beginning to sprout. An informed people would prevent a usurpation of the democratic form of government. At midnight he boarded the train for Chicago. He had been elected a member of the state central committee of the new party, and henceforth his paper would have inside information on future activities. Thus the party and the paper might grow together, each helping the other. What was more, Charles Ray had made up his mind that Abraham Lincoln warranted pushing to the front—perhaps into the United States Senate.

VII The Election of Buchanan

EDITOR Ray scanned the newspapers to learn the popular reaction to the Bloomington Convention. Lincoln's Springfield seemed strangely cold to the new party and its platform. Southern Illinois, influenced by adjacent slave states, was frankly hostile to both. Ray determined to do everything in his power to change this sentiment and to arouse the people. Senator James Henry Lane of the extralegal free-state government of Kansas, who had escaped an indictment for treason, was in Chicago. Ray invited him to the *Tribune* office. The tall, spare, big-boned man was remarkably like Lincoln in build. His face was clean-shaven but leathery and deeply lined; his lips were stained slightly with tobacco. Lane, like Ray, had been a Democrat who deplored Pierce's subservience to the slave-power. Lane had a reputation for being able to move an audience to ecstasy much as Lincoln had done at Bloomington. He agreed to speak in Chicago, and Ray announced that a grand meeting of Republicans would be held at Metropolitan Hall on May 31.

Chicago was different from conservative downstate Illinois. The people were interested in reform politics and congregated by hundreds to hear Lane. All seats in the "Met" were taken and the aisles packed, so the presiding officers moved the crowd to the steps of the courthouse, where thousands could stand and listen in the street. Word had just been received from Missouri that the slavemen had placed cannon along the Missouri to turn back any free-state settlers who might come to the aid of the antislavery cause. One party of Illinoisans had been stopped. Their friends in Chicago advocated equipping gunboats to keep open the Missouri.

News of this civil war in Missouri brought the nation to the verge of hysteria. The Republican mass meeting in Chicago opened with the singing of patriotic songs. Then several orators expatiated about the outrages. Finally Senator Lane electrified the audience with his eloquence. He reminded the crowd that he was a veteran of the Mexican War and had fought to extend the privileges of American democracy into dictatorial Latin America. He described the heroes of that war, citing Illinois's own General J. J. Hardin, who had given his life for his country, and William H. Bissell, gubernatorial candidate, who had once been challenged to a duel by Jefferson Davis. "It did not occur to me [then]," he said pointedly, "that I should be indicted for treason because I loved liberty better than slavery."

Lane held up a copy of the statutes of Kansas and read carefully the laws abridging freedom of speech and the press which had been passed by the proslavery legislature. These enactments and the deaths of the free-state Kansas patriots who had protested them were chargeable directly to President Pierce, Lane said. He and his administration must be held accountable. Lane confessed that he had voted for the Kansas-Nebraska Bill, thinking that a fair contest between the North and the South would follow. He had not visualized the tyrannous usurpation of republican government to which the slave-power had stooped. Lane said also that as presidential elector from Indiana he had cast his ballot for Pierce but that he was now completely disillusioned.

Charles Ray watched the upturned faces. Never before had he seen an audience instilled with such rapt frenzy. Lincoln's "lost speech" at Bloomington had left the people in a trance. This speech keyed them to fighting fervor. Lane closed by calling for contributions to help defend American principles in Kansas. He asked for enlistments of men who would fight for right or would supply money to send others. In no time tall hats were brimming with bills and change. Workmen, highly paid in the fast-growing city, emptied their pockets; sailors tossed in their accumulated wages; newsboys, their pennies. Someone started the crowd singing the "Marseillaise." They marched away, filling the streets with the roar and roll of the revolutionary song. Ray's emotions were stirred by this popular demonstration of the people's determination to uphold time-worn American rights against a reactionary government. He turned to the *Tribune* building, climbed the two flights of dark stairs to his office, and wrote a long article for the paper. He prophesied that the meeting had inaugurated a new era in American history. The people, knowing at last the magnitude of the slavocracy's tyranny, would submit no longer.

"Senator" Lane traveled east to lecture to other audiences. The National Kansas Committee set to work in earnest to help settlers enter Kansas by a northern route across Iowa and thus circumvent the military forces in Missouri. Almost every county in northern Illinois held mass meetings to raise money for horses, wagons, and cattle to send to Kansas. Young men, farmers, and politicians volunteered to enlist with their guns and plows. All were determined to win the election of 1856 for the new Republican Party. Trainloads of emigrants with covered wagons on flat cars chuffed out of Chicago for the West.

On June 2, 1856, the Democratic National Convention met in Cincinnati. Delegates admitted that Franklin Pierce had been unsuccessful in his attempt to reconcile the slavocracy with the interests of Northern party members and nominated James Buchanan as a new compromise man.

On June 17 the Republicans met in Philadelphia for their first national convention. The illegal methods used in Kansas to perpetuate the Democratic Party promised to be the big issue of the presidential campaign ahead. Congressman John Sherman, fresh from his duties on the investigating committee in Kansas, mingled with the delegates, telling his experiences west of the Missouri. Several Kansans who were present at the sack of Lawrence perpetrated by the Missouri, Alabama, and South Carolina companies told about their experiences. Martin Conway, the slim, red-headed boy orator who had resigned from the "Bogus" Legislature, nominated John C. Frémont as the first presidential candidate of the Republican Party, and the delegates approved his nomination. Frémont was a popular hero known to schoolboys across the nation—schoolboys who were now casting their first ballots. His father-in-law was Thomas Hart Benton, whose enmity with David Rice Atchison, leader of the Missouri troops, was well known. For vice-president the name of Abraham Lincoln was offered, but he was soon voted down in favor of New Jersey's William L. Dayton. In a national gathering Lincoln was as yet unknown, but Charles Ray had made up his mind about the Illinoisan's ability and determined to sell him to the nation.

Lincoln began to spend much of his time campaigning for the Republican ticket. As the party grew stronger in various communities, he spoke at organization rallies, and Charles Ray reported the events with gusto. Invited to the village of Princeton in northern Illinois, Lincoln learned while driving north in the first week in July that a district convention had nominated Owen Lovejoy for Congress. He was dismayed over the selection of this rabid Congregational minister instead of his own personal friend, Leonard Swett, a calm and competent attorney, perhaps the most brilliant in the state. Lincoln believed that Republicans must not be considered wild-eyed radicals intent only on abolition and the overthrow of the Southern social system. To enlist Swett in their cause would do much to gain the support of the moderate liberals. Lincoln knew that crowds rallied to see and hear Lovejoy—the man who had taken a solemn oath over the body of his murdered brother to avenge his death. As a preacher, Lovejoy was immensely popular. He appealed to the emotions rather than to the intellect. Lincoln was familiar with his oratorical technique. At one meeting, when a proslavery mob had threatened his life if he dared speak, Lovejoy was reported to have stood up fearlessly and asked the mob to be a jury to decide a case he wished to put to them. This silenced the audience, and Lovejoy began in his soothing voice:

On a plantation, in the distant Southland, in the low miasmatic swamps, there was a woman. She was young, handsome, and under God's law had as much right to live and control her own actions as any of us. She was of one-eighth African and seven-eighths white blood, just like your blood and mine. The overseer of the plantation where she was held in bondage sought to persecute her because she would not assent to his advances. She escaped into the swamps. Bloodhounds were set on her trail. She boarded a little steamboat which plied on a small river which emptied into the great Father of Waters. In the fullness of time she landed at the first station in Illinois [name not given], and proceeded from station to station. Finally she arrived in Princeton. I myself, Owen Lovejoy, was the keeper of that station at Princeton. She came to my house hungry and told me her story. She was fairer than my own daughter, proud, tall and beautiful. She was naked, and I clothed her; she was hungry, and I gave her bread; she was penniless and I gave her money. She was unable to reach the next station and I sent her to it. So from station to station she crossed the Northland far from baying dogs on her trail, and out from under the shadow of the flag we love and venerate into Canada. Today she lives there a free and happy woman.

As Lovejoy reached the end of this simple recital, women sobbed and men swore. He lowered his eyes to his audience again and thundered:

"As you shall answer to God, what would you have done?

Get up. Rise, men, and give your verdict." It goes without saying that Lovejoy's emotionalism had won the crowd.

Lincoln realized that such impassioned oratory drew tears from audiences and votes for the party. He soon changed his mind about accepting Lovejoy as the congressional candidate, and decided what Ray had already learned—that a crusade must be emotional. When Lincoln returned to Springfield, he expressed his views in a letter to Henry C. Whitney: "It turned me blind when I first heard Swett was beaten, and Lovejoy nominated; but after much anxious reflection, I really believe it best to let it stand."

In August Lincoln left the state to speak at Kalamazoo, Michigan. The concourse was tremendous, with eight bands in a gigantic parade. Orators at four rostrums all spoke at once—a four-ring circus—and newspaper correspondents could attend only the most important gatherings. Lincoln, according to reports reaching Ray, reiterated the *Tribune* doctrine that slavery was the great issue of the campaign. He appealed to members of all parties who loved liberty, to "strike and strike again! So sure as God lives, the victory shall be yours."

News from Kansas helped the slavery crusade. Redpath and other journalists traveled west with the overland emigrants through Iowa. The Democratic administration had ordered the United States Army to stop them on the border. Some were halted, but on the unfenced prairie many got through. At every wagon camp the prospective settlers preached to one another about the tyranny of the slave-power and what they intended to do to it. Arriving in Kansas, they quickly destroyed the three proslavery blockhouses—Forts Franklin, Saunders, and Titus—that had been built around Lawrence. Colonel James A. Harvey, with a battalion of Chicagoans, made a name for himself by participating. John Brown and his sons were also prominent in the fighting. Missouri newspapers along the border called on their proslavery readers to cross the state line and restore the old order. "Civil

War has begun," they shouted. The South was implored to send reinforcements.

Charles Ray announced in the *Tribune*: "Kansas is now in a state of open war. . . . It is not a war in which the interests of Kansas are alone at stake, but the cause of freedom in the whole country." He urged all lovers of democracy to go west or finance others to go, to buy carbines, and to send ammunition. He considered the emergency too critical for the people to wait meekly until the November elections but insisted that they go or send aid, now—today.

President Pierce, having failed to maintain order with either of the two governors he had appointed, sent a third, John W. Geary, with authority to use the United States Army to put down the free-state men. Geary was a handsome military fellow, six feet, five inches tall. He had been mayor of San Francisco when that city was in the hands of the vigilantes and knew how to handle lawless elements.

The Missouri army, not waiting for Governor Geary and the United States troops, entered Kansas in three columns. Two of them headed for Osawatomie, where they hoped to capture Old John Brown. The third column marched toward the free-state town of Lawrence. The first column was surprised and put to flight in southeast Kansas by James Montgomery, a Campbellite preacher, and his free-state followers. The second column reached Osawatomie, drove Old Brown from the cabins, burned the settlement, and returned to Missouri. The third column, under Senator Atchison, was met halfway to Lawrence by free-state volunteers under Senator Lane. Both sides skirmished and retreated. The *Tribune* lauded the Kansans' valor with Lincoln's words: "Strike and strike again! So sure as God lives the victory shall be yours."

Feeling their own strength for the first time, the free-state army marched over to besiege the proslavery capital at Lecompton, Kansas. Some Missourians were still there. The United States Army now interfered, insisting that there be no open warfare and promising to see that the Missourians went home. Four days later Governor Geary arrived. A Democrat like his predecessors, he had come to administer President Pierce's orders. He discounted the incendiary articles he had read in the *Chicago Tribune* and other Republican journals as purely political propaganda. He intended to enforce the laws. He had hardly reached the capital when free-state messengers came to him stating that the Missouri army, after retreating a short distance, was now marching on Lawrence. Incredulously the governor ordered out four hundred dragoons and four cannon. In his carriage he drove the ten miles to the free-state village and found the citizens prepared for war. He promised to protect them if they would lay down their arms. Then he drove away, hunting the alleged enemy.

He found the Missouri army, 2700 men strong, under command of Senator Atchison. The senator denied invading a neighboring state. His men had come, he said, to apprehend an "organized band of murderers and robbers"—the free-state men who refused to be governed by the proslavery politicians.

Governor Geary, like the two proslavery governors before him, was unwilling to submit the people to such tyranny. Though he knew the senator's power in Washington, Geary dared ask him to go back to his own state, and Senator Atchison obeyed. The governor drove along the road behind the retreating army—an experience which convinced him that James Redpath's articles for the *Tribune* were no exaggerations. Governor Geary, the proslavery Democrat, then deserted his party as his predecessors had done. He learned that the so-called posse, out to apprehend the "organized band of murderers and robbers," were acting in that capacity themselves. At one farm he saw with his own eyes the owner lying in his field, mortally wounded by the Missourians, who had stolen his team of horses. He had been shot down protesting the robbery. The governor interviewed the fellow and learned that he was the sole support of a large family and depended on his team to cultivate enough ground for a livelihood. Governor Geary, a veteran of the Mexican War, was used to sudden death, but not to murder and robbery by members of his own political party.

Back in the capital at Lecompton, the governor investigated further into his territory's government. He found that the jail was filled with free-state men held on trivial charges. No man, it seemed, could expect justice unless he belonged to the proslavery wing of the Democratic Party.

Tribune correspondents reported these developments to Charles Ray, who used them to good advantage in his Illinois antislavery campaign. Nevertheless it was difficult for many people to abandon their inherited party allegiances. They deplored Pierce's administration but seemed to have confidence that Buchanan would act differently if elected. Dr. Ray studied the entire state. The northern section seemed safe for the Republicans, the middle doubtful, and the southern end hopelessly Democratic. As a member of the state central committee, Ray sent speakers to the doubtful areas. He also arranged for huge parades and barbecues. Artillery roared welcomes to visiting delegates, and brass bands escorted them through the streets. At Peoria, on one occasion, a float held thirty-one young women dressed in white, except for one in mourning to represent Kansas. All were embarked on a bunting-draped boat named the *Constitution,* drawn by eight white horses.

Rival newspapers belittled these demonstrations and called Ray a Black Republican, saying that if his party won, every white man's daughter might have to marry a "nigger." They persistently asserted that the Republicans were antiforeign and pointed to Bissell as an invalid too ill to serve as governor. The duel with Jeff Davis, they said, would prevent him from taking the oath of office without committing perjury, for dueling was forbidden by the state's constitution.

Ray ignored the personal attacks, but he revealed the fact that Bissell's opponent, Colonel William A. Richardson, had himself taken part in several affairs of honor. That discovery ended the attacks on Bissell's dueling record. Ray's effort to get the German vote was a harder job. He prepared circulars in the German language and sent them to key points for distribution. As Lincoln worked with him, the two men became better acquainted. The Springfield lawyer, stumping the state, helped mightily by noting German communities which had not received folders or had forgotten to pass them at rallies. The foreign vote had become crucial, and Lincoln, in Bloomington, on September 13, 1856, wrote Ray: "Last evening I was scared a little by being told that the enemy are getting the Germans away from us in Chicago. Is there any truth in that? Write me here."

Dr. Ray thought not. He was more uncertain about the Germans near St. Louis. The Know-Nothing Party had been powerful down there, and many Germans still believed that the Know-Nothings had joined the Republicans. He enlisted a German, Frederick Hecker, to speak for the Republican Party around Belleville. He urged poor Germans to take a trip south into a slave state and note the condition of white working people in a slave economy. Hecker's house was burned, and Ray gave it wide publicity as the work of Know-Nothing fanatics. He also called attention to the burning of the house of a German named Fuchs because he dared speak out in favor of the Republican Party. Ray pointed out that house burning conformed to the Democrats' policy of intimidation and suppression of the press. Ray was encouraged to hear from his assistant editor, John C. Vaughan, that the Know-Nothings where he was campaigning were determined to defeat Buchanan because he depended on the German vote. Those Germans must be convinced that the Republicans were not Know-Nothings. They must be won to the new party. Watching always for news that would convince them that it was the Democrats who were antiforeign, Ray published an account of the murder of a downstate minister by a Democratic mob, merely because he was a German and, as such, must be an abolitionist.

Even though constantly concerned with local problems, Ray never neglected to tie the Illinois campaign to the general national movement against slavery. He learned that Buford's expedition to populate Kansas with Southerners had failed miserably. He sent a reporter to interview him and quoted Buford as saying that he had lost from $24,000 to $50,000 of his own money and was thoroughly discouraged. His "soldiers" had deserted as soon as their support money stopped. Some had joined the free-state settlers. Others were straggling back to their Southern homes. Buford felt particular bitterness against the Border Ruffians. "If there is a scoundrel on God's footstool greater than the rest," he said, "it is David Rice Atchison."

Ray also published with delight a statement of Senator John Bell, Whig from Tennessee, who said, "If resistance to such oppression be treason, so help me God, I would have been a traitor." Back in Massachusetts, Ralph Waldo Emerson had joined the crusade, warning all lovers of democracy: "We must learn to do with less, live in a smaller tenement, sell our apple-trees, our acres, our pleasant houses."

As election day approached, a whispering campaign among the Democrats repeated a story that invalid Bissell's brain was "softening." Ray received so many reports that he feared the tale had been believed by many people. To stop it he decided that the candidate must deliver a campaign speech and convince the skeptics that his mind was sound even if his body was not. Bissell agreed to deliver a political message from his reclining chair on the porch of his Belleville home. Ray reprinted the speech for immediate distribution throughout the state. Let politicians in every precinct quote from it as conclusive evidence of Bissell's mental capacity and also as the full text of the party's platform.

On election day Dr. Ray watched the returns with as much

apprehension as he had ever felt for the progress of a patient. This was the first Republican election nationally as well as in Illinois. The count would reveal the new party's strength. To Ray's disappointment, Buchanan won, but he was a minority president. Unless the Democrats changed their policies, they would probably lose four years hence. The figures showed encouraging trends. Although Buchanan had carried Pennsylvania, his home state, he had lost New York. Had the Republicans won Pennsylvania, they would have been within six electoral votes of victory. The Know-Nothing Party had shrunk to inconsequence nationally, with only eight electoral votes, but their number prevented Frémont from winning in Illinois. However, the Illinois Republicans showed amazing strength by electing Bissell governor. Four years hence, if the Republicans held their present gains and carried Pennsylvania and Illinois, they would elect the president. That was plain to any man, and a candidate selected from either Illinois or Pennsylvania had the best chance of carrying the nation in 1860. Ray must have noticed, also, one sinister election return. In Missouri the vote had been proslavery, elevating to the governorship the anti-Benton, pro-Atchison Trusten Polk.

With Illinois unquestionably headed for freedom's ranks and a hopeful national contest in the offing, the Republican politicians planned a great celebration in the Hall of Representatives at Springfield in January. Charles Ray decided to participate. In the meantime he was busy reporting local news and taking part in civic activities at home. The Chicago Historical Society had always interested him, and he attended its December meeting. On this occasion it was announced that the Society had recently acquired the Illinois muster rolls from the Mexican War and also the military journal of the troops engaged in the removal of the last of the Indians from Illinois after the Black Hawk War.

In the middle of January, Charles Ray went down to Springfield, as planned, to attend the political celebration. Registering at the St. Nicholas Hotel, he walked over to the capitol and greeted friends on the portico. Upstairs in the Hall of Representatives, the meeting was called to order by Springfield's Republican newspaper editor, Simeon Francis, and Gustave Koerner was elected permanent chairman—a courtesy to the state's German voters who were considered so important in the party's victory.

Koerner was a highly educated *doktor* with degrees from Jena and Heidelberg. He had participated in the revolution of 1833 and had fled the *Vaterland* to save his life. In southern Illinois he now exerted great influence among German immigrants. Like most of them, he had originally espoused the Democratic Party. He had served as a justice on the Illinois Supreme Court and as lieutenant governor. In the recent campaign he had made many speeches for the Republican Party, assuring his fellow Germans that the new party was not antiforeign, merely antislavery, a principle all liberal Germans should endorse. He had married Sophie Engelmann, whose brother had warned Charles Ray about the Know-Nothing plot to discredit Bissell for the gubernatorial nomination.

With Koerner installed in the speaker's chair, a galaxy of secretaries was elected, among them three newspapermen—Charles Wilson, Paul Selby, and Charles Ray. Next, speeches were delivered by Abraham Lincoln, Richard Yates, and others. Ray noted that the tall Springfield lawyer was living up to his expectations. Two years hence he should be good material for the Senate, if Trumbull's supporters stayed with their promise to support Lincoln's nomination. When Ray returned to Chicago he wrote about the celebration in glowing terms and, a fortnight later, was rewarded by Governor Bissell with an appointment as commissioner for the Illinois and Michigan Canal—a post considered one of the state's best political prizes.

VIII Lincoln for Senator

WITH the Republicans strong in Illinois and gaining nationally, the *Tribune* became a voice of importance. Editor Ray saw plainly that his denunciation of the slave-power was bearing fruit. He must step up his labor in this vineyard. He subscribed to the leading proslavery journals and began clipping pertinent passages from them. To a statement from one of these papers, claiming that the South would have seceded from the Union if Frémont had been elected, Ray replied that it was all bluff. He quoted another paper as saying that "capitalists, money makers and money seekers of the North" feared disunion. Therefore it behooved the South to threaten it in order to get concessions. Three weeks later Ray reprinted a similar editorial and followed it with: "They who threaten disunion are pretenders simply—they neither mean what they say, nor, if they do, have the ability to accomplish what they wish."

This was all right for politicians in want of a better complaint, but Charles Ray knew that future threats were more effective political ammunition than past lamentations. With a new administration promising to improve conditions, the *Tribune* must wait for the Democrats to commit a new blunder. Then in January 1857, the proslavery party laid itself wide open for another attack. When their partisan legislature met in Kansas for its second session, it was plain to all members that the settlers were overwhelmingly free-state and in the next election would vote the incumbents out of office. Two methods of saving slavery still remained. The present proslavery legislature could pass an act for the drafting of a state constitution and specify that no vote on the organic act be taken by the people. In case this device failed, another fraudulent election could be tried.

Governor Geary, already angry at the lawlessness of the proslavery army, determined to thwart such political tricks. He promptly vetoed a bill for a constitutional convention, and when President Pierce criticized him severely he resigned. Thus Pierce showed his true colors, and the proslavery, or Lecompton, constitutional convention was approved. James Buchanan, when he took the oath of office in March, would have to show whether or not he would be dominated by the proslavery wing. Would he or would he not let the majority rule in Kansas? Immediately after his inauguration, editor Ray found out.

A slave named Dred Scott had sued for his freedom during Pierce's administration. Dred claimed that his master had taken him into a free state and into free territory and thus had made him free. The case had been tried in Missouri and finally went to the Supreme Court of the United States. The Chief Justice, Roger Taney, was a Democrat, a kindly and serene old man with one foot in the grave and the other in the proslavery wing of the party. Buchanan learned shortly before his inauguration that Taney and a majority of the Supreme Court had denied the Negro's plea on the assumption that slavery was recognized by the Constitution and therefore Congress had no authority to keep it out of the territories. In short, the free-state Kansans had fought and won a victory only to have it nullified by the Supreme Court when squatter sovereignty failed to support slavery. "Heads we win, tails you lose" was the rule by which the slave-power played the game.

The Republican Party had grown mightily as a crusader against the injustice of proslavery ballot-box stuffing reported in Kansas. Ray believed that the party would thrive doubly if this latest usurpation were properly publicized. The prospect of sure victory for the free-state settlers had deprived the editor of a target for his opposition shafts, but the slave-power, with this decision, had set up another for him to shoot down. Ray was also delighted to see conservative industrialists who had not voted for Frémont joining the Republican ranks. The future of the party seemed bright indeed. At about the same time, Ray's wife confided that there was to be a third addition to the family. Surely life was rewarding.

On March 17, 1857, Chief Justice Taney's entire opinion on the case of Dred Scott was printed in the *Tribune*. Two days later Ray published the dissenting opinion of Justice John McLean. Let readers compare the original words, pro and con, and judge for themselves. On March 19, Ray told his readers that the remedy was the ballot box. Lovers of freedom, he said, should vote as a unit and elect legislators who would send a Republican senator to Congress. Lincoln's name had not yet been mentioned. Looking beyond the senatorial election, Ray added:

> Let the next President be a Republican, and 1860 will mark an era kindred with that of 1776, and the country and the Constitution be ruled and considered by men kindred in American principle with Washington, Jefferson and the Fathers.

President Buchanan, soon after the announcement of the Dred Scott decision upholding slavery in Kansas, sent a new governor, Robert J. Walker, to administer the territorial laws. Walker was another Democrat who presumably understood the Northern and the Southern viewpoints. He did not want the job, but President Buchanan and Senator Douglas persuaded him to take it. So Walker set off to accomplish the seemingly impossible task of preserving a slave dictatorship and at the same time administering a democratic government. Before leaving for Kansas, he exacted a promise from the President that democracy be protected there and that the majority be allowed to rule in the territory—a promise any chief executive would be obliged to grant whether or not he sincerely intended to live up to it.

As soon as Walker arrived in Kansas, he announced that the existing legislature, whether bogus or not, must be respected as legitimate. He stated that the Kansas climate did not seem suitable for slaves, but insisted that the Dred Scott decision permitted them there until the people, organized as a state, voted to exclude them. The free-state voters had a recognized majority and Walker urged them to assert their wills at the polls. He promised that the election count would be fair and hinted that handsome railroad subsidies might be had by co-operating with him.

Walker's plan did not meet the approval of Buchanan's proslavery cabinet, but that was an inter-party quarrel in which the *Tribune* could only applaud the plucky governor and urge the settlers to uphold their rights. Then, before the elections were held, a financial panic struck Chicago. Subscriptions to the *Tribune* declined rapidly, and Ray experienced his first real worry over money since he had bought into the paper. The basic cause of it all seemed to be Chicago's too rapid growth. With great prosperity, the city had been able to support seven daily newspapers, fifteen weeklies, and six monthlies, glutting the market. Of 1350 businesses of all kinds, 117 failed during the year. Twenty thousand unemployed workers faced starvation in the muddy streets. Mayor Wentworth created some employment by hiring men at seventy-five cents per day to tear down shanties on the sand dunes along the lake. He prevented a riot between the workers and shack owners by enticing the latter away to see a civic-sponsored dog fight. Municipal soup kitchens and a program of public works were considered, but neither was resorted to. Ray blamed the depression on the Democrats. He pointed out that Buchanan was doing nothing to save the economy, nothing but courting the slave-power, as Pierce had done. Let Illinois send a Republican senator to Congress and times would change!

Ray and Joe Medill both taxed their ingenuity to rebuild circulation. The opening of a new counting room on the first floor of their Clark Street building was announced on May 28. They hoped that curious sightseers would buy a paper or subscribe. Ray sent agents into the country to organize anti-slavery clubs. The *Tribune* would serve as an association organ for them, keeping members posted on the crusade's progress and suggesting new activities. This was the plan he and Fairchild had tried with their temperance paper in Springfield in 1845. One *Tribune* agent came back with a thousand new subscribers, but the plan was, on the whole, unsuccessful.

Ray, however, would not give up. For the new club members he prepared such topics for discussion as the horrors of slavery and its danger to American democracy. He understood the journalist's technique of focusing on individuals instead of abstractions. Lincoln was his favorite in Illinois, but in the national scene he singled out the picturesque Jim Lane of Kansas, who had set the mob in Chicago wild with his oratory. Ray published anecdotes about Lane and his speaking tour in the East. When the Kansas correspondent of the *Cincinnati Gazette* reported that Lane had turned up surreptitiously in the West, Ray reprinted the entire dispatch. Club subscribers read the following and waited for the next installment, which they knew would be more stimulating:

The most exciting news at this town is that Jim Lane is in the territory. He was a passenger on the St. Mary, the boat I was on. He had taken deck passage and was disguised. I noticed an uncouth looking old codger with stogy boots, green blanket coat and prodigious pair of green spectacles on. His disguise was so complete that persons who had known him intimately in Indiana did not recognize him even in conversation with him. . . . I commenced a conversation with him and after talking awhile discovered it was Jim Lane. . . . He got off at Wyandotte last evening in company with a refugee from Kansas named Ritchie. He shouldered a knapsack and made tracks, he said, for Lecompton but he will hardly venture there. I presume he went directly to Lawrence.

With readers waiting for Lane to start some sensational escapade in Lawrence, Ray turned his attention to local matters. On July 4, 1857, the cornerstone of the University of Chicago was laid. Senator Douglas attended the dedication. He had given the institution ten acres of land for their buildings. The ceremonies opened with prayer by the Reverend J. E. Roy, who dared ask God's mercy "for our poor colored brethren in bondage, even though Judge Douglas himself is present among us." The principal speaker, Isaac N. Arnold, also attacked Douglas' policy on the slavery issue, in spite of the donor's presence on the platform behind him. Next day Ray lampooned the Little Giant in the *Tribune* under the heading: MEPHISTOPHELES.

This made amusing reading and everybody knew that the fall elections in Kansas would test the courage of the Buchanan administration to resist slavocracy. The President was now claiming no responsibility for conditions out there. He had inherited them from his predecessor, he said. Moreover, he had promised Walker that the will of the majority would be respected by the Federal government. Walker had convinced the settlers that this was so. They had agreed to countenance the proslavery legislature until they could vote it out of existence. The whole nation waited to see if the President would keep his word. For Dr. Ray the suspense was broken in September by the birth of a third child, Paul, at the Ray home on the corner of Ohio and State (then Wolcott) streets.

Meanwhile Ray was learning that his job as canal commissioner was not a sinecure. Many lengthy and important decisions were required of him. Former governor Joel Matteson was building a new home, finer than the executive mansion from which he had just moved and directly across the street from it. True he was a wealthy man, but he was also cashing

$200,000 worth of canal scrip which the commissioners did not know to be outstanding. This financial tangle took a lot of Charles Ray's time. In addition, a man named David Leavitt was asking the commission to approve a $40,000 fee due him for floating a loan of $1,600,000 for the canal. Charles Ray approved the request. Rivers and canals were still considered the most important form of transportation in the West, although their prestige was being questioned. A steamboat company had just sued the Rock Island Railroad for building a bridge across the Mississippi. One of its ships, the *Effie Afton,* had rammed the bridge and burned to the water line. Was the railroad responsible for obstructing traffic on a waterway? The case promised to be important in the competition between water and rail transportation. Steamboats had made St. Louis. Railroads were making Chicago. Ray's friend, attorney Norman Judd, represented the Rock Island. Abraham Lincoln came up from Springfield to serve with him. The newborn Republican Party was lining up on the side of corporations that stood for progress, whether against steamboats or against slave labor. Ray could remember when he believed in the superiority of water transportation, had even invested, to his sorrow, in Mound City real estate. However, he had changed, deserting the old Democratic Party to join what he considered more progressive people. As the *Effie Afton* case continued, Ray reported the full testimony every day, filling three or four pages of the paper. Lawyer Lincoln was always pictured as an earnest and gracious pleader.

This case ended with a hung jury—indecisive, but many people had to admit that the day of the steamboat was threatened precisely as the day of the slave was threatened in a changing world. With the news value of this legal contest squeezed dry, Ray turned his attention again to Kansas. From all reports, Walker's promise of an honest election count was having its effect. Perhaps the settlers were encouraged by the presence of Jim Lane. In any event, they turned out en masse to vote for their legislators, and there was no invasion from Missouri. So far, so good, but when the votes were counted some districts showed unquestionable evidence of fraud. The proslavery machine had been up to its old trick again—not an invasion this time, but ballot-box stuffing. In the Oxford precinct of six houses, 1628 votes had been tallied. In McGee, on an Indian reservation, fourteen votes had been cast in June, but now, in October, 1266 were reported. The proslavery votes in these two districts were enough to change the entire complexion of the state legislature. John Calhoun, a staunch Democrat from Illinois, had gone west in time to be elected chairman of the proslavery, or Lecompton, constitutional convention. This assembly had recessed for the election, and the notorious Calhoun might be responsible for this cheating to win for slavery. Charles Ray knew all about him. He intended to investigate and give the facts to *Tribune* readers.

Governor Walker, true to his word to the free-state settlers, threw out the questionable returns. A proslavery judge immediately issued mandamuses for the governor to certify the fraudulent ballots. One candidate in the disputed area, the infamous Sheriff Jones, dared enter the governor's office with a gun and demand his certificate. What more could Ray ask as an example of the slave-power's determination to rule by dictatorial methods?

Governor Walker proved to be a man who could not be intimidated. Jones's gun did not look dangerous to him, and the ex-sheriff slunk away. The lame-duck legislature, defeated in this last trick, knew now that their only hope lay in the constitutional convention still in session. As the last proslavery organization remaining in Kansas, this convention determined to resort to its desperate prerogative. It would draft a proslavery constitution and submit it to Congress without first securing approval by the people.

To prevent this outrage, the eloquent Jim Lane began to fan the settlers to the verge of frenzy. He urged Governor Walker to avert a revolution by calling a special session of the newly elected free-state legislature in order that it might terminate the convention's nefarious scheme. Walker, now furious at the proslavery-machine's domination, called the special session, and President Buchanan recalled him from office. Like Pierce, Buchanan feared popular government in Kansas. The slave oligarchy must rule. Once more the Republican Party had a cause.

The *Chicago Tribune* printed column after column protesting the imposition of a constitution on a state without the consent of the governed. The convention chairman, John Calhoun, realized that something must be done. He offered a remedy, a slippery one which would deceive none but the most undiscerning. He said that the solution had been suggested to him by the great compromiser of the Senate, Stephen A. Douglas. Why not let the people vote on the constitution "with slavery" and "without slavery"? Ray saw through this subterfuge—a typical Douglas compromise. The people were to be forced to approve the organic act by voting only for or against one clause in it, though a majority obviously disapproved of the entire document. Charles Ray turned the *Tribune's* heaviest artillery against this outrage, and as the time for a vote on the peculiar constitution approached, he sent a special correspondent to Kansas to report the ballot.

On election day 6226 ballots in favor of the constitution "with slavery" were counted, 569 for the constitution without it. Ballot-box stuffing had been resorted to again, and there seemed reason to believe that 2720 of the 6226 votes were fraudulent. The small total number of ballots showed that a great majority of the free-state men had not voted. How could they, when they disapproved the constitution whether or not it sanctioned slavery? Of all the tricks brought forward by the slave-power to make a travesty of democracy, this was the worst. A large batch of ballots, the basis of the questionable returns, was found in a candlebox belonging to Calhoun.

Charles Ray asked for the candlebox for display in Chicago as an example of the Democrat's trickery. The candlebox was then sent east to other Republican centers. "Candlebox Calhoun," the convention's chairman was called henceforth by the *Tribune*.

Even Democratic newspapers across the North protested foisting on the people of Kansas a constitution that they did not want. Republicans crowed. The Democrats had accused the Republicans of manufacturing "Bleeding Kansas" for political appeal. Now it was the Democrats themselves who were splitting on the wrongs done that state by the slave-power. Douglas had been back in Illinois during the summer of 1857. Attending political rallies and listening to speakers at the University of Chicago dedication, he had learned the magnitude of his constituents' opposition to further association with the proslavery wing of the party. Unless he took a strong stand now, he might lose his seat in the next election. Confronted with this dilemma, he broke with the administration and stood firmly on his old platform of popular sovereignty. If the people of Kansas did not want the Lecompton Constitution, he would not vote to force it on them.

President Buchanan still hoped to appease the South. He would force Senator Douglas to follow the administration's wish or lose his patronage. Even the most powerful senator might thus be brought into line. Charles Ray greeted this defection in the Democratic Party with an article captioned: "LO! THE HEADMAN'S AXE." He was not prepared for Douglas' next move. The Little Giant sent one of his lieutenants to the *Tribune* office to ask if Ray would support Douglas in case that Democratic chieftain bolted his party and ran for senator on the Republican ticket.

The temptation to accept Douglas' offer was great. The Little Giant had a tremendous personal following in Illinois. With the assimilation of Douglas' organization, the Republican Party would be supreme. The *Tribune* still suffered from the financial depression, and mortgages were coming due. If the paper failed, new owners might abandon the antislavery crusade. Subscriptions from Douglas' followers were almost sure to be sufficient to save the paper. On the other hand, supporting Douglas for the senatorship meant sacrificing Lincoln and others who had given up safe political ties to help the new movement, and with the party in the hands of old-line politicians there was danger that it might be steered quickly off its progressive course and back into the old reactionary rut. Ray told Douglas' representative that he would have to consider the offer. When his visitor left, Ray wrote to Senator Trumbull, whose seat Lincoln had been promised:

> We are almost confounded by his [Douglas'] anomalous position and we do not know how to treat him and his overtures to the Republican Party. Personally, I am inclined to give him the lash, but I want to do nothing that damages our cause or hinders emancipation in Kansas.

A few days later Congressman Washburne himself stamped up the stairs to the *Tribune* office. Horace Greeley had sent him from Washington, he said. The New York editor was sure that the Republican Party would profit mightily by taking Douglas into the fold. Already the *New York Tribune* was eulogizing the Little Giant, building up his stature as a man who put principle above party.

The Chicago editors pushed aside their papers to discuss the decision they must make, a decision vital to their own personal finances and to the future of the Republican Party. Half of the group rationalized the substitution of Douglas for Lincoln. The other half argued doggedly for the Springfield attorney who had waived his opportunity so graciously in 1855. Charles Ray, as editor-in-chief, held the deciding vote, and he cast it against the Little Giant. When the conference ended, Ray wrote another letter to Senator Trumbull:

> Tell our friends . . . who may be more zealous than discreet, that we in Illinois have not delegated our powers to them and that we may not ratify bargains that they make—in a word, that among the inducements which they hold out to the "distinguished Senator" to ensure his continuance of his fight with the Administration, they must not hold up the Senatorship as the prize of his defection.

Then, taking a fresh sheet of foolscap, Charles Ray wrote an editorial for tomorrow's paper. In part it said:

> If the Republicans of Illinois should now sink all party differences and reelect Mr. Douglas, their party would be so disintegrated that the state would be lost to freedom in 1860, or if saved, saved only because he [Douglas] allowed it to be saved. The Republican Party would be wholly at his mercy.

Douglas, a lone wolf now, expelled from the Democratic pack and unacceptable to the Republicans, tested his strength against the administration on March 23, 1858. On that day the United States Senate voted on the Lecompton Constitution and accepted it by a vote of thirty-three to twenty-five. Evidently the slave-power still ruled in the Senate without Douglas, but a few days later the House voted down the proslavery document. President Buchanan was beaten at last. He had continued to appease the slave wing of his party until he lost so many of his Northern supporters that his power was gone. His next move, a threat of war against Spain over Cuba, brought further scorn from his political foes. This belligerent manifesto was proclaimed to be nothing but an effort to divert attention from domestic defeats. Charles Ray summed up the whole unhappy situation in a March editorial:

> The deceit, bad-faith, and double dealing which have characterized the Sham Democracy North and South, have at last their legitimate results. The organization is split from summit

to base. . . . The cause of the rupture dates back to 1853. . . . The heresies of that monomaniac John C. Calhoun . . . dressed up anew in ambiguous phrase—with Northern and Squatter Sovereignty aspect for the North—with a nigger-driving look for the South— . . . were embodied in the Kansas Nebraska bill. . . . So enamored have the people been with the Democratic name, and so fearful, in the event of a Democratic defeat, that they would be forced to take negroes for wives and accept mulattoes for children that they have failed or refused to see the swindle by which the Democratic victories have been won.

In April 1858, a friend of Douglas came to Ray with a new proposition. If the *Tribune* would back the Little Giant for Congress, he would withdraw from the senatorial race and leave Lincoln a clear field. Once more Ray was sorely tempted. By accepting this more moderate proposition the *Tribune* might gain the Douglas subscribers it needed to prevent the paper's collapse. On the other hand, for Douglas to consider such a surrender showed him to be badly frightened. Perhaps he had lost his following. Ray decided not to commit himself at this time. He preferred to watch the political barometer.

In June 1858, the Republicans held their state primary convention in Springfield to nominate a senator. Lincoln's aspiraation would be achieved or lost at this meeting. Ray, though busy with financial matters, gave the meeting all the attention he could spare. The Cook County delegates included Charlie Wilson, John Wentworth, Isaac N. Arnold, and Norman Judd. Charles Ray knew that "Long John" Wentworth was scheming for the nomination. "Long John," as much an enemy of Ray's as Douglas himself, was a big, bluff fellow. Wags said tailors "surveyed" him for his breeches. In a crowd he did most of the talking, and since he owned a newspaper—the *Daily Democrat*—people listened and usually gave him what he wanted. Ray had known about this plot of Wentworth's for some time. He had discussed it with Judd and other party leaders. Lincoln's friends also had learned that the Trumbull men who had pledged to support Lincoln were now wavering, making excuses. How those politicians might act when the time came to vote was anybody's guess. Ray and his fellows had planned with Judd to surprise the opposition before they organized—the old game used to get Ray elected clerk of the Illinois Senate in 1855. The details were carefully worked out before the delegation left Chicago, but Wentworth, sitting and talking with the men, was ignorant of their plan against him.

The convention opened next morning, with Richard Yates presiding. The roll was called, and, before any nominations were made, a Chicago delegate marched down the aisle with a banner inscribed: COOK COUNTY IS FOR ABRAHAM LINCOLN. This unusual proceeding was also unparliamentary but a "planted" delegate from another county arose and with assumed dignity proclaimed: "I wish to amend this banner by substituting a word I hold in my hand." The man then unrolled a scroll containing the word ILLINOIS in large capitals. The Cook County delegation—even "Long John"—accepted this amendment, and with a roar of applause the convention agreed: ILLINOIS IS FOR ABRAHAM LINCOLN.

That evening, shortly after the town lamplighter had made his rounds of the square, Lincoln was scheduled to accept the nomination formally in the statehouse, with a speech outlining the party's platform in the ensuing campaign. The words Lincoln uttered might make or break the Republican Party in Illinois. Ray, back in the *Tribune* office in Chicago, waited apprehensively. Before midnight an incomplete story came through from Horace White announcing the success of the intrigue and listing the other nominees. Ray headlined the story: THE GREAT REPUBLICAN STATE CONVENTION—EVERY MAN FOR LINCOLN. He followed this with a couplet:

Sound the loud timbrel o'er Egypt's dark sea.
Jehovah has triumphed; His people are free.

Horace White closed the dispatch with, "Mr. Lincoln, as I close this letter, is addressing an immense audience." Lincoln's address did not come through until the next day. Then a copy, carefully edited by Lincoln himself, was released for publication. Conservatives who feared Lincoln too radical on the slavery issue read:

A house divided against itself cannot stand. I believe this government cannot endure permanently half *slave* and half *free*. I do not expect the Union to be *dissolved*—I do not expect the house to *fall*—but I *do* expect it will cease to be divided. It will become *all* one thing, or *all* the other.

Did this mean that the Republican Party had shifted its position from opposing the extension of slavery to seeking its abolition in the slave states? Lincoln was careful to say no. The Republicans did not demand abolition in the South, but the Democrats were insisting on extending slavery into the North. To prove this, he summed up the recent Democratic acts: Stephen A. Douglas' Nebraska Bill, the arbitrary orders of Franklin Pierce and James Buchanan, the violation of all democratic processes to force slavery on Kansas, and Roger Taney's decision in the Dred Scott case. Then, to fix the pattern of the slave-power's aggression in the popular mind, Lincoln declared:

When we see a lot of framed timbers, different portions of which we know have been gotten out at different times and places and by different workmen—Stephen, Franklin, Roger and James, for instance—and when we see these timbers joined together, and see they exactly make the frame of a house or a mill, all the tenons and mortices exactly fitting, and all the lengths and proportions of the different pieces exactly adapted to their respective places, and not a piece too many or too few—not omitting even scaffolding—or, if a single piece be lacking, we can see the place in the frame exactly fitted and prepared to yet bring such piece in—in *such* a case, we find it impossible to not *believe* that Stephen and Franklin and Roger and James all understood one another from the beginning, and all worked upon a common *plan* or *draft* drawn up before the first lick was struck.

Ray pondered Lincoln's address with some misgivings, but with admiration too. Lincoln had cleverly put Douglas on the defensive. He must not be allowed to run for Congress but must, instead, be set up as a whipping boy for Lincoln. The Little Giant, with his national reputation, would thus be forced against his will to carry Lincoln's light before the world. A series of joint debates between them would serve the press adequately and Charles Ray, reporting for the *Tribune*, would see to it that Lincoln received his due. Ray's first move was to force Douglas to participate in such a debate or leave himself vulnerable to the taunts of enemies who could say, with reason, that he feared Lincoln's logic. Only one possible obstacle stood in the way: the *Tribune* might not survive. Ray and Medill discussed their pending obligations. Then they worked out a plan which saved the paper's life—and made Abraham Lincoln.

IX The Lincoln-Douglas Debates

THE PLAN to alleviate Ray's and Medill's financial embarrassment was to consolidate with the *Democratic Press*, which now had a circulation about equal to the *Tribune's*. If the papers combined, much duplication of work could be eliminated, and the services of the *Press's* talented writers, John Locke Scripps and William Bross, would be retained. Scripps was a dignified, professorial man, who had taught natural philosophy before becoming a reporter. A quiet fellow, he had two aims in life—to further the abolition of slavery and to edit a successful newspaper. The Scripps-Howard chain derives its name from his family. Ray had known Scripps since the old *Jeffersonian* days. He had written leaders for him to publish in the *Democratic Press* when Scripps's health broke during the Kansas-Nebraska excitement.

Bross differed from Scripps by being an extrovert. Pompous and assertive, he was a strict Presbyterian usually addressed as "Deacon." He had shaggy eyebrows, a rugged face, and a deep voice which constantly foretold the splendid future of Chicago. These two additions to the staff seemed enough alone to pull the *Tribune* out of its predicament.

Bross was a born promoter—as great as Chicago ever had, which is saying a lot. He liked to point out that the Northwest was a territory larger than the twenty-three older states east of the Mississippi. He wrote:

It contains the largest and richest deposits of lead and copper that exist on the globe. . . . Where the buffalo now range in countless thousands, must, after all, become the greatest corn-growing sections of the Union. There, too, will be reared the countless herds of cattle and hogs to be driven to Chicago and packed in as beef and pork to feed the Eastern States, with an abundance to spare for all nations of Europe.

Bross could look out his office window at the stone and brick houses standing in the mud among squalid shanties and declare that this place was the great business center of the future. "No other country in the world has ever witnessed such progress," he said.

Although Bross and Scripps were valuable additions to the *Press and Tribune*, as the combined paper was called, Ray continued to do most of the political reporting. The others handled general news, commerce, and civic promotion. The paper's chief goal now that Lincoln had been nominated for the Senate was to elect him—a slightly involved procedure, for senators were chosen by the legislature. It was necessary, therefore, to elect legislators pledged to Lincoln. On June 29, 1858, Ray opened the campaign by writing Lincoln to ask for a brief biography "of the next U. S. Senator." He added: "All we want is dates, place of nativity, parentage, trials, disadvantages &c &c—all of which will make, if we are rightly informed, a thrilling story." In the same letter Ray told Lincoln about the consolidation of the papers and the new nine-column format.

Charles Ray was loading his columns for the campaign when the *Chicago Times* opened fire with a blast at Lincoln's Mexican War record. He had been in Congress at that time and had voted against the war. Lincoln replied to this charge quickly enough, and the *Press and Tribune* published his complete voting record, which showed that he had opposed the war, truly enough, but after it was declared had always voted for the soldiers' necessary supplies. With this defense on record, the *Press and Tribune* took the initiative and defined Lincoln's position on the present issue of slavery—more important, surely, than an incident dating back more than a decade.

"In my opinion," Lincoln was quoted as saying, "neither the general government nor any other power outside the slave states, can constitutionally or rightfully interfere with slaves or slavery where it already exists." Lincoln went on to say that efforts to extend slavery into the territories or into the free states "shall be fairly headed off, the institution will then be in the course of ultimate extinction."

Here was the essence of Lincoln's position on slavery. Quite naturally the slave-power took violent exception to the "ultimate extinction" of their basic source of labor. The Southern press howled protests against this threat. Ray clipped the most pertinent, added suitable prefatory remarks, and sent them to the printers. A news note from the *New Orleans Delta* seemed particularly to the point:

> Somebody named Lincoln, who in the eyes of his friends is an unborn Samson of the Free Soilers, was the choice for the United States Senate. The *Chicago Tribune*, that Iago of a journal which supported Lane of Kansas, though knowing him to be one of the greatest knaves of the Union, grows jubilant on the doings of the convention. . . .
>
> Everywhere in the West, antislavery leaders survey the field, raise themselves in their stirrups and swing high the black banner, confident of success in the great battle of 1860.

The Southerners' prophecy proved true. This senatorial campaign would be very important in the presidential selection two years hence, and the *Press and Tribune* intended to speak with authority in both elections.

Douglas arrived in Chicago from Washington to open his campaign on July 9, 1858. His supporters met him at Michigan City to conduct him to the Windy City in a special train. As the cars rattled into Chicago, cannon boomed a welcome. A hilarious crowd waved banners and exploded fireworks. In the evening Douglas spoke from the balcony of the Tremont House. He extolled the advantages of local self-government—popular sovereignty—as the solution to the slave controversy and excoriated Lincoln's "house divided" speech as the words of a warmonger.

Next day the *Press and Tribune* devoted three and a half columns on page one to Douglas' speech—wider coverage than was given by the Democratic papers. The paper also described the crowd, the processions, bands, runaway buggies, and all the attendant excitement. Here was a new kind of journalism—giving the devil his due. An extra edition was advertised for distribution downstate. Farmers in isolated villages now read all about the meeting, felt that they had been a part of the crowd, and became vitally interested in the campaign. An editorial added slyly: "The Hon. A. Lincoln will reply to Senator Douglas this evening. His speech will be a masterly dissection and exposure of the many sophistries and misrepresentations crowded into that of Judge Douglas. Let everybody turn out to hear him."

Lincoln did dissect Douglas' speech unmistakably. He pointed out that all the alleged blessings of popular sovereignty had been wiped out by the Dred Scott decision, which nationalized slavery regardless of the opinions of local groups. He said that if the "house divided" doctrine precipitated a war, it would be brought on by the South, and the theory that the United States must be all slave or all free was not a plank of the Republican platform, but merely a personal prophecy of his own.

Charles Ray devoted four columns on page one to Lincoln's speech. Once again he described the crowd and admitted that it was smaller than Douglas had drawn. He called special attention to the German Club of the Seventh Ward, which had marched to the meeting. Let foreigners note this and forget the oft-repeated falsehood that Know-Nothingism and Republicanism were the same.

For rural distribution Lincoln's and Douglas' speeches were printed by the *Press and Tribune* side by side in a new weekly edition. Farmers were told to put the paper behind the clock on the mantel until Saturday night, then read at their leisure. "Comparison of [the] speeches," the editor said, "would show Lincoln's masterly refutation of Douglas' points."

Lincoln and Douglas both remained in Chicago for a few days. Douglas planned a triumphal tour through the state in a special train dedicated to "the champion of popular sovereignty." A twelve pounder was mounted on a flatcar to boom his arrival in each town. At the *Press and Tribune* office Lincoln, Judd, and Ray planned a counter campaign. Northern Illinois was considered a Republican stronghold. Southern Illinois was hopelessly proslavery. The contest, therefore, must be waged in the central area. The editors agreed that Lincoln must follow Douglas, stand in the crowds in the dust and heat, listen to the remarks of the bystanders, and call a meeting of his own for a reply on the next day. The *Press and Tribune* would print his speeches and give them wide publicity.

This plan was tried during the hot, stifling days of July 1858, but it failed to bring the results anticipated. Only dregs of the crowds appeared on the second day, and since these people were Lincoln voters already, nothing was gained. Douglas, in his opening speech, always put Lincoln on the defensive and was never vulnerable to attack himself. Lincoln's managers saw plainly that they were being defeated. They must devise some way to get Lincoln on the same platform with Douglas. Let Douglas' cannon and banners draw the crowds, then let "Old Abe" have an even chance to speak with him. Charles Ray sounded out Douglas' managers on the possibility of a joint debate. The Little Giant was not enthusiastic.

Why give up the offensive and spend his lavish campaign funds for the benefit of a rival? Even Lincoln seemed diffident, but Ray drove ahead with his plans. He must make Abe Lincoln a popular figure, and he must force the Douglas men to recognize him as a potential equal. On July 18, Ray wrote Lincoln the following letter, asking once more for the short biography which he wanted to publish:

My Dear Sir:

It is my suspicion that Abe Lincoln was not born with a silver spoon in his mouth and that suspicion, more than anything else impelled me to make the request I did. Mathias Mount in Mackinaw whom you know very well used to tell me—I know not with how much truth—of your joint adventures in rail-splitting and the like, for wages that would seem ridiculously small. He told me enough to make me desirous to learn more and I take it that the public, to whom you are now an object of concern, have the same curiosity that I feel. In my way of thinking you occupy a position present and future prospectively that need not shrink from the declaration of an origin ever so humble. If you have been the architect of your own fortunes, you may claim the most merit. The best part of the Lincoln family is not like potatoes, under ground. Had you not better reconsider your refusal? . . .

Yours very truly,
C. H. Ray

With this letter in the mail Ray resorted to the political trick of anticipating an action and thus forcing its consideration. Boldly he printed for all his readers to ponder:

We understand that the Republican State Central Committee have requested, or will shortly request, Mr. Douglas to canvass the State in company with Mr. Lincoln, in order that both speakers may address the people at the same places on the same day. This is the usual, almost universal style of conducting a political campaign, and it has been justly held that the candidate who refused to speak in that way had no better reason than cowardice for declining the challenger.

Douglas was now neatly trapped. The challenge to his courage was known throughout the Northwest. Meanwhile Ray's trouble with Lincoln continued. The Springfield candidate still seemed reluctant to step into the doorway the *Press and Tribune* had opened for him. Ray wrote again to Lincoln:

> You certainly owe it to yourself and not less certainly to your party who have honored you by an unanimity of choice that is without parallel except in the histories of Clay and Benton and Calhoun, to leave nothing undone which may promise to give you a vote. The reputation you have already acquired by entering the lists against a "Giant" will be permanent by success which no false delicacy must keep you from trying to win by any legitimate means in your power. You have a chance which comes to but few men in each generation. It is for you to make the best of it.

Ray urged Lincoln again to send him the biographical notes in order that he could write more about him in the *Press and Tribune*. Already, Ray said, Lincoln had become known even in rural New York, where people were more conservative and farther from railoads than they could be anywhere in Illinois. On trains, in hotels, everywhere, Ray had been asked questions about this man who dared challenge Douglas. They wanted to know his age, profession, appearance, and every possible personal detail.

The publicized challenge was finally accepted by Douglas on August 3, 1858. An exchange of letters specified arrangements for debates in the state's seven congressional districts. Lincoln's opportunity had come at last. He went into retirement to prepare his speeches. The *Press and Tribune* reorganized its staff in order that it might lead all other newspapers in reporting the campaign. To transcribe the arguments word for word, a shorthand expert, Robert R. Hitt, was employed.

The first debate was held at Ottawa on August 21, 1858, but the audience began to arrive the night before. Farmers came in wagons and on horseback. The hotels and private houses were crowded. Many people slept in their own bedding at the livery stables. Soon even these accommodations were filled, and latecomers camped by their carriages along the river bottoms or beside the Illinois and Michigan Canal. Their campfires at midnight resembled an army bivouac. In the morning the crowd thronged the dusty streets and public square. Douglas had brought his charming wife to town. Other women had come by dozens to enjoy the gaiety. Booths for the sale of lemonade and watermelons lined the streets. Peddlers offered painkillers and ague cures. Jugglers tossed balls, then passed hats for coins. Beggars and pickpockets pushed their way through the throng. Brass bands made the air pulse with "Columbia the Gem of the Ocean."

According to the rules for the debate, Douglas was to open with an hour's speech and Lincoln would have an hour and a half for reply. Then Douglas might close with half an hour. The Little Giant, who excelled in political offensive, began by attacking his opponent. He accused Lincoln of being a Whig who had turned abolitionist. To impress the stigma of extreme antislaveryism on him, Douglas said that Lincoln had taken part in an abolition meeting in Springfield in 1854. He read the radical platform adopted there.

Lincoln could only reply that he was not present at the meeting and did not know about the resolutions. He seemed uncertain and confused. The debate ended in Douglas' favor with many people believing that Lincoln had been fairly trapped, although his supporters carried him from the platform with a show of bravado. Hitt, taking shorthand notes on the Little Giant's speech, accepted the resolutions as genuine and transcribed only the opening lines, planning to copy them in entirety when he returned to the *Press and Tribune* office.

Back in Chicago, he asked a clerk to hunt up the record of the 1854 meeting. The paper was found in the files, but the resolutions Douglas had quoted were entirely different from those which had been adopted. Hitt strode over to the editor-in-chief's desk with this information. Ray called his colleagues to a hurried conference. The texts were laid out on the table. Someone remembered that the resolutions which Douglas quoted had been passed by a radical meeting at Aurora. Ray snatched a pencil and began an article on the "forgery." He headed the column: DOUGLAS' OTTAWA SPEECH PROVED TO BE A LIE AND A FRAUD.

With this "scoop" finished and in print, he noticed that the *Times* had garbled Lincoln's Ottawa speech, making the most of his confusion and emphasizing beyond all reason his abolition principles. Thus the discovery and exposure of the forgery was pertinent and well timed.

Charles Ray looked forward to following up his advantage in the next debate. He planned visiting Lincoln and coaching him for the contest, but an emergency in New York called him east. Before leaving he wrote Washburne:

My dear W.

I shall not go to Springfield. I am under the bitter necessity of going to New York tomorrow and of course cannot be back in time.

Tell old man Houghton to howl on that Douglas forgery, fraud and lie at Ottawa. We have got him on that sure, and we must make it a sufficient answer to all his charges during the campaign. Before the fight is over we will characterize every lie as one of Douglas' finding in Platform of the "State of Aurora." That's the note.

When you see Abe at Freeport, for God's sake tell him to "Charge Chester! Charge!" Do not let him keep on the defensive. Let him be fortified with his proofs and commence thus: "I charge so and so, and prove it thus!"

"I charge so and so, and prove it thus!" and so until the end of his hour, charging in every paragraph. Let him close the hour with a charge, and in his half hour following, let him pay no attention to Douglas' charges, but lump all his together and fling them at his head, and end up by shrieking a loud vote for Freedom! We must not be parrying all the while. We want the deadliest thrusts. Let us see blood follow every time he closes a sentence.

They (the Ruffians) feel like hell to-day. That forgery has cowed them. They won't say a word. Is it not a wonder that nobody at Ottawa detected it? The reply ought to have been then and there. It would have crushed him.

Tell old man H also to keep that mutilation of Lincoln's speech before the people; it is shameful—outrageous! The little cowards.

I am as you see warmed up, and before the canvass is over, I will give 'em some awful licks. The fight will be somewhat bitter if it keeps progressing as for ten days past. But, who cares? We are in for the war.

Yours Sincerely,
C. H. Ray

Within a week Douglas' action was known in the most remote villages in Illinois, and papers across the nation discussed the forgery which Ray had reported. Douglas tried to explain, saying that he had been innocently mistaken, but the political press refused to give him the benefit of the doubt. His own partisans admitted that their champion had been struck a body blow. Greeley came out against him in the *New York Tribune* and wrote to Lincoln and Herndon that Douglas was "like the man's boy who (he said) didn't weigh so much as he expected and he always knew he wouldn't."

The second debate was scheduled at Freeport on August 27. People realized that it would be most important. Lincoln's backers had studied the weaknesses of the first contest. They knew now what to expect and coached Lincoln on the necessity for taking the offensive, "Charge, Chester! Charge!" The

Press and Tribune engaged a special train of seventeen cars to carry the crowds from Chicago. A corps of reporters from the metropolitan press covered the event. Ray had not returned from New York, but he penned a question for Lincoln to ask Douglas to expose the sophistry of his popular sovereignty. Douglas' reply was destined to be the most important utterance of his life, for it permanently split the Democratic Party and assured the election of Lincoln as President of the United States two years hence. A comparison of the question Ray suggested and the one Lincoln submitted is therefore important.

Ray selected the District of Columbia as an example of a territory ruled by Congress. He wanted Lincoln to say that, if elected senator, he would vote for abolition in the District in case a majority of the residents wanted it. Could Douglas, favoring the Dred Scott decision and counting on Southern support, say as much? (At Ottawa Douglas had asked if Lincoln stood "pledged to abolition in the District of Columbia" without qualification.)

Lincoln evaded Ray's statement but planned another. With deadly skill he formulated a question which Douglas could not answer without antagonizing either the South or his own Illinois constituents. He would have to take one side or the other. The question might hurt Lincoln himself in southern Illinois if he dared ask it. On the train to Freeport he showed it to Medill. The editor read:

> Can the people of a United States Territory, in any lawful way, against the wish of any citizen of the United States, exclude slavery from its limits prior to the formation of a state constitution?

Medill, who did not know that the query may have originated with Ray, considered it unwise. Freeport, he said, was strongly antislavery and also Democratic. Douglas would give an affirmative answer and the people there would applaud and vote for him as one of themselves.

Lincoln put the paper back in his pocket and looked out the window at the telegraph poles flicking past, the rolling green pastures, and the wheat stubble brown in the August sun. He had been urged not to make the "house divided" speech and had dared to do so. What advice should he take now?

That night, at the hotel in Freeport, Medill told Judd and Washburne to implore Lincoln not to give Douglas the opportunity to come out against slavery by asking the question he had formulated—at least to wait until the debates moved farther south, where the sentiment was stronger for protecting slavery. In the lower counties Douglas might make a reply in favor of slavery that could then be used against him in northern Illinois. Lincoln was urged to emphasize nothing but the forgery charge in the next day's debate.

In the morning the speakers moved out to a grove where a platform had been erected. A drizzling rain veiled the countryside, but reports said that as many as 15,000 people had assembled. It was Lincoln's turn to open the debate, and when he rose from his chair and lifted his hand for silence, "Deacon" Bross shouted from the back of the crowd: "Hold on, Lincoln, you can't speak yet. Hitt isn't here and there is no use of your speaking unless the *Tribune* has a report"—typical Bross advertising. The vast throng must know that the *Press and Tribune's* published account would be meticulously transcribed.

"Ain't Hitt here?" Lincoln replied, entering into the game. "Where is he?"

"If Hitt is in this crowd he will please come forward," Bross boomed. "If he is tell him Mr. Bross of the *Chicago Press and Tribune* wants him to come here on the same stand and make a verbatim report for the only paper in the Northwest that has enterprise enough to publish speeches in full."

Hitt piped from the tightly packed crowd that he could not move through the press of people. What should he do? With a shout he was lifted into the air, and Mr. Hitt was propelled forward over the heads of the audience.

This circus act completed, Lincoln raised his hand again for silence and began to speak. Like Douglas at Ottawa, he took the initiative by asking embarrassing questions. Regardless of his advisers' disapproval, he read the fateful question: "Can the people of a . . . territory in any lawful way . . . exclude slavery from its limits?" The Dred Scott decision had said not. Already Douglas had dared split with Buchanan over the Lecompton Constitution. Would he go one step further and repudiate the slaveholders' Supreme Court decision?

Douglas replied boldly:

> It matters not what way the Supreme Court may hereafter decide as to the abstract question whether slavery may or may not go into a Territory under the Constitution, the people have the lawful means to intoduce it or exclude it as they please, for the reason that slavery cannot exist a day or an hour anywhere, unless it is supported by local police regulations. Those police regulations can only be established by the local legislature; and if the people are opposed to slavery, they will elect representatives to that body who will by unfriendly legislation effectually prevent the introduction of it into their midst. If, on the contrary, they are for it, their legislation will favor its extension.

Democrats in the audience who had backed Douglas' popular sovereignty as well as their party's Dred Scott decision, negating popular sovereignty by insisting that slavery be permitted in territories, cheered Douglas' clever logic. Here was a man who could reconcile contradictory principles. The *Press and Tribune* reporters saw through this at once and in the next edition complained: "Let Mr. Douglas be one thing or another, fish, flesh, or fowl, and not be dodging and skulking about, sometimes one thing, sometimes another, and sometimes both at once." The bait on Ray's hook was now well set in the Little Giant's gills.

Douglas' Freeport speech was printed word for word in the *Press and Tribune* and soon copies reached the South, where a great protest arose. The slave-power did not want the Little Giant's popular sovereignty unless it would fix slavery in every locality. They had favored his principles when they thought popular sovereignty would extend their peculiar institution. Now they feared that it would not do so, and Douglas was hailed as a betrayer of the South. Ray, having returned to Chicago, again took up his pen to attack Douglas. In editorial after editorial he reminded his readers that the Little Giant had continually played double in order to gain the presidency:

> The theories in which he was nursed taught him that such a prize was only to be sought among the slave breeders of Virginia and slave drivers of Alabama. He has put in pawn successively his manhood, his conscience, his constituents and the Senatorship in behalf of the ambition which devours him.

"Well, Mr. Douglas," another editorial added, "your agency will soon be over. Only five more debates, and you can go to the obscurity that yawns for you."

From Freeport the debaters moved to towns in the other congressional districts in Illinois – Jonesboro, Charleston, Galesburg, Quincy, and Alton. Constantly Lincoln stressed the ridiculousness of the Freeport doctrine that "a thing may be lawfully driven away from where it has a lawful right to be." Lincoln also maintained that Douglas tried to injure him with the abolitionist resolutions after he knew them to be false. He drew a hearty laugh from the crowd when he said that Douglas reminded him of the fishmonger's wife whose drowned husband's body was brought in full of eels. When asked what she wanted done with the corpse, she replied,

"*Take the eels out and set him again.*" That, Lincoln said, was what Douglas was doing with those forged resolutions. He was setting them again after he knew them to be dead.

Lincoln was also careful to show that the Republican Party was not abolitionist. It was the South that wanted to extend slavery into the North, not the North that wanted to wipe out slavery in the South. To strengthen this contention he pointed to the Dred Scott Decision, which might, if analyzed artfully, be construed as establishing slavery in the free states. Choosing the words carefully, he said:

> I submit to the consideration of men capable of arguing, whether as I state it in syllogistic form the argument has any fault in it:
>
> Nothing in the Constitution or laws of any State can destroy a right distinctly and expressly affirmed in the Constitution of the United States.
>
> The right of property in a slave is distinctly and expressly affirmed in the Constitution of the United States;
>
> Therefore, nothing in the Constitution or laws of any State can destroy the right of property in a slave.
>
> I believe that no fault can be pointed out in that argument; assuming the truth of the premises.

The premise, of course, had been affirmed by the Dred Scott decision which the Democrats and Douglas affirmed. Charles Ray printed this syllogism in full, and it is not surprising that newspapers in New England were soon claiming that the decision legalized slavery in the free states—a usurpation that might force any freedom-loving people into war.

Between the scheduled debates Lincoln and Douglas both spoke in scores of other towns. In all, they addressed meetings in fifty-seven counties of Illinois, in the open air except in two instances. Seven speeches were delivered in pelting rain. Again and again, they repeated their two doctrines, and the *Press and Tribune*, at great expense, devoted columns to the speeches and debates, informing the entire Northwest. One editorial announced:

"Old Abe" gathers strength as he goes along. He is like one of those long-winded racers that run the last heat and the last mile faster than the first and don't get fairly warmed in the work until they are on the last half of the race.

In another leader Ray wrote:

The fact is Douglas has been grossly overestimated as a debater, both by himself and the public. An uncommon fertility of quibbles, an opulence of sophistry, and a faculty of obscuring the issue from the people—in which he stands pre-eminent among men—constitutes his entire capital.

While Douglas' sun was setting, Lincoln and the *Press and Tribune* were rising together, as Ray had planned at the Bloomington Convention—each helping the other and both making a financial sacrifice. But while they grew, Lincoln's logic, as printed in the *Press and Tribune*, became Republican Party dogma. The entire nation watched and listened to those debates in the Middle West.

As the time for election approached, both sides, as is usual in politics, predicted victory. The *Press and Tribune* kept close watch on the various districts. They sent speakers to doubtful towns and complained that the Democrats—with $80,000 to spend on the campaign—were sending floaters to vote in some areas. The *Press and Tribune* warned readers to beware. The price of freedom was eternal vigilance. Vote, vote, by all means vote, and prevent this election from being lost by negligence. In doubtful precincts, committees must be appointed to watch for fraud.

November 2, 1858, was the crucial date. Bustling Chicago, with its hundred trains coming and going every twenty-four hours, broke ground that day for its first streetcar tracks.

Many people seemed too busy to vote, but Ray's precinct workers brought them to the polls in droves. Early returns from the city showed a Republican majority. Evidently the foreign vote had been won. Reports from downstate were conflicting. On November 4 the result was still doubtful, but on the next day the sad news had to be admitted. Even though the Republicans had polled a total of 125,430 against 120,609 for Douglas' supporters, the apportionment of the state gave the Little Giant a majority of the legislators who would elect the next senator. More encouraging, however, was the fact that the party had polled more votes than in the Frémont campaign two years ago. The *Press and Tribune* conceded:

We are beaten, but not disheartened or overawed. The principles and policy for which we have contended and shall still continue to contend, commend themselves with such convincing power to our judgment and conscience that we cannot be false to them if we would. . . . Now is the time to put the elements of the next and the great campaign in motion. . . . We promise nothing, except to be true to our professions, and to leave nothing undone that will make the *Press and Tribune* worthy of your continued support.

Certainly the *Press and Tribune's* campaign had paid off politically, though not financially. Even after the consolidation, the expense of promoting the debates and furnishing speakers in doubtful districts had placed a heavy burden on the paper. Three days after the final returns had been tallied, the *Press and Tribune* owners called together their creditors and told them that they could not meet the next payments and that unless given more time they would assign their assets. The creditors wanted their money instead of the paper. They looked over the plant, the new presses, the constantly expanding circulation, and the obligations amounting to only $65,000. They decided to renew the mortgage for another three years at ten per cent—which did not seem large to Charles Ray. Three years extended the life of the paper until after the presidential election of 1860. What more could a crusader ask? Surely the cause would be triumphant by that time and the paper financially sound as well.

Dr. Ray returned to his desk in the best of spirits. A letter came to him from defeated candidate Lincoln. Abe wanted two copies of all the *Press and Tribunes* which had carried his speeches in the debates. He said that he planned to clip and save the speeches in a scrapbook. He did not say what he intended to do with the scrapbook but he ended the letter with:

I believe, according to a letter of yours to Hatch you are "feeling like h—ll yet." Quit that. You will soon feel better. Another "blow-up" is coming; and we shall have fun again. Douglas managed to be supported both as the best instrument to *put down* and to *up-hold* the slave power; but no ingenuity can long keep these antagonisms in harmony.

Yours as ever,
A. Lincoln.

Ray, with three years' life guaranteed for the paper, looked eagerly forward to the next "blow-up." He dipped his pen into the inkwell and wrote a long creed for the continuation of the struggle:

We shall be very sorry, very sorry indeed, to believe that Illinois is a pro-slavery State; but whether it be or not, we owe to our fathers, our country and posterity, a war against the pro-slavery Democracy, here and elsewhere, to be terminated only with our lives—and we mean to discharge the debt with such power as has been given us. We are defeated—not for the first time, perhaps not for the last. The seed of Republicanism planted in this great contest must spring and ripen into its proper fruit; if not now, then in the next year or the next twenty . . . and what remains to be done when we have ceased to be, we shall bequeath fervently to our children. This is the spirit which animates Republicans from Maine to Oregon. They want no Senators, no Presidents at the price of their principles. They will try again and a hundred times again. The cause which animates them—will outlive the mountains.

X "You Are Strongly Talked of for the Presidency"

THE *Press and Tribune* greeted Lincoln's defeat arrogantly on November 5, 1858, by saying:

So long as life, liberty and the pursuit of happiness are left us, the Republican party is enlisted with all its energies for the battle of the Right against the Wrong. As said John Paul Jones, of heroic memory, when asked if he had struck his colors: WE HAVE ONLY BEGUN TO FIGHT.

Five days later Ray again wrote about the campaign and Lincoln's part in it:

Mr. Lincoln is beaten. . . . We know of no better time than the present to congratulate him on the memorable and brilliant canvass that he has made. . . . He has created for himself a national reputation that is both envied and deserved; and though he should hereafter fill no official station, he has done the cause of Truth and Justice what will always entitle him to the gratitude of his party and to the admiration of all who respect the high moral qualities, and the keen, comprehensive and sound intellectual gifts he has displayed. . . . His speeches will become landmarks in our political history. . . . Mr. Lincoln, at Springfield, at peace with himself because he has been true to his convictions, enjoying the confidence and unfeigned respect of his peers, is more to be envied than Mr. Douglas in the senate! Long live Honest Old Abe!

On November 21 the newly elected Douglas met Ray face to face. The Little Giant looked up at his big enemy and talked with apparent cordiality and frankness. A professional fighter, Douglas displayed none of the hatred he must have felt. He stated unequivocally that he would seek no peace with the Buchanan Democrats and, being unacceptable to the Republicans, he intended to continue the fight for his "great principle"—that the Supreme Court could sanction slavery in territories but that local laws could keep it out.

Ray looked critically at the little man as he talked. Douglas' egotism showed in his expensive clothes. Courage bristled from his energetic figure. He told Ray that he planned to vote for the protective tariff advocated by the *Press and Tribune*. He stated also that he did not expect to be a candidate for President in 1860. The proslavery wing of the party, he said, would scheme to prevent that.

Charles Ray was not so sure that Douglas had given up all hope. The call seemed to him like another overture to the Republicans. Ray was certain that the new party must begin grooming its own choice for President before Douglas pulled some political rabbit from his sleek high hat. The most likely presidential candidates were Senators Seward, the New York Whig, and Chase, the Ohio Democrat. Thomas Hart Benton of Missouri had died. St. Louis Republicans might advance Edward Bates in his place. As a Western man, Bates should poll Western votes. Abraham Lincoln did not seem to be considered by many pollsters. His defeat at the hands of Douglas had hurt his chances. It was useless to point out that he had won the greater number of votes. The fact remained that he had lost the senatorship. "President-making," Dr. Ray wrote on March 29, 1859, "is a dangerous and thankless business. . . . The day for the nomination of the Republican candidate has not yet arrived." Ray considered a discussion in the press premature at this time. "The hour and the man will come together," he said. Talking over prospective candidates with the staff, Ray noticed that Medill seemed to favor his old friend, Salmon P. Chase. Ray, himself, preferred Lincoln but was not yet sure of his presidential stature. In any event he wanted a Western man. In July he still had no candidate and seemed willing to permit the East to offer its best man as soon as possible, "putting him into a press in which he will be squeezed to death long before the convention is called." Then the West might come forward with its dark horse and win.

The looming nomination of 1860 colored Charles Ray's every thought during 1859. Municipal elections in Chicago, Quincy, and Rockford, all normally Democratic, went Republican, and the politicians noted the significant change. The normal Democratic vote in Ottawa also changed as the result of a much-publicized fugitive slave rescue.

Early in the year a Negro had been adjudged a free man in Ottawa and immediately thereafter was kidnaped and spirited away by slave catchers. The citizens were still outraged about this event when they learned that a second Negro, alleged to be a slave, had been captured down at Jonesboro, Illinois. Judge John Dean Caton, at Ottawa, issued a writ of habeas corpus to give the black man an impartial trial in the North. The Negro was brought upstate by the jailer and the slave's owner, a Missouri planter. As the train came through Bloomington, Judge David Davis met it and warned the slave owner that the upstate men had been in an ugly mood since that last Negro had been kidnaped. The judge advised him to desist from going farther north. The slave owner and the jailer, however, believed that they had the law of the land behind them and stayed on the train.

At the railroad station in LaSalle, seventeen miles out of Ottawa, the downstate men had to change cars. The slave was taken out with his arms trussed by a rope. A trace chain dragged from one leg. The jailer led him with a "plow line" of the length commonly used for livestock. In southern Illinois people laughed when a Negro was treated like an animal—they thought it taught him to know his place. In LaSalle the downstate jailer's humor did not make anybody laugh. A man on the sidewalk asked the Negro, "What are you up for, fellah?"

"What crime have you committed?" another asked.

The jailer raised the end of the chain to strike the black man and keep him from replying. However he decided not to do so when he saw that a large crowd had congregated. Judge Davis had been right. These Northern farmers were in an ugly mood. The sight of clanking chains, roped arms, a felon's guard around a man who had committed no crime except to run away from slavery infuriated them. The downstate men were glad to get back on the train once more. The jailer took the chain from the slave's leg and loosened the rope around his arms. Later he explained: "The fact was, it was a pretty sour crowd around here. I allowed they would feel a little better to have it off."

The slaveholders did not like the looks of things as the train trundled along the last leg of the journey. They realized that they were very far from home, among strangers in a strange land. The train stopped next at Ottawa. A crowd was waiting on the platform. The slave men got off. The crowd parted and let them through. They marched away, with the crowd following, grim and silent. Stovepipe hats bobbed among the broad-brimmed beavers. The slaveholders felt miserable. This steel-trap silence "got a fellah" worse than the hubbub back at LaSalle. Then they heard a voice tell the black man, "Never mind, boy! You needn't be scared—you're all right."

News of the unusual trial had spread across northern Illinois, and Ray sent a correspondent to Ottawa. According to reports and grapevine telegrams which soon filtered through to Chicago, the mob was sullen and intense. Anything might happen. People said that the planter was a "nigger ketcher" who would steal the black man before his trial. A few philanthropists raised $500 and offered it for the slave. The owner held out for $1000. On the morning of the trial a crowd of curious onlookers lined the public square. The courthouse steps were packed. Inside, some two hundred men jammed the halls. The elderly slaveholder was not molested as he elbowed through the crowd to Judge Caton's chambers. The planter sat down beside the judge at one end of a long table. The deputy and the Negro stood by an open window. The whole room was filled with grim men with eager, squint-eyed, bearded faces. Bald heads gleamed pink and white above sunburned cheeks.

The judge was a large man weighing over two hundred pounds. He examined the papers and said that the Negro was the lawful property of the planter. A slight movement started through the crowd. The old planter could stand the suspense no longer. He got up, tottered out, and sat in the fresh air on the courthouse steps, frightened, sick, and weak. Judge Caton looked at the waiting crowd. He knew many of the men personally and he told them that he hoped there would be no interference with the execution of the law. He had issued the writ of habeas corpus for the upstate people in order that the Negro might be brought north for a fair trial. The papers indicated conclusively that the Negro belonged to the planter. Now if the people did not abide by the court's decision, he would never issue another writ to bring a man to a country where the law was not respected.

The judge got up and stalked out. The Negro stood by the window with the deputy. Everyone was silent. Judge Caton looked at the familiar faces in the crowd and noticed an "intensity of expression." As soon as he had left the room somebody jumped on a chair and called on all good law-abiding citizens to aid in carrying the Negro back to slavery. The crowd broke into an uproar. There was a rush for the door. A voice shouted: "If you want your liberty, run."

Men standing on the board sidewalks across the square saw a frightened black man jump the courthouse fence and dart under the drawn curtain of a waiting carriage. Peter Meyer, a saloon man, ran into the street and grabbed the horses' bridles, jerking them to a stop. A man named John Hossack snatched the lines from Meyer's hands and swung his fist at him. The horses reared, then plunged forward, and the carriage spun out of sight with the driver standing on the front boot lashing with his whip. People on the sidewalk and in the street cheered and waved their hats. The elderly planter and his friends slipped out of town as quickly and as quietly as possible.

Back home in Missouri the planter regained his courage. He did not mind the loss of one slave, he said. It was the principle of the thing. He immediately sold four "sound hands" and said that he was prepared to sell four more and use all the money to get back the escaped "boy."

John Hossack, the man who had rescued the Negro, was highly respected in Ottawa. Born in Scotland, he was now a citizen of the United States. He had come west to work on the Illinois and Michigan Canal and had made a small fortune. He abhorred slavery and believed sincerely in the Declaration of Independence. However the Fugitive Slave Act provided for the return of escaped slaves, and Hossack was arrested for violating this law. He asked for a change of venue, and his trial was set for February 28, 1860, in Chicago. Charles Ray knew that the blood of martyrs would nourish the Republican Party and he looked forward to Hossack's trial with great interest.

As yet the *Press and Tribune* had not endorsed a candidate for President. On June 15, 1859, Ray received the following letter from Lincoln.

Gentlemen:

Herewith is a little draft to pay for your Daily another year from to-day. I suppose I shall take *The Press & Tribune* so long as it, and I both live, unless I become unable to pay for it. In it's devotion to our cause always, and to me personally last year I owe it a debt of gratitude, which I fear I shall never be able to pay.

Yours very truly,
A. Lincoln.

During the summer Lincoln made a number of speeches in Illinois and took a trip to Wisconsin to deliver an address at that state's agricultural fair. Ray gave him constant publicity in the *Press and Tribune* and printed his Wisconsin speech in full, but he told his readers frankly that the newspaper's one great concern was to select a presidential candidate for 1860 who would be absolutely sound on the Republican platform. Ray pointed out that the Republicans must nominate a man of courage and "old-fashioned integrity." He must have an acceptable attitude toward slavery and must be radical enough to suit the abolitionists and moderate enough to reassure the conservatives. Without such a man, he warned, the Republican Party might split and die as the Democrats were doing.

Douglas had followed his re-election to the United States Senate with a triumphal trip through the South, ostensibly for his health. He traveled with his charming wife to help ingratiate him with prominent slaveholding politicians. To his dismay, he learned that Southerners had read the *Press and Tribune* or extracts from it. The slave-power was familiar with his Freeport doctrine, which maintained that local communities might keep out slavery, and they considered Douglas a traitor. Southern Democrats insisted that the next candidate for president must be a man who would insure the protection of slavery in all the territories. But Douglas always had a compromise up his broadcloth sleeve. He expressed approval of the acquisition of Cuba in order that slavery might expand down there if it couldn't in the Western territories.

Returning to Washington, the Little Giant failed to patch up his disagreement with President Buchanan and he quarreled with Jefferson Davis. In desperation, Douglas turned to his Northern constituents. In a last effort to keep them from joining the Republican Party from which he had been excluded, he wrote an article for *Harper's Monthly* explaining that his principle of popular sovereignty took the fangs from the Dred Scott Decision without surrendering to the slave-power.

This final effort of Douglas to reach the ears of Northern Democrats gave Lincoln an opportunity to answer him publicly once more. The Springfield lawyer made arrangements to speak in both Columbus and Cincinnati, Ohio. In the *Press and Tribune,* Ray greeted the announcement of the speech in the latter place with, "Well done, Cincinnati! You are paying merited respect to an honest man!" Abe's honesty was becoming more and more a symbol in the contest against the corruption of the Buchanan administration. Ray liked the name "Honest Abe" and used it with increasing frequency. Soon other Republican papers took up the sobriquet. With a constant flow of eulogies, Ray promised to print Lincoln's Ohio speeches, and, as he did so, he continued to remind readers that a Western man must be the next candidate for President of the United States. He still suggested no names, but he wrote:

> Is it not high time that the WEST claimed her political rights in the Government? Or is she merely a vassal or colony of the cotton, negro-breeding, and the importing portions of the Union? . . . The vast interests of the mighty West demand recognition in the administration of the Government. It is not enough that the West should be allowed to furnish a Western candidate with *Southern principles.* Let us have a Western statesman, who will remember there is a West, whose interests are entitled to a full and equal care and attention at the hands of the Executive and Congress.

Ray sent Hitt to report Lincoln's Ohio speeches. Let everyone read the *Press and Tribune* for a verbatim account. Already the paper's circulation had become the largest in the Northwest—and the once worrisome debts were being paid off rapidly. On September 16 Lincoln spoke at Columbus, attacking Douglas' *Harper's* article. He made popular sovereignty ridiculous, saying:

What is Judge Douglas' Popular Sovereignty? It is, as a principle, no other than that, if one man chooses to make a slave of another man, neither that other man nor anybody else has a right to object. Applied in government, as he seeks to apply it, it is this: If, in a new territory into which a few people are beginning to enter for the purpose of making their homes, they choose to either exclude slavery from their limits, or to establish it there . . . there is no power or right to interfere. That is Douglas' popular sovereignty applied.

Lincoln had hardly returned from Ohio and settled back in Springfield when the nation was jarred by distressing news from the East. Old John Brown, with some twenty men, had captured the Federal arsenal at Harpers Ferry and had liberated and armed a few slaves, calling on others to rise. A slave insurrection was one of the worst horrors Southerners could conceive and they immediately blamed this on the Republican Party.

Horace Greeley, Dr. Ray, Joseph Medill and the other leading editors had praised Jim Lane and John Brown when they fought for civil rights in Kansas. Lincoln had been more cautious, as befitted a politician groping his way into a strange field, but the Douglasites persisted in classing him with the most extreme supporters, calling him a "Black Republican abolitionist." Lincoln had always denied being an abolitionist, maintaining only that he objected to the further extension of slavery.

Now, however, the Republicans' man, John Brown, had been caught starting a Negro revolt. The entire party was sure to be blamed. Charles Ray dashed off an editorial condemning the violence but putting the final blame on the slavocrats, who had driven old Brown from Osawatomie, burned his house, and killed his son. Atrocities in Kansas, Ray said, had been sufficient to stir up sentiment for retaliation everywhere. Subscribers to the *Press and Tribune* read:

The news from Harpers Ferry, in which the insurrectionary attempt of a handful of blacks, aided by two or three white men, is related, will produce a profound sensation in all the slave-holding States. Osawatomie Brown, who seems to have been the head and front of the movement, figures not unexpectedly to us in this purposeless and senseless riot. Since the death of his son Frederick, who was shot down at his own door in Kansas by a Missouri mob tenfold more revengeful and bloody than that which now fills Virginia with terror, and since the old man witnessed, on the same occasion, the destruction of the property he had been a life-time in accumulating, he has been a monomaniac. He has supposed himself divinely appointed to free all American slaves by some violent and decisive movement. . . .

Three days later Ray wrote again:

Let the fear and trembling that have run through the Old Dominion and which will hereafter haunt the pillow of every slaveholder in the land, be charged to the account of those who have set the causes in motion. Let the Democracy of the North—particularly of the Northwest—who, under the lead of Douglas, have stopped at nothing to degrade Freedom and elevate Slavery, bear the burdens which their causeless criminality has imposed upon them. Republican skirts are clear.

With this in print Ray wrote a short note to Lincoln, saying:

We are damnably exercised here about the effect of old Brown's wretched *fiasco* in Virginia, upon the moral health of the Republican party! The old idiot—the quicker they hang him and get him out of the way, the better. You see how we treat it—I hope we occupy the right ground.

Then Ray added a significant note: "Do you know that you are strongly talked of for the Presidency?—the Vice-Presidency at least?"

XI "Old Abe Must Have Lost Our Notes"

Two weeks after Charles Ray wrote Lincoln, telling him that he was "talked of for the Presidency," the *Press and Tribune* began to discuss possible presidential nominees. The state election returns had just been counted and the Republicans showed remarkable strength. The paper stated:

We premise that no man has any *claims* on the Republican party for a Presidential nomination that are worth talking about. . . . The right of each in the premises is measured, *first* by his ability to administer the government on Republican principles; and, *second*, by his strength in the manner of electoral votes. . . .

What man can carry the five Northern States which Frémont lost, or a sufficient number of them to make a majority of the electoral college? The States are New Jersey, Pennsylvania, Indiana, Illinois and California. . . . Here is the question in a nut-shell. The representatives of the four doubtful states [omitting California] in the national Convention will throw some light upon it. They will exercise an influence on the result quite out of proportion to their numerical strength. . . . We have the utmost faith that the decision will commend itself fully to the judgment of all sections of the country.

Probably all the editors of the *Press and Tribune* saw at this time that Lincoln had the best chance to carry the four important states, but still they refrained from saying so editorially. However on November 19, 1859, Ray reprinted a column from a Pennsylvania paper which suggested the names of Senator Simon Cameron for the presidency and Abraham Lincoln for the vice-presidency, to assure the votes of Pennsylvania and Illinois. These two, the paper maintained, would swing the election. Ray added to the reprint the comment that the ticket should be the other way.

We fancy the Republicans of the Northwest will insist upon turning it end for end, so that it may read LINCOLN for PRESIDENT and Cameron for Vice President. . . . We make these suggestions not to insist that the Republican party of the Union shall nominate Mr. Lincoln for the Presidency, but to state what sort of a ticket we should prefer.

Charles Ray spent several weeks in Springfield in the winter of 1859-1860. Officially he went down on Illinois and Michigan Canal business. His duties as commissioner were giving him more trouble than ever. A scandal had arisen from the cashing of the scrip by Ex-Governor Matteson. Evidence indicated that this "paper" had already been turned into the state and paid for. The hearings were long and involved. Lincoln had given Ray legal advice on other canal matters, and Ray undoubtedly conferred with him on this problem. Recesses in the hearings enabled Ray to learn the attitudes of Lincoln's personal supporters on political questions.

In December Lincoln left for Kansas on a speaking trip along the Missouri. He was out there when news reached Chicago that John Brown had been hanged. Bells tolled in the city, and ministers offered prayers for the martyr's soul. The *Press and Tribune* received a long telegaphic account of the execution and published all the details. On the day after the hanging Lincoln was in Leavenworth, addressing a hostile audience of Southern sympathizers who had already threatened to help the slave states secede in case the Republicans won the next election. Lincoln said to them:

> [You say] if the Black Republicans elect a President . . . you will break up the Union. That will be your act, not ours. . . . Old John Brown has just been executed for treason against a state. . . . If constitutionally we elect a President, and therefore you undertake to destroy the Union, it will be our duty to deal with you as old John Brown has been dealt with.

While Lincoln was speaking in Kansas, the *Press and Tribune* editors met with Norman Judd, chairman of the Republican state central committee, and other party leaders to plan a campaign for Lincoln's nomination. The first step was to get the national convention to meet in Chicago. A Western city was sure to be chosen in recognition of the potential vote in the new states. Both Indianapolis and St. Louis wanted to play host to the convention. The national committee was scheduled to meet at the Astor House in New York and consider the invitations. Since Medill was going east to serve as Washington correspondent for the *Press and Tribune* the editors of the paper decided he should attend the New York meeting. They also decided that Judd must go east too with the formal invitation for the national committee.

At the Astor House, in December 1859, the committee considered the bid from Indianapolis and turned it down because that city lacked sufficient hotel accommodations. St. Louis' invitation was declined because Missouri, as a slave state, was certain to be carried by the Democrats. Judd and Medill both assured the committee that Chicago could take care of large crowds. That booming city, with its hundreds of immigrants arriving daily, was accustomed to handling great numbers. Crowds were the city's usual diet. Moreover, Illinois would be neutral ground for a contest between the supporters of Seward, Chase, and Bates. Lincoln was not considered an important candidate.

The Eastern delegates believed the politicians' convincing talk. They wanted to see the Wonder City and agreed to hold the convention there. Medill wired the good news and on December 22, 1859, *Press and Tribune* readers were informed of the decision. Ray did not add that this circumstance gave the *Press and Tribune* editors an opportunity to be king-makers, but certainly he must have enjoyed an especially merry Christmas. Everything that he had promised Jane was coming to pass and more, too. New Year's Day was snowy in Chicago, and Charles Ray looked from his office window through a trembling curtain of falling flakes at sleighs slipping along the white streets, bells jingling. He knew that the year ahead was to be crucial for the nation, perhaps for civilization. In his position he might be instrumental in the nomination and election of a president who would put to rest for all time the issue of slavery.

With Chicago selected as the place for the convention and Abraham Lincoln as the *Press and Tribune's* candidate, Charles Ray began publishing articles about the platform on which he hoped the Republican Party might win. He demanded a protective tariff, a homestead act, a Pacific railroad, improvement of rivers and harbors, and reciprocal trade with Cuba, instead of Douglas' proposed annexation. Above all, the nation must clean out corruption and favoritism in government. With this in mind he wrote:

The leaks whereby the treasury is exhausted and the government reduced to bankruptcy must be sought out and closed. The jobbing and nepotism, the peculation and robbery, which have made the national Administration a reproach where our American newspapers go, must be exposed and corrected. The relation which the government bears to other powers—our European as well as American neighbors—must be settled on a just and honorable basis, and in such a way that filibustering and piracy will not have a leg to stand on. The improvement of our rivers and harbors, upon some constitutional and economic plan, must be undertaken. The freedom of the public lands to actual settlers, must be accorded as a measure of justice to the landless and to the Western States, and as a guaranty of the freedom of the territories now unoccupied.

As Ray expounded the Republican platform and the virtues of Abraham Lincoln in the West, Medill, in Washington, talked continually in favor of Lincoln for the presidency. This publicity elicited an invitation for the little-known Illinois lawyer to come to New York and speak in the Cooper Union Institute. Charles Ray announced Lincoln's acceptance of the request with a long editorial on February 16, 1860:

It appears to be a foregone conclusion that the nomination of the Chicago Convention will be conferred upon no one who does now [*sic*] unite in himself the essentials of requisite qualification, devotion to the distinctive principles of the Republican party, and availability [i.e., a resident of Illinois, Indiana, Pennsylvania, or New Jersey].

We have no hesitance in saying that as respects the first two essentials, Abraham Lincoln, of Illinois, is the peer of any man yet named in connection with the Republican nominations, while in regard to availability, we believe him to be more certain to carry Illinois and Indiana than anyone else, and his political antecedents are such as to commend him heartily to the support of Pennsylvania and New Jersey.

A campaign for the popularization of Lincoln in these two states had been started by the Illinois state central committee in December 1859, when Jesse Fell published, in the Pennsylvania *Chester County Times*, a Lincoln autobiography claiming Quaker ancestors in the East.

Ray's task now was to emphasize Lincoln's popularity beyond Illinois and the Northwest. His memorable campaign against Douglas in 1858, Ray said, had given Republicans throughout the Union the opportunity to become familiar with "his admirable personal qualities, his entire devotion to the distinctive principles of the party, his rare abilities and his broad, statesmanlike views on national political questions." Ray devoted columns of the *Press and Tribune* to reminding the Cooper Union audience that Lincoln was a presidential possibility. How extensively the *Tribune* was read in the East, except by editors, is of course conjectural, but Ray never relaxed his publicity. Lincoln's outstanding characteristics were delineated under four headings:

1st. A gentleman of unimpeachable purity of private life. His good name is not soiled by a single act, political, social, moral or religious, that we or his friends need blush to own as his. In all of his relations to his fellows he has not yet been guilty of that thing upon which an enemy can place a finger and say, "this is dishonest," or "this is mean." Herein he is the peer of the most unspotted man of the Republic—the living likeness, full length size, of the best of the eminent characters who laid the foundation of the government.

2d. A man of, at once, great breadth and great acuteness of intellect. Not learned in a bookish sense, but master of great fundamental principles, and of that kind of ability which applies them to crises and events. The masterly canvass which he made with Douglas, and his later speeches in Ohio, mark him as one of the ablest political thinkers of his day.

3d. Right on the record. An Old Line Whig . . . acceptable to Pennsylvania and New Jersey—candidate of the party which in itself is an embodiment of the principles and measures necessary for the perpetuity of the Union and the preservation of our free institutions—he would enter the field acceptable to the Opposition of all shades of opinion, harmonizing all interests, conciliating all jarring elements—the master of the position, a guarantor of success.

4th. A man of executive capacity. Never garrulous, never promising what he cannot perform, never doing anything for show or effect, laboriously attentive to detail, industrious and conscientious, he would see to it that no want of promptness, attention or industry on his part should defeat the reforms in the administration of national affairs which Republicanism is pledged to inaugurate.

Extracts from this lengthy eulogy were copied by many newspapers across the nation and may fairly be said to have been the first description of the candidate's character to circulate outside Illinois. Easterners reading it would look forward to Lincoln's Cooper Union speech with new interest. Ten days later Joe Medill wrote from Washington that the East was becoming interested in this man. His name was mentioned for the presidency "ten times as often as it was one month ago."

Dr. Ray was careful to be undogmatic about the selection of Lincoln, stating that the *Press and Tribune* would accept the selection made by the convention. However, on February 23, he reprinted the autobiography which Lincoln had written for the Pennsylvania *Chester County Times*. Next day Ray also suggested that the state committee rally to the name of Lincoln and form clubs to work for his nomination. In case Bissell, Trumbull, or some other favorite son were selected, the same machinery could be used for the nominee.

We take it for granted that LINCOLN is the first choice of every Republican in the State. . . . When Mr. Lincoln wants the vote of Illinois, he will receive it by unanimous consent. If this be so, let us organize at once and in his behalf!

Down in Springfield Lincoln realized that his destiny hung, to a large extent, on his Cooper Union speech. On the impression he made in New York the East would judge his soundness as presidential timber. He worked hard on the ideas and wording of his proposed oration. Then, finally, he stuffed a suit and extra shirt into his carpetbag and went to Chicago to discuss his speech with the *Press and Tribune* editors. Medill had just arrived from Washington. Lincoln asked Ray and Medill to read his speech carefully, polish the language, suggest better turns of phrases, and delete or add where it seemed advisable. Easterners, after all, might not agree with Westerners on the Republican platform. Lincoln, with this great opportunity at Cooper Union, wanted to say exactly the right thing. He left the two editors, promising to call for the speech next day and to consider their suggestions.

Medill and Ray hastily finished the work on their desks and sat down together. This they knew to be Lincoln's big speech. First one then the other read from the manuscript while the listener took notes. They stopped to discuss the impact of certain points, suggested additions, and scribbled memoranda in the margins. That evening each took part of the speech home to reconsider.

Ray knew that a short play with the babies refreshed a man's mind and brushed the cobwebs from his thinking. It was always relaxing to listen to Jane's household problems, to look at the new bonnet and shawl she thought becoming. Then Ray returned to the manuscript. At night in bed he pondered Lincoln's phraseology, reflected how to give it more strength, and jotted down ideas for a better method of presentation. At the office in the morning Medill said that he too had been thinking about Lincoln's work. Together the two editors read Lincoln's speech again and added more suggestions. In midmorning Lincoln bounded up the steps, two at a time. His face was aglow at the prospect of the trip ahead. Ray and Medill complimented him on the speech and said they had proposed some changes in the margins. Lincoln thanked them heartily, folded the papers, and clattered down the stairs.

The editors turned to the day's work. Ray wrote an editorial printed on February 27, exalting Lincoln as the Republican Party's best candidate. He said:

Mr. Lincoln's record, both political and personal, is without a line of which any Republican need be afraid or ashamed.

> . . . His growth in the Antislavery belief has not been the result of any quickening hot-house process, but the ripening of his convictions. . . . No government dollars would, if elected, stick to his fingers, or be appropriated to partisan purposes. . . . Is not Lincoln the man for the hour?

Next day the *Press and Tribune* printed another article boosting Honest Abe, but almost a week elapsed before Ray heard about the reception of Lincoln's Cooper Union speech. Then he learned that the hall had been filled with many notable people and that Abe had held them spellbound. William Cullen Bryant had introduced the Westerner. Horace Greeley, using Lincoln's own notes, printed the speech in the *New York Tribune*. Ray clipped the transcription for reprinting in the *Press and Tribune*. With great interest he and Medill read the familiar language, the typical Lincoln simplicity, that they had hoped to polish. Lincoln had been forthright and to the point. According to his own copy he had said:

> If slavery is right, all words, acts, laws, and constitutions against it, are themselves wrong, and should be silenced, and swept away. If it is right, we cannot justly object to its nationality—its universality; if it is wrong, they cannot justly insist upon its extension—its enlargement. All they ask, we could readily grant, if we thought slavery right; all we ask, they could as readily grant, if they thought it wrong. Their thinking it right, and our thinking it wrong, is the precise fact upon which depends the whole controversy. Thinking it right, as they do, they are not to blame for desiring its full recognition, as being right; but, thinking it wrong, as we do, can we yield to them? Can we cast our votes with their view, and against our own? In view of our moral, social, and political responsibilities, can we do this?

Medill looked at Ray. This wasn't their language, it was Lincoln's. Was it in later paragraphs that they had changed some of his sentences? They read on:

Wrong, as we think slavery is, we can yet afford to let it alone where it is, because that much is due to the necessity arising from its actual presence in the nation; but can we, while our votes will prevent it, allow it to spread into the National Territories, and to overrun us here in these free States. If our sense of duty forbids this, then let us stand by our duty, fearlessly and effectively. Let us be diverted by none of those sophistical contrivances wherewith we are so industriously plied and belabored—contrivances such as groping for middle ground between the right and the wrong, vain as the search for a man who should be neither a living man nor a dead man—such as a policy of "don't care" on a question about which all true men do care—such as Union appeals beseeching true Union men to yield to Disunionists, reversing the divine rule, and calling, not the sinners, but the righteous to repentance—such as invocations to Washington, imploring men to unsay what Washington said, and undo what Washington did.

Ray must have looked at Medill with a strange twinkle in his blue eyes, then continued reading:

Neither let us be slandered from our duty by false accusations against us, nor frightened from it by menaces of destruction to the Government nor of dungeons to ourselves. Let us have faith that right makes might, and in that faith, let us, to the end, dare to do our duty as we understand it.

Dr. Ray put down the paper. "Medill," he said, "old Abe must have lost out the car window all our precious notes, for I don't find a trace of one of them in his published talk here."

Medill laughed, without humor, and said, "This must have been meant for one of his waggish jokes."

Both men had to admit though that the country lawyer had written with penetrating force. He would be his own boss, his own master—a characteristic which might, or might not, help him win the election for the Republicans.

XII The John Hossack Case

LINCOLN had not returned from his Cooper Union speech when the case of John Hossack, accused of helping a fugitive slave escape, came to trial in the United States District Court in Chicago. The city was seething with anticipation of the Republican Convention. The old Sauganash Hotel on the corner of Lake and Market was being torn down to make room for an assembly hall. The Wigwam, as the vast structure was called, would have a frontage of 180 feet, a depth of 100 feet, and seats for 5000 people, with standing room for an equal number. According to the plans a gallery was to encircle three sides of the auditorium. The speakers' platform was to be four feet high, one hundred and forty feet long, and thirty-five feet deep, with committee rooms at each end. All accredited delegates would sit on this platform. A slight elevation in the center would be occupied by the chairman and his secretaries. Alternate delegates, holders of special tickets, and the public would sit in the parquet and balcony. Thus all the delegations would be part of a grand dramatic performance to be enacted before the audience.

The split between Douglas and the Democratic administration gave the Republican Party a great advantage in the coming election, and many people believed that the next President of the United States would be nominated in this great flimsy building. Hundreds of people came daily to watch its construction while they gossiped about the Hossack case.

Chicago was reckoned an abolition town—just the place to acquit John Hossack or to nominate Abraham Lincoln for the presidency. At least two churches in the city were terminals of the underground railroad. From here Great Lakes vessels carried fugitives to freedom in Canada. A swivel-eyed Scot, Allan Pinkerton, operated a detective agency in Chicago. A former member of the police force, he had the inside track on matters of difficulty with "the law." He was also an ardent abolitionist, and he took conscientious pride in being superintendent of the underground railroad's embarking depot. Chicago was notoriously lawless—full of transients and immigrants, all presumably opposed to slavery and the Fugitive Slave Act.

Charles Ray saw the importance of properly reporting the Hossack case. Wasn't the antislavery sentiment in the city strong enough for a jury to ignore the Federal law, as the mob had done at Ottawa? Ray watched for demonstrations of popular opinion. Five eminent attorneys had been employed to defend Hossack. Among them was Isaac N. Arnold, who shared Ray's interest in the Chicago Historical Society. He had been a prominent antislavery advocate for a decade and understood every angle of the Fugitive Slave Act. Surely he could present Hossack's case in such a way as to convince not only the jury but also the mob in the streets. As the day of the trial approached, a mass meeting convened at Metropolitan Hall and passed resolutions denouncing any court or any law, Federal or state, that would punish a man for helping a fellow man gain his liberty.

Seeing this rising tide of popular indignation, Charles Ray wondered if United States District Attorney Henry S. Fitch would prosecute the case himself or employ additional counsel. The defense attorneys were popular men, hard to beat. They were stimulated by the knowledge that they were being watched by streets full of fickle citizens and wily politicians alert for every shift of sentiment for or against the nomination of Abraham Lincoln. To win against this handicap and get a conviction of John Hossack seemed well-nigh impossible. But when Charles Ray learned that Fitch had employed Alfred Arrington to assist him he knew that the prosecution would be vigorous and the case might well be the best story of the year, barring only the presidential nomination in May and the election in November. Arrington was a Southerner who had come to Chicago recently to practice law. Already he had established a reputation for swaying juries as effectively as Owen Lovejoy could inspire an abolition meeting. What success would this orator have in immigrant-packed, normally antislavery Chicago?

A tense crowd congregated for the trial. The planter who had lost the slave, the Jonesboro jailer, Judge Caton, and Peter Meyer the saloon man, all testified and were cross-examined. Charles Ray, in a spectator's chair, had to admit that the defendant's guilt was self-evident and that a conviction seemed certain. However, he was a bit dubious when Isaac N. Arnold summed up the defense in the following words:

> Gentlemen, in the nineteenth century of the Christian era, in the Republic of the United States, in the free State of Illinois, a man of unblemished character—a man known and beloved in a city which his intelligent industry has aided to build up, and his high moral qualities have contributed to adorn—sits at the felon's bar of this Court, and is on trial as a criminal.
>
> And the offense—the *crime* alleged against him, and for which he is thus arraigned—is that he has aided a fellowman in his effort to obtain his liberty. It is charged to be a crime in that Republic whose foundations were laid in these great principles of liberty, equality, and the rights of man, of which the Declaration of American Independence is the fullest and noblest national expression, to aid a fellowman in seeking to secure for himself that blessed boon of liberty to which every human being is by virtue of his manhood entitled.

Charles Ray considered the case well stated and was still more pleased when the defense pointed out the repugnant sections of the Fugitive Slave Act. No trial by jury was required to deprive a free Negro of his liberty. If a Southerner found a bale of cotton in the North he had to prove ownership before a jury, but if he found a Negro he could deprive him of the highest of all rights, his freedom, on the writ of a government commissioner, with no sanction of court or judicial officer. The defense counsel continued:

> My word for it, gentlemen, if this law gave a right to have the question of a man's freedom tried before a jury of twelve men, under all the solemn sanctions of a court of justice, determined by legal and competent evidence, given openly and with that right of cross-examination of witnesses so essential to the discovery of truth and the exposing of falsehood and fraud, and the fact that the man was a slave were established by the verdict of the jury—my word for it . . . such judgment would enable the claimant to go from one end of this State —aye, of this whole country—to the other without interruption or molestation.

Having established the repugnance of the Fugitive Slave Act, Arnold appealed to the Chicago jury by explaining that the unwritten law in a court of justice superseded all statutes. Next he pointed out certain irregularities of the papers. Surely John Hossack, when at Ottawa, was justified in suspecting that an illegal arrest of the Negro was being perpetrated. Counsel closed by warning the jury to guard themselves against the compelling oratory of the prosecution. Lawyer Arrington, he said, possessed powers of eloquence to charm juries and cloud the issue. His poetic citations from Shakespeare and the classics, his profound erudition, sometimes wooed men from their better judgment.

The last defense attorney sat down. Charles Ray thought Hossack's chance of acquittal a good one. He watched Arrington stand up and walk before the jury box. What reply would he make? Outside the roar of a marching Republican club prevented counsel from speaking. Charles Ray hoped that those hoodlums would help nominate Abraham Lincoln on a platform pledged to end slavery. Arrington smiled as he waited for the parade to pass and the noise to subside. Then he bowed to the defense counsel. His opponent, he said, and his voice was very low, had complimented him on his erudition, his ability to quote classics. Arrington smiled at the jury:

> I confess, as his powerful and persevering argument unfolded its logic, one little passage of the immortal poet did strike me. . . . "A rose by any other name would smell as sweet." But perhaps they deny this poetic truth of Shakespeare to be applicable to the negro, or the negro race. And I must say that another slight quotation ran through my mind excited by the law of association which psychologists term contrast—the line where Lady Macbeth exclaims, "all the perfumes of Arabia will not sweeten this little hand." And that I am quite certain is pertinent to the negro.

Ray wondered how this sarcasm would affect the jury. Arrington's next move in the prosecution was to discuss the Negro's place in society. He showed that Louis Agassiz, professor at Harvard, had demonstrated the black man to be inferior to the white because his brain "development never goes beyond that of a Caucasian in boyhood." From this statement Arrington went on to say that no objection was made to restraining boys and denying them certain liberties until they reach man's estate. This restriction on liberty had not seemed inconsistent to the signers of the Declaration of Independence. Boys must pass through a period of tutelage; so too, in the grand economy of history, the black man may also be developed.

"Slavery is a necessity," he said, "an indisputable condition without which he can never emerge from the night of barbarism." The word "Liberty," Arrington continued, was fine in the abstract, but the liberty displayed by the Paris mob in the French revolution or by the black savages in the Santo

Domingo slave revolt of 1791 proved the danger of allowing liberty to a maniac. The Revolutionary Fathers believed literally in the Declaration of Independence and the clause that all men were created equal, but they saw the necessity of qualifying the Declaration of Independence with the Constitution—a supreme law that provided for the return of fugitives from labor. Ray knew this to be convincing argument. Conservatives who disapproved of slavery yet disapproved still more of upsetting the South's economy might subscribe to this doctrine and undo the *Press and Tribune's* long campaign for freedom of the slave.

Lawyer Arrington walked over to his table. He picked up a copy of the Constitution of the United States. "The prinsiple of life to our federal organization," he said, showing the impressive document to the jury, "the bond of its unity, the basis of its being. Cancel that, and the entire system ceases to exist."

Arrington read Article IV, Section 2, of the Constitution, which related to the return of fugitives from labor, then said:

> I ask you, gentlemen, when and by whom was that high law made? The spirit of seventy-six has been invoked to aid the defense. Did the eloquent counsel remember that the men of seventy-six, fresh from the strife of the Revolution . . . enacted that law?

Next Arrington picked up a leather-bound statute book. He opened it and read the provisions of the Fugitive Slave Act of 1793, then stepped back before the jury :

> I beg now to show you that that law is precisely similar to the law under which you are to convict this defendant. . . . It was the same immortal men of seventy-six that placed that law upon the statute book; and it was Washington that sanctioned it and signed it. When, therefore, they declaim against the present law as hard and cruel, and when they libel [this planter]

as a miscreant and man-stealer, because he sought his property in a mode recognized by the Constitution, let them recollect whose dust they spurn.

The act of 1850 was cited next as the product of "the grand names of Clay and Webster." Then Arrington turned to another source:

You have often heard of the Ordinance of 1787. You have listened again and again to the praises of the men who gave this vast north-west to the dominion of freedom. Now, the sixth article of the ordinance is as follows:

". . . Any person escaping into the same from whom service or labor is lawfully claimed in any of the original states, such fugitive may be lawfully reclaimed, and conveyed to the person claiming his or her labor or service as aforesaid."

And this law, too, was passed when the echoes from the thunders of revolutionary cannon were still ringing in the valleys and over mountains where our fathers lived and died.

Arrington outlined the development of the Constitution. He scoffed at states' rights as a political expedient of a minority that would inevitably lead only to chaos. He condemned the recent decision of the Supreme Court of Wisconsin which had nullified the Fugitive Slave Act on the basis of states' rights. Such an interpretation was mere repetition "of the heresies of the arch heretic, Calhoun." The true constitutional doctrine of the Fathers, Arrington thundered, could be found in the political thinking of the "High Priest of the Republican Party" himself:

A man of incorruptible integrity; a statesman of great practical power, and in many traits of character resembling Henry Clay, and more than all, as pure a patriot as ever lived. . . .

Abraham Lincoln, the highest authority with the best section of his party, in his fine Freeport speech had the noble daring, the truthfulness of heart, and the great moral heroism to announce that he was in favor of "an efficient fugitive slave law." Gentlemen, after that you cannot entertain a fear of excommunication. . . .

In conclusion, gentlemen, let me say again for the last time, . . . it is the voice of your fathers from the dust of their glorious graves which demands a vindication of their memory. . . . I implore you, gentlemen, to do your duty, . . . for the sake of that Union which gives us and our children a name among the nations of the earth.

The jury filed out of the courtroom. Charles Ray admitted that Arrington had made the best possible case for slavery. Would these twelve men, picked at random from the streets of Chicago, see the sophistry in his argument? At six o'clock they returned and the foreman read this verdict: "We, the Jury, find the defendant GUILTY, as charged in the indictment." This surprising verdict was accepted by the city without protest. The *Press and Tribune* lauded the mob's forbearance and pointed out that a Southern mob would not have shown similar respect for the law. With this commendation of the people's conduct the editor printed a ringing call:

In ten weeks our standard bearer will be in the field. In the meantime a Republican Central Club should be organized in every county seat with branch clubs in every township and precinct. These clubs should make it their special business to see that a good live Republican newspaper is in the hands of every citizen who will need one. The Northwest has two states to redeem from the hands of the slave power, and it behooves every true patriot to buckle on his armor and prepare for the contest.

Illinois and Indiana must be wheeled into the Republican

column. The Northwestern states—children of the Jefferson Ordinance of '87—must be a unit for free soil. . . . It will be a re-assertion of the central idea upon which the struggle of the Revolution was won.

On March 15 the *Press and Tribune* said: "Mr. Lincoln is our candidate—has been so from the beginning, and will be so until the Convention takes from us the right as partisans to press his claims."

On March 22 the editors stated:

We do not know that we urge [Lincoln] with his approbation or consent. We have never had a word from him or any of his friends authorized to speak in his behalf, oral or written, in which his desire for the Presidency was even hinted. We have no scheme to further—no enmities to gratify by placing him above others in the struggle. Our desire is for the nomination of a representative man with whom success is not merely problematical but certain. That man we believe to be Abraham Lincoln.

Lincoln himself arrived in Chicago that day. He had come from Springfield to participate in what became known as the Sand Bar case. Title to the land which had formed by accretion along the lake front was involved. Lincoln stayed in town two weeks, visiting in Evanston and speaking at Waukegan. Everywhere he was greeted as the likely nominee for the presidency. The *Press and Tribune* published Lincoln's Cooper Union speech in a brochure for wide distribution. His supporters in Ohio announced that his debates with Douglas, as transcribed by the *Press and Tribune*, were being published in a bound volume of 268 pages, some to be distributed in paper covers, others to be handsomely bound in cloth. Sculptor Leonard Volk, a cousin of Stephen A. Douglas, had recently returned from studying abroad at the senator's expense. He had finished a bust of his distinguished relative and asked Lincoln to "sit" for a life mask. Volk said later that Lincoln seemed preoccupied during the sittings. To prevent his clothes from being spattered by the plaster of Paris, Lincoln had stripped to the waist, laying aside his shirt and rolling down the upper part of his union suit. On one occasion he had suddenly remembered an appointment, put on his shirt without replacing his underwear, and hurried down the stairs. Boys—*Press and Tribune* newsboys, no doubt—spied the long sleeves dangling below the skirts of Lincoln's coat and shouted after him. Volk said that he heard someone bounding up the stairs, two at a time. Into the room burst Lincoln, laughing but embarrassed. He had come back to dress properly.

Late in April the Democrats met in a national convention at Charleston, South Carolina. By the first week in May it was plain that the party was due to split over the slavery issue, as so many people had prophesied. This meant that the Republican nominee would surely be elected president. The Illinois Republicans were highly elated when they convened in Decatur on May 9, 1860, for the purpose of nominating state officers and endorsing a candidate to present to the national convention in Chicago next week. The enthusiastic assemblage first nominated Richard Yates for governor. Other state candidates were selected. Then John M. Palmer offered a resolution for the nomination of Abraham Lincoln, the delegates to vote as a unit. Richard Oglesby asked for the floor. He had recently been defeated on the Republican ticket by a Macon County Democrat. "Mr. Chairman," he boomed, "I would like to move that an old Democrat of Macon County be allowed to make a contribution to this convention."

The offer was approved by acclamation. Then some old settlers in working clothes walked down the aisle, carrying fence rails which supported a banner inscribed:

ABRAHAM LINCOLN
The Rail Candidate
For President in 1860

Two rails from a lot of 3,000 made in 1830 by Thos. Hanks and Abe Lincoln—whose father was the first pioneer of Macon County.

The hall rocked with applause until part of the canvas roof collapsed. On the platform Abraham Lincoln pointed to the fluttering banner and said, "I suppose I am to reply to that. I cannot say whether I made those rails or not, but I am quite sure I have made a great many as good." Again the crowd cheered: Hooray for an ex-Whig who represented the working man and who was being supported by dirt farmers!

George Schneider, German editor who favored the forthright Seward for president because Lincoln was not sufficiently outspoken in his antislavery views, returned to Chicago convinced that "Seward has lost the Illinois delegation." Charles Ray was delighted with this indication that the Germans would back the *Press and Tribune* candidate, and he perfected his plans for the nomination of Abraham Lincoln.

Outside Illinois, Lincoln's chances seemed slim indeed. Ray paged through all the eastern periodicals, noting the lists of possible candidates. Only *Harper's Weekly* included his name. Perhaps the editors had been impressed with the Rail Splitter's reply to the article Douglas had written for *Harper's Monthly* and knew his hidden power. Perhaps it was as well that Easterners did not suspect the magnitude of the *Press and Tribune's* preparation for Lincoln's nomination.

Better-known candidates might be unprepared to cope with the popular enthusiasm which Ray hoped that he had engendered in the West. Less than a week now would tell! Dr. Ray must have glowed with happiness—ruddy cheeks aflame under blue eyes and curly hair. He loved the excitement of a fair fight, and the *Press and Tribune* would lead the fray. The campaign was bringing the paper a very profitable business. Ray's fearless editorials had attracted thousands of readers, and Medill's careful management had conserved the firm's income. All the debts would be paid soon, with interest, and the owners planned to move into more spacious quarters.

To greet the convention guests, the *Press and Tribune* office was decorated with fence rails. One hung at the main entrance to the counting room, and two others swung from the ceiling. Ray liked to tell curious visitors that the fence rail had become the symbol of Lincoln's candidacy. Ever since the Lincoln-Douglas debates the *Press and Tribune* had been portraying him as a workingman, a rail splitter, to get the labor vote. In that campaign Douglas had traveled from his special train to speaking platforms with a cortege of carriages. Lincoln had followed in a covered wagon hauled by oxen. This had seemed good politics. For years the commercial and banker Whigs had been striving for the poor man's vote by campaigning with coonskin caps and hard cider. The fence rail seemed a better symbol in this election, because the Whigs were still a distinct party, even though the Republicans had absorbed many of them. All the other candidates—Seward, Chase, Cameron, and Bates—were big businessmen or high-ranking government officials. The masses might well crowd them back into their ivory towers and cry for the humble mauler of rails. Certainly Charles Ray had laid all the necessary plans for such a popular reaction.

XIII Lincoln's Nomination

A WEEK before the Republican National Convention met in Chicago, the *Press and Tribune* began preparing readers for the great event. Leonard Volk used the life mask he had made of Lincoln as a model for life-size busts which he offered for sale at $10.00 each. He sent Dr. Ray a cabinet-size bas-relief—the rarest of all Volk sculpture today. Ray praised the artist's work in the *Press and Tribune* and hoped that Lincoln supporters who came to the convention would purchase copies.

The Wigwam was completed, and on Saturday, May 12, 1860, a committee of leading citizens dedicated the huge building. Charles Ray devoted five columns to the ceremony. He described the wonders of the barnlike structure and its enormous seating capacity. He urged political-minded farmers throughout the state and from near-by Indiana to come and take part in the convention. Norman Judd, railroad attorney, arranged for special excursion prices on the fifteen railroads converging on the city. Board and room at the best hotels was advertised at from $1.00 to $2.50 per day.

The *Press and Tribune* had been educating its readers for years to take part in the drama soon to be enacted. The Hossack case had served as a prologue to the main performance. Small crowds had attended that trial. Let hundreds of country people come to Chicago now and impress Eastern delegates with the magnitude of the West's voting importance.

Political spokesmen were the first to arrive. They engaged rooms for headquarters, discussed critical situations, and arranged tentative deals. Charles Ray, listening to everybody, became sure that William H. Seward was the greatest rival Lincoln supporters must face. Soon trainloads of delegates and their friends rolled into the railroad stations. Organized troops from various precincts—Wide-Awake clubs, the *Press and Tribune* called them—escorted delegations to their lodgings and gave them copies of the paper endorsing Lincoln's candidacy.

The city had dressed itself in gala attire. Billowing banners were suspended across the thoroughfares. Store and house fronts were draped with flags. Omnibuses were bandaged with bunting. Crowds in holiday mood marched through the muddy streets, cheering, waving to friends on the wooden sidewalks, and flaunting standards inscribed with the names of their favorite candidate—Chase, Cameron, Seward, or Lincoln. Explosions from miniature cannon and sputtering rockets called attention to unusual displays.

The hotels soon filled. Many private houses accommodated roomers. Chicago's business district was in a turmoil, with 40,000 visitors thronging the streets. The city had quadrupled in size in the last decade, but had never experienced anything like this. Gambling rooms and keno parlors along Randolph Street were packed. Country people stood in front of the open doors, wondering and asking what was going on inside. Chicago's best streets were being raised above their old muddy level. Victorias and barouches carrying gamblers and their fancy companions lurched through the muck, jostling black-curtained hacks. The shouts of teamsters and the popping of whips sounded like gunfire amid the buzzing crowds. Many of the houses in town stood on stilts waiting for the new ground level to come up to them. Some of the wooden sidewalks were poised precariously on high piles. Others, at lake level, were reached by descending wooden stairs from adjacent buildings. Along this rickety and rattling scaffolding of causeways the professional political managers watched hundreds of organized ward heelers march and cheer.

The *Press and Tribune* announced the arrival of all important delegations and prominent individuals. A half-dozen trains full of delegates chuffed in from New England. The Pennsylvania delegation all wore white hats labeled CAMERON. From New York came a special train with an army of several hundred plug-uglies ready to march and cheer for Seward. They were lodged at the Richmond House in charge of the famous and popular prize fighter, Tom Hyer. A peculiar cap worn by active sportsmen had been named for him. New York's political boss, Thurlow Weed, was managing Seward's candidacy.

Seward's chief enemy was Horace Greeley, editor of the *New York Tribune*. He came to Chicago as delegate from Oregon, though he had never lived there. His influence was powerful with the independent New York delegates who, as erstwhile Democrats, opposed Seward's Whig background. Greeley was a fresh pink-and-white fellow with a bald head above blond whiskers. He had a clean dairy-barn look that attracted farmers. His newspaper and Ray's were as influential as any Republican organs in America. Yet Greeley, with all his importance, was a democratic chap, who could usually be found standing on a street corner in the center of a crowd, talking rapidly. Thurlow Weed would stride past him–suave, smiling, pretending not to notice. Seward certainly was the most popular candidate. Cameron, with the big Pennsylvania vote behind him, probably stood second on the list of favorites.

Previous to the opening of the convention, the New York delegation invited the public to a grand rally in the Wigwam. Twelve thousand people packed into the building designed for only five. They stood in the aisles, leaned against the walls, clutched the pillars. The meeting opened with a presumably routine motion by William D. ("Pig Iron") Kelley of Pennsylvania, who preferred Cameron for the nomination. Having gained the floor, he talked hour after hour as the bored audience slipped away. At midnight, when he finished, only a scant thousand remained to listen to the New York orator's appeal for the nomination of Seward.

Down the lamp-lighted street, at Lincoln's headquarters in the Tremont House, Charles Ray sat with portly Judge David Davis, Leonard Swett, Richard Oglesby, Norman B. Judd, Jesse Fell, Billy Herndon, and John M. Palmer. A giant bowie knife, seven feet long, was on display to ridicule Southern chivalry, but none of the Illinois delegates felt facetious. The chance of success in the convention looked unusually dark to all of them. A straw poll taken from arriving contingents showed a majority in favor of Seward. The Illinois delegation, with twenty-two votes, had been instructed at the Decatur convention to cast a unit ballot for Lincoln, but already some of the members hinted that they might vote independently. Eight of them openly admitted that Lincoln's chance was hopeless. Seward would win, and it behooved Illinois to profit by starting the ball rolling in his direction. Other Illinois delegates were still undecided, timid, interested only in being on the winning side.

Charles Ray showed his stature in this group of vacillating men. Fearlessly he spoke out for Abraham Lincoln. Seward, he conceded, might win the nomination, but he had been too radically outspoken against slavery to carry the election. Greeley's *Tribune* would fight him to the last ditch. The delegates from New Jersey, Pennsylvania, and Indiana all admitted that Seward could not carry their states. Without these, he could not muster enough votes to win. In such a situation, why desert Lincoln to bet on a sure loser? A few other Illinoisans talked with the same confidence, and the strong characters in the group, lawyers used to defending causes with all their might, resolved to stand firm and do their utmost for the nomination of Lincoln.

To the smoke-filled room Ray pointed out that New Jersey wanted to nominate William L. Dayton, who had been candidate for vice-president in 1856. Pennsylvania had paraded for Cameron. Ohio delegations were marching and shouting for their Salmon P. Chase. Horace Greeley of the *New York Tribune* wanted Edward Bates of St. Louis. The problem before Lincoln's handful of backers was to convince these delegates that they could not nominate their candidates nor elect them if they were nominated. Bates's alleged affiliation with the Know-Nothings would lose him the foreign vote. Chase was too extreme an abolitionist for moderates. Dayton was tinged with defeatism since he had lost the election for vice-president in 1856. The backers of these men admitted that Seward could not be elected. Thus the Illinoisans could point to Lincoln as the man around whom all must rally.

The little group of Lincoln supporters determined to begin their campaign by converting certain key men in each state delegation. To win entire blocs was impossible, but a few individuals pledged to Lincoln could be used as levers to pry others from their solid allegiance to some native son. Indiana seemed the easiest mark, and Ray left the room and went down through the crowded lobby to the Indiana delegation's headquarters.

The Hoosiers admitted that they probably could not win the nomination for one of their own men. They were willing to negotiate. What could Illinois offer them? Men and places were discussed. Ray suggested a seat in the cabinet for Caleb Smith and the post of Indian Commissioner for William P. Dole. The delegates agreed to trade on this basis, giving all their twenty-six votes to Lincoln. Ray hurried back to Lincoln's headquarters. Bursting into the crowded room where David Davis sat, his legs apart below his bulging vest, Ray said, "We are going to have Indiana for Old Abe, sure." Medill turned his intense, dedicated face toward his partner. "How did you get it?" he asked.

"By the Lord," Ray replied, "we promised them everything they asked." Other scouts came in, reporting promises of a small scattering of votes from other states—two here, four there. The chance of victory for Lincoln looked better, though far from certain. In the excited crowd of men Ray dashed off a note marked "Profoundly private" to Lincoln, down in Springfield. It said:

My dear Lincoln:

Your friends are at work for you hard, and with great success. Your show on the first ballot will not be confined to Illinois, and after that it will be strongly developed.

But you need a few trusty friends here to say words for you that it may be necessary to be said. Dare you put yourself in the hands of Judd, David Davis, and, if there is no better man, Ray? A pledge or two may be necessary when the pinch comes.

Don't be too sanguine. Matters now look well as things stand to-day. I had rather have your chances than those of any other man. But don't get excited.

Yours faithfully,
C. H. Ray

In his haste the editor placed a three-cent stamp on the envelope upside down. Reporters saw him hurrying in and out of headquarters during half the night. They watched half a dozen other political caucuses. The *New York Herald* correspondent sent east a dispatch stating that the contest had narrowed down to Seward, Lincoln, and Ben Wade. The *Boston Herald* reporter notified his paper: "Abe Lincoln is booming up to-night as a compromise candidate, and his friends are in high spirits."

On the morning of May 15, 1860—the day before the convention was scheduled to assemble—the *Press and Tribune* appeared in the streets with a leading story headed: THE WINNING MAN, ABRAHAM LINCOLN. Crowds in hotels, after the hectic night, read further:

We represent our candidate, because he is that honest man, that representative Republican, the people's candidate, whose life, position and record are so many guarantees of success—because he is that patriot in whose hands the interest of the government could be safely confided.

Next day, Wednesday, May 16, 1860, a thousand delegates and alternates took their seats, while nine hundred reporters watched and scribbled notes. The balconies filled with women in flowered bonnets and gay paisley shawls. Many had worked far into the night decorating the bare building with banners and rosettes of flags. The raw, wooden joists were wreathed with masses of greenery. On the walls hung paintings of Justice and Liberty. Portraits of American statesmen by George A. Healy stared at the milling throng. On the platform Republican notables shook hands. Spectators in the pit and gallery watched them and identified those whom they recognized.

There were Thomas Corwin of Ohio, the orator with irresistible brown eyes; Carl Schurz, a fidgety German with a lantern jaw; and Thaddeus Stevens, crippled and savage but very influential in Pennsylvania politics. People whispered that he loved the Negro so much that he had lived with a female one. Elderly Frank Blair was on the platform, too. He had been prominent in politics since Andrew Jackson's time. His two sons, Frank, Jr., and Montgomery, both mature politicians in their own right, were with him. George Ashmun and tall, bearded Gideon Welles had come from New England. Cassius M. Clay, the Kentucky antislavery fire-eater who had fought proslavery advocates with knife and pistol at many hustings, stood out from the throng. Andrew H. Reeder was there, too, champing his false teeth, still bitter about being expelled from the governorship of Kansas because he had insisted on majority rule. Moving graciously among the notables was tall, suave, bowing Thurlow Weed, always with a good word for his worst enemies. Weed had a burning ambition to get the nomination for Seward at any cost.

The chair for the presiding officer was a huge polished stump presented to the convention by Michigan. Another chair was made of thirty-four kinds of wood, each from a different state, Kansas being represented by weeping willow. The presiding officer's gavel was made from a fragment of the battleship *Lawrence*, famous for Commodore Perry's defiant statement from the quarter-deck, "Don't give up the ship."

By prearrangement Judd and Medill seated the Pennsylvania delegation between the Illinois and Indiana contingents, where they could be dealt with if the situation became critical. When everyone was in his place the assemblage was called to order by the chairman of the Republican National Committee, who introduced temporary chairman David Wilmot of Pennsylvania—an unassuming man famous for the Wilmot Proviso designed to restrict slavery in all territories acquired in the Mexican War. In a brief speech he told the assembled Republicans:

> We oppose the new dogma by which the Constitution carries slavery into our Territories. We will read the Constitution as our fathers read it. . . . Freedom follows our flag, not slavery.

This was greeted with a cheer, and Wilmot called for nominations for permanent chairman. Congressman George Ashmun of Massachusetts was elected by acclamation, then committees were appointed. Ray heard the name of Gustave Koerner read with the list of those who were to prepare the party's platform. Would the Illinois German insist on the Decatur articles that he and Lincoln had written in 1856? The next important order of business was the adoption of rules for making nominations.

The first test of strength between the factions would come now. Seward's supporters insisted that the nomination should be made by a majority of the delegates present. Others maintained that a majority of all delegates be required. It was believed that the former rule would insure Seward's nomination and, amid great confusion, the assembly adopted it.

This was discouraging to Lincoln's supporters, but Ray noticed that the vote was close. In fact the rule might not have passed at all if order had been maintained. Lincoln's chances had been hit a body blow, but the violence of those opposed to Seward was encouraging. The day's session adjourned with the nomination still an open question. Greeley wired his *Tribune* that Seward seemed most likely to win.

Walking from the hall, Thurlow Weed greeted the Illinoisans cordially. He overwhelmed them with kindness. Few men could be more gracious to an enemy. He explained that balloting for the nominee would start tomorrow or the next day. He had already received pledges for Seward from Massachusetts, Michigan, Minnesota, Wisconsin, and California. Victory seemed assured, Weed said in his suave way, but for the good of the party and of the cause, he wanted to put Lincoln on the ticket. Would Honest Abe be available for vice-president? The less determined Illinois delegates, flattered by notice from the great man, said that they did not know. They hurried to Lincoln's headquarters in the Tremont House with the proposition. Some of them thought it best to accept. While they argued, Judge David Davis stormed in.

He had been interviewing the New Jersey delegation. Weed had made them the same sort of proposition he made the Illinoisans—Seward for president, their own Dayton for vice-president. Davis said that Palmer must come with him at once and talk with the Jerseyites. Davis turned with a grunt and puffed away. Walking was an effort for a man of his weight, but the errand seemed important. At the New Jersey headquarters Palmer explained that Illinois' votes would win or lose next fall's election. The Republican Party in Illinois included 40,000 former Democrats who had deserted Douglas.

If the national ticket was composed of two former Whigs, Seward and Dayton, the party would not carry Illinois. To win, the ticket must have a former member of both the Whig and Democratic parties. The Jerseyites seemed impressed, but they were noncommittal.

Thursday, May 17, was one of harrowing anxiety for Charles Ray. He started the day with a special *Press and Tribune* "convention supplement." So far Lincoln could count only on Indiana's twenty-two votes and a few others. The Pennsylvania contingent admitted that their fifty-four votes were insufficient to nominate a candidate, and Cameron's bad reputation as an unscrupulous placeman kept them from enlisting others in his behalf. For them the time had come to make the best deal they could. They were pledged to vote on the first ballot for their native son; after that they were open to conviction. Charles Ray knew this, but no proposition had been agreed upon when the delegates took their seats for the opening of the day's session.

The platform committee reported and Ray was pleased to hear the provisions which he and Lincoln had drawn at Decatur adopted with what he considered little fundamental change. Other routine business was transacted. Then a shrewd motion for adjournment was pushed through, and nominations were postponed another day. The delegates crowded out into the streets for a last effort to trade votes and come to some agreement. Tomorrow's session would settle the question. A correspondent for James Gordon Bennett's *New York Herald* wired his paper:

> The friends of Seward are firm, and claim ninety votes for him on the first ballot. Opposition to Seward not fixed on any man. Lincoln is the strongest, and may have all together fifty votes. The various delegations are still caucusing.

In the Illinois headquarters in the Tremont House, the vacillating delegates watched their stubborn colleagues for signs of faltering. Agreement on Lincoln seemed more hopeless than ever, and the opportunists wanted to profit by being on the bandwagon for a winner. Ray, almost desperate now, went to the Pennsylvania headquarters to ask their price and came back with the good news that they would settle for a seat in the cabinet for Cameron. Jesse Dubois wired his old friend Lincoln for a commitment and received a reply. "I authorize no bargains and will be bound by none."

"Damn Lincoln," Dubois swore when he read it.

Leonard Swett, the polished attorney, said, "I am very sure if Lincoln was aware of the necessities——"

Lincoln's former law partner, the skinny, skeptical Logan, spat and exclaimed: "The main difficulty with Lincoln is——"

Judge David Davis spoke authoritatively. "Lincoln ain't here," he said, "and don't know what we have to meet, so we will go ahead as if we hadn't heard from him, and he must ratify it."

Davis beckoned to Ray and they walked upstairs to the Pennsylvania delegation's rooms to close the deal Ray had discussed. Joe Medill waited in the lobby for a report on their progress. He knew that Lincoln counted on Pennsylvania's vote. When the two of them had appraised the prospects of nomination, Lincoln had said, "I want that big Pennsylvania foot brought down on the scale." Surely he would ratify any agreement his friends made.

At midnight Medill saw Davis and Ray coming downstairs from the conference. "Damned if we haven't got them," the judge said.

"How did you get them?" Medill asked.

"By paying their price"—a reply similar to the one Ray made when he returned from the Indiana headquarters.

Medill turned to Ray for more details. "We promised to put Simon Cameron in the cabinet," Ray said. "They wanted assurance that we represented Lincoln and that he would do what we said."

That had been a difficult assurance to give, but the Pennsylvanians felt that the editor of the *Chicago Press and Tribune* and the district judge of the law circuit in which Lincoln practiced could surely be depended upon.

"What have you agreed to give Cameron?" Medill persisted.

"The Treasury Department," Ray replied.

"Good heavens! Give Cameron the Treasury Department? What will be left?"

"Oh, what is the difference?" Ray shrugged his broad shoulders. "We are after a bigger thing than that; we want the Presidency and the Treasury is not a great stake to pay for it."

(It is important to note that this incident was recounted by Medill years later, when he was no longer friendly with Charles Ray. It seems possible that he was mistaken in some parts of the conversation, for Ray and David Davis, as will be shown, quarreled bitterly over carrying out this agreement.)

On the night of May 17, 1860, many lights burned in Chicago conference rooms until dawn. The morning *Press and Tribune* headlined a column in bold type: A LAST ENTREATY. The convention was due to assemble at 10:00 A.M. In the streets Seward's exulting plug-uglies marched behind blaring bands. Some supporter of Lincoln's who had access to a printing press turned out many extra admission tickets to the Wigwam, and while Easterners watched the Seward demonstration in the streets, Lincoln supporters quietly filled the building, taking most of the seats and standing room. On top of the Wigwam Lincoln men placed a cannon. Another was mounted on the Tremont House.

Charles Ray came with the Illinoisans, hoping to hold them in line and see that promises were kept. Influential men from several states had agreed that if Lincoln made a good showing after the first ballot they would urge their respective delegations to vote as units for him. In deadly silence the meeting was called to order. The packed hall was stiflingly hot. Hundreds of palm-leaf fans, hats, and folded newspapers waved in front of perspiring faces. Nominations began at noon. William M. Evarts presented the name of William H. Seward. New York's delegation roared approval. The applause made some Illinoisans fear that the trick to take all the seats and keep out Seward supporters had failed.

Next Norman Judd asked to be recognized. "I desire," he shouted, "on behalf of the delegation from Illinois, to put in nomination, as a candidate for President of the United States, Abraham Lincoln, of Illinois."

Five thousand people jumped to their feet with a wild yell that, according to one observer, would have drowned out "a thousand steam whistles, ten acres of hotel gongs, [and] a tribe of Comanches." When the noise abated, a voice roared for "the man who can split rails and maul Democrats—Abraham Lincoln." Once more the Wigwam shook with cheers and the stamping of feet on board floors. Women in the balconies waved handkerchiefs and little flags. Indiana seconded the nomination. "Abe Lincoln has it by the sound now," a voice bawled, "let us ballot."

Other nominations were made—Cameron, Chase, and Bates among them. Then the voting commenced. Illinois delegates, with paper and pencil, began to tally the count. Ray believed that Lincoln would poll at least a hundred votes, obliging the pledged delegates to urge their colleagues to vote en bloc on the second ballot. But would they make good their promises? The roll call, as it droned along, showed Seward forging steadily ahead almost two to one. He closed with 173½. Lincoln had polled only 102, with four votes from Pennsylvania. Two hundred and thirty-three were necessary to nominate. Other candidates received approximately fifty votes each. If the Pennsylvania delegates did as they had agreed to do and cast their ballots for Lincoln on the second roll call, their fifty additional votes would give Lincoln an increase which might start a landslide. Then if Chase's Ohioans would switch their votes, too, Lincoln would have enough to beat Seward. But neither of these states, along with Illinois, had sufficient votes to nominate Lincoln.

While the pollsters were tallying their sheets, the Pennsylvania delegation rose and walked to one of the committee rooms at the end of the platform. Ray, looking over the sea of moving fans, could only surmise what would be decided behind the board wall. Were they repudiating their agreement or going ahead with it? The clerk was calling the roll for the second ballot when the Pennsylvanians reappeared. Not one of the delegates gave any sign that revealed their decision. Finally Pennsylvania was called, and a voice roared above the rustling crowd, "Pennsylvania casts her fifty-four votes for Abraham Lincoln."

The hall was silent for a moment. The fans stopped, then a tumult of voices broke over the drone of the tellers. Waving hands, papers, and hats boiled up from the pool of faces. The New York delegation sat stupefied, unbelieving. The final count on this ballot gave Lincoln 181, Seward 184½. Both were a long way from the 233 necessary for nomination. Imperturbable Weed showed disciplined calmness.

A third ballot was called. Joe Medill walked over and sat among his Ohio friends. He had worked with many of these politicians, building the Republican Party with his Cleveland newspaper. To D. K. Cartter, big, pock-marked, stuttering Ohio politician, Medill whispered, "If you can throw the Ohio delegation for Lincoln, Chase can have anything he wants."

"H-how d-d' ye know?" Cartter stammered, as suspicious as the Pennsylvania delegates had been of David Davis' and Charles Ray's promises.

"I know, and you know I wouldn't promise if I didn't know," Medill replied.

Cartter knew Medill's power as part-owner of the great *Chicago Press and Tribune*. He was a man who capitalized on his infirmity, displayed his stammer for the amusement of an audience. The convention had become acquainted with his face. Now he sat stolidly while the third ballot was called. Lincoln's count passed the 181 votes he had received on the second tally. Surely he was the winning man! Hundreds of pencils added each new block of votes given him. The number reached 231½—only 1½ more needed to nominate. Cartter jumped onto his chair and waved for recognition. Without doubt a dozen other delegates wanted the honor of clinching the nomination, so Medill's promise may have amounted to little. "I rise (eh), Mr. chairman (eh)," Cartter stuttered and all faces turned toward the coarse countenance looming above the Ohio delegation, "to announce the change of four votes of Ohio from Mr. Chase to Mr. Lincoln."

That nominated the Rail Splitter, and the avalanche began. Under a torrent of cheers, Maine tossed in ten votes for Abe; Massachusetts added ten. Delegates from Missouri, Iowa, and Kentucky all changed their ballots. Thurlow Weed nodded wanly to Evarts, who shouted that New York voted for Lincoln, making it unanimous.

Above the chaos a man at the skylight on the roof signaled the result to the crowd packing the streets below, and ten thousand throats roared with delight. Men threw away their hats, hugged each other, wept and laughed in one another's beards. All the bells in town began to toll. Whistles on river and lake steamboats, on locomotives, and in factories screamed. Thurlow Weed pressed his hand hard against his moist eyes. He had struggled from a poverty as debasing as Lincoln's. He had worked as hard for success and now had lost the goal of his lifetime. The victor's manager, giant Judge David Davis, wept with joy. As the crisis passed, he put his arms around a friend and sobbed like a child.

The convention nominated Hannibal Hamlin of Maine for vice-president and adjourned shortly afterward.

In the meantime Charles Ray wired Lincoln in Springfield: "I congratulate you shall you be up tomorrow answer." The meeting with Lincoln would be important. Ray and Medill would have to tell him that the Pennsylvania contingent was waiting for his commitments to be made good. Other state delegations were departing hourly for their homes, but New York's Thurlow Weed was still lounging around the hotel lobbies. He seemed to be waiting for something. Ray decided to send Lincoln a second wire. It said: "On consultation the Penna. folks say do not come here until after New York has gone home." This wire was signed by C. H. Ray, J. Medill, and J. L. Scripps.

The nomination had completely surprised, disappointed, dizzied the professional politicians. New combinations, new organizations would be necessary to consolidate their power. Lincoln's Illinois promoters had suddenly attained national importance.

As darkness settled over Chicago, lanterns were hung on the fence rails in the *Press and Tribune* counting room. Over the main door a glowing transparency proclaimed to all passers-by: FOR PRESIDENT—HONEST OLD ABE—FOR VICE-PRESIDENT—HANNIBAL HAMLIN. Companies of Wide-Awakes, with torches dripping on their oilcloth capes, stopped before the office to give three cheers. Then they marched up Clark Street behind blaring bands. Charles Ray was tired to the point of exhaustion, but he was very happy as he wrapped up an editorial written in the grand manner of that day's political oratory. Its text sounds startlingly hypocritical in the light of all the political deals made for Lincoln's nomination. These negotiations have troubled defenders of Lincoln's political purity, and the deeper they are probed, the more confusing they become. Over two weeks before the convention Lincoln himself wrote an Indiana delegate to come early and negotiate with Davis. During the convention, as has been seen, Lincoln sent word to his managers saying that he would be bound by none of their deals. After the convention he complained, "I cannot begin to fill all the pledges made in my name." The question is clouded further by a personal letter written soon after the convention by Leonard Swett, an Illinois delegate who knew as much as any man about the political promises made at the convention. In this letter Swett said, "The nomination is from the people, and not the politicians. No pledges have been made, no mortgage executed, but Lincoln enters the field a free man." However, twenty-five years later Swett said for publication that Cameron was "indebted to Davis and me"—not the reverse.

Charles Ray's editorial harmonizes perfectly with Swett's first statement. At the time, both men evidently felt themselves guiltless of unseemly negotiation, while similar offers of deals by the established Seward machines were considered grossly unethical. Excessive devotion to a cause makes most people insensible to the penetrating cold of logic. So with enthusiastic sincerity Charles Ray wrote:

Ever and anon there springs from the bosom of the people, a man qualified to meet the people's highest wants in great emergencies—a man who by reason of his many virtues, his moral heroism and his commanding qualities, is recognized by all classes as one endowed and anointed for a great work. His credentials bear the impress of a power whose fiat is irresistible, and his progress toward the appointed goal is as sure as the march of destiny. Scorning adventitious aids, trampling under foot every suggestion of mere policy, with heart all athrob with pure and lofty aspirations and generous aims, he moves right onward with the assured tread and the unquailing eye of a born conqueror. Of the people by birth, with the people by association and by a community of interests and ideas, what wonder that they should always hold him closely to their hearts, and, in their hour of greatest need, hail him as their leader and sure deliverer?

Such a man is ABRAHAM LINCOLN, and the whole philosophy of his present position is embraced in that fact. No other man in the nation stands so near to the popular heart to-day; and in the exigencies to which corrupt rulers have brought our Government, and amid the perils which on every hand threaten our free institutions, the people turn instinctively to him, as the man for the occasion—as one who had been led by Providence through all the experiences of lowly life, through labor and privation, through struggles and sacrifices, into self-reliance, into honest simplicity of life, into nobleness and purity of character, into a love of justice, of truth and of freedom, that he might be fitted for the work.

For no fact stands out more clearly than this—that ABRAHAM LINCOLN is indebted to the people—not to the politicians—for his nomination. From every part of our country where freedom is cherished, the voice of the people came up in unmistakable tones, calling for the nomination of honest old ABE:—Neither personal effort, neither private pledges, neither promise of office nor of patronage were used ["by Lincoln," certainly should be added] to secure the end. They are wholly ignorant of the character of ABRAHAM LINCOLN who suppose him capable of any of these things. Men peculiarly fitted for great occasions are sought for and called to their work by the spontaneous unbought suffrages of the people; and never was the fact more signally illustrated than in the nomination of ABRAHAM LINCOLN.

And now that he stands before the country as a candidate of the people's own choosing, it requires no gift of prescience to foretell the result. As surely as the sun shall rise upon election day, just so surely will the people of this nation place the man of the people at the head of government.

XIV Time for a Change

DR. RAY and his coeditors on the *Press and Tribune* prepared to run the final heat of this race. The policy of printing general news was continued with the old vigor, but more than half of each issue henceforth dealt with politics. HONEST OLD ABE—RAILS AND FLATBOATS—LOG CABINS AND HARD CIDER COME AGAIN! the banner lines read on May 19, day after the adjournment of the convention. Not a day must be lost until the November elections. The leading editorial announced:

The age of purity returns. After a succession of Presidents, who have not only been subservient to the interests of the Protagonists of Human Slavery, but corrupt to a degree alarming to the truest friends of Republican institutions, the nomination of Abraham Lincoln—Honest old ABE—is a guaranty that the country, wearied and outraged by the malfeasance of those invested with Federal power, desired a return to the sterling honesty and Democratic simplicity which marked the Administrations of Jefferson, Madison, Adams and Jackson. The party has not mistaken the man selected for a standard bearer.

. . . We refer to one matter with pride and congratulation. Mr. LINCOLN has, by his own motion, never been a candidate for President of the United States; hence he has no pledges to redeem, no promises to make good. The uprising in his favor has been spontaneous—the outgrowth of a widespread conviction of his fitness and availability. . . . That during the past week, in which there have been so many temptations to lead him into the practices which are unfortunately so common with politicians of less rectitude, he has in terms of just indignation refused all offers of votes which are based upon promises of future rewards, we have reason to know. With the spirit becoming an honest man, he rejected them all.

Does this mean that Lincoln had refused to honor his "managers' " deals when he first met them after the convention? In any event, at this stage of the game Lincoln was not guilty of paying political rewards, and the editorial has the same quality of truth as the former one announcing Lincoln's nomination.

In the same issue, Ray printed a 4000-word biography of Lincoln and announced that a more complete one was being prepared for separate publication. The job of writing this biography was assigned to John Locke Scripps. As the basis for this account, he planned to use a copy of the brief autobiography which Lincoln had written for Jesse Fell, but Scripps expected to go to Springfield to get additional data.

The *Press and Tribune* also printed the words for a new song to be sung to the tune of the *Star Spangled Banner:*

O, say have you heard from Chicago today,
As the news has flashed onward from station to station;
O, what is the name that the winged lightnings say,
The Republican choice for the head of the Nation?
See the rockets red glare,
Soaring high in the air:
And freemen rejoice
For a victory there!
Is it Seward or Lincoln whose banner shall wave
To lead on the hosts of the free and the brave?
Now hear you that sound as it comes on the wind,
Is it thunder of cannon, that news is proclaiming?
'Tis the honest, the able, the giant of mind,
It is Lincoln, 'tis Lincoln! all hearts are exclaiming

The first blow is given,
Our fetters unriven:
The Union stands firm
In the free light of Heaven.

On May 22, 1860, the *Press and Tribune* told its readers about Lincoln's formal notification of his nomination:

In the evening, the delegation accompanied by forty or fifty outsiders, walked up to Mr. Lincoln's house and were at once ushered into his presence. The parlors of the residence, small but neatly and tastefully furnished, were thrown together by the opening of the folding doors, and he stood at the bottom of the back parlor, gracefully bowed as the delegates entered and after a moment's delay motioned Mr. Ashmun to proceed....

At the close of this ceremony, the gentlemen went into another parlor across the hall where Mrs. Lincoln received them "with that grace and intelligence which have made her a distinguished ornament of the excellent society of the capital."

The *Press and Tribune* printed vivid reports from various towns describing the celebrations with which they greeted the news of Lincoln's nomination. Most were replicas, on a lesser scale, of the Chicago festivities. The paper took pains to say:

To-day ABRAHAM LINCOLN stands before this nation, the most striking living embodiment of the genius of our free institutions that the country has ever produced; and the masses from whom he sprung will not fail to vindicate their favorite son from the contemptible flings of the organs of the pro-slavery, purse-proud aristocracy.

Opposition papers struck unmercifully at Lincoln's record. They reiterated the old charge that Lincoln had voted against the Mexican War. They accused him of having bought, when in Congress, a pair of boots and charging them to the government as stationery. They blamed him for corrupt trading to secure the nomination and declared that he had promised government positions to various factions in case he won. The *Press and Tribune* struck back, denying these charges. Its old article listing Lincoln's voting record during the Mexican War was reprinted. The story about using government funds for boots was exploded like an iridescent soap bubble. The accusations of dickering for the nomination were refuted by Lincoln's own statement that he had not asked for the nomination and was not bound by any pledges.

The *Press and Tribune* devoted its entire resources to winning the campaign. Reporters set to work writing about Lincoln from every angle. A Republican textbook of ninety-four pages was published. Lincoln's speeches, along with Owen Lovejoy's, were printed to familiarize the people with the horrors of slavery. Feature articles described the slave trade and the South's recent demands for reopening it. A separate brochure containing the official stenographic account of the Republican National Convention's proceedings was printed, and copies were sold for five cents each. Dozens of other pamphlets were run off by the *Press and Tribune* printers. Each plank of the Republican Party's platform was discussed at length in the paper's columns. The platforms of the Douglas and the radical proslavery Democratic parties were printed together with the Whigs' so that readers could compare all three. Squatter sovereignty and the terrors of Democrat rule in Kansas were recounted.

Between writing stints, Ray and Medill sat for hours studying a map of Illinois and discussing which of the doubtful sections would be influenced by speakers they might send. No other large paper in the nation was so close to Lincoln and the heart of the Midwest in this campaign. The *Press and Tribune's* expanding wealth, circulation, and talent were all dedicated to the cause. In the senatorial contest of 1858 the editors had learned that northern Illinois was sure to vote for Lincoln. On the other hand, the extreme southern tip, bordered by the slave states of Kentucky and Missouri, was sure now, as then, to favor the radical proslavery wing of the Democratic Party and vote for John C. Breckinridge, who had been nominated by the Southerners. Douglas' popular sovereignty solution of the slavery issue was too lukewarm for the voters down there. Central Illinois still held the balance of power between the two sections and must be won by the Republicans. That was Lincoln's home, but Douglas had also resided there for many years.

The *Press and Tribune's* immediate objective was to prevent a political alliance between central and southern Illinois. Ray, with his gift for sensing the grievances of a region, wrote editorials designed to arouse the men of the central area. He had lived at Springfield long enough to know the tender spots to be probed. He also pointed out to the Germans settled in south-central Illinois that the Democrats had absorbed the Know-Nothing Party and that the Republicans could best represent their interests. Ray instructed local political leaders to make the campaign rallies and speeches holidays for the country people. Folks must be invited to come and have a good time, to form clubs, practice marching, and sing campaign songs. Special editions of the *Press and Tribune* which reached 20,000 farmers carried editorials headed: "ORGANIZE IN ILLINOIS. Organize in every school district where a Republican can be found and victory is certain."

This was later qualified by:

In every School District in which three Republicans can be found, let there be a Republican Club, whose duty shall be the enumeration of the voters and the designation of their political preferences, the circulation of newspapers and documents, and by quiet, noiseless exposition of the beneficence of Republican doctrines, the creation of a belief in the necessity of a Republican triumph. A representative of each school district club should be a member of the town committee, and the chairman of the different town committees should be the effective planning, working force, for the county.

A unique feature of the *Press and Tribune's* organization for the campaign was the extension of Wide-Awake marching clubs, originally used to meet delegations at the Chicago convention. Military companies were a popular fad of the age. Germans, fresh from the European revolutions, enjoyed drilling in gymnastic societies. The Irish had organized to protect themselves from rioting Know-Nothing fanatics. These organizations quickly adopted the Wide-Awake oilcloth cape and glazed military fatigue cap with its brass or silver eagle in front. Each man carried a rail with a small swinging lantern and an American flag bearing the names of Lincoln and Hamlin. Affluent companies wore uniforms of blue, red, or silver gray.

Young Elmer Ellsworth, reading law in Lincoln's Springfield office, began training a company in gaudy Zouave uniforms. He perfected a zig-zag movement in imitation of a rail fence. The precision of the men's footwork earned the company wide renown. With it Ellsworth traveled across the North, giving exhibitions and firing the hearts of youthful watchers to organize drill companies of their own. Before the summer passed at least half a million young men—some too young to vote but not to march—had joined Wide-Awake organizations. They drilled daily and staged frequent parades in their home-town streets. When not in formation, club members wore distinctive badges depicting Lincoln mauling rails or steering a flatboat. Lincoln medals were circulated by business firms to advertise soap, tea, wagons, etc. Canes were also distributed, all allegedly made from rails split by Abraham Lincoln.

Dr. Ray made it a point to describe the activities of these

organizations in detail. He made the *Press and Tribune* their Bible, but always he kept up the paper's standard as a disseminator of news. Between reports of concerts in the Wigwam, a review of Whitman's *Leaves of Grass,* and descriptions of a tornado that swept from Iowa into Illinois, the paper reiterated that the time had come for a change in government, too long in the hands of the Southern slave oligarchy, that it was time for the North to take charge, improve the country with river dredging, railroad construction, etc. Democrat spending was a constant issue. Lincoln, an editorial said, could be counted on to save the country from the effects of Democrat profligacy. The editors pointed out that when the Democrats came to power there were twenty-four millions in the national treasury and that now the country was sixty millions in debt.

The *Press and Tribune* conducted a straw vote in Illinois and on June 18 declared that Lincoln had carried the state. Southern Illinois replied with riots. Down there the Democratic machine was reported to be intimidating local newspaper editors. Many publishers had sold their presses rather than see them destroyed. Outside papers, like the *Press and Tribune,* were the only Republican sheets circulated in "Egypt." Ray reported this new infringement on the freedom of the press—exactly what might be expected of slavocrats! He reminded readers that schoolteachers in southern Illinois had been dismissed in 1856 for voting the Frémont ticket. Clergymen who had preached freedom for all men had been threatened with tar and feathers.

On the same day that the *Press and Tribune* announced its victorious straw vote, John Locke Scripps wrote Abraham Lincoln:

My dear Sir,

I am hard at work on the biography and now need the remaining notes which I trust Nicolay will be able to send me without delay.

Since I returned from Springfield, it has been thought best, provided satisfactory arrangements can be made, to bring the work out in New York. Parties have been written to on the subject and Medill will go down to New York and complete arrangements should the answer seem to make it advisable. In that event, I will complete the MS here and take Springfield in on my route to New York.

Very truly yours,
J. L. Scripps.

On June 27, 1860, the *Press and Tribune* summarized the Republican platform once more. The party's position on slavery and abolition was repeated again in the following words:

The fight now going on in this country is not one which affects Slavery in the States where it is established by law, or which touches, except remotely, the question of emancipation. It is a struggle which arises out of a new interpretation of the Constitution which the South has procured from the Supreme Court, and which the North opposes. This interpretation assumes that the fundamental law of the Republic recognizes *property in human beings;* and that assumption the Republicans deny, hence the combat.

The object of the South, according to the *Tribune*, was to acquire legal permission to take slaves into any territory and thus inevitably degrade free labor. "The Republicans aim at the preservation of the Territories to free labor and then settlement by free men. Beyond this they do not go."

With this in print Ray wrote on the same day a personal letter to Lincoln saying:

It is early yet; but it will do no harm to begin to consider what shall be the quality and cut of your inaugural suit. It does not seem to me that you have anything else to do in the campaign which Breck and Lane have taken off your hands. The rest are overplanning with joy and thankfulness at the turn of events, and I cannot, though worked half to death, refrain from stopping to congratulate you upon the prospect of your election and the consequent rescue of the country from the hands of the spoilers. You will go into power under the most favorable auspices. The Southern men to get a Northern vote will be forced to assume Union ground from which they cannot recede; and your inauguration will be followed by a calm which nothing but the infernal folly of the radicals can disturb. . . .

Yours very truly,
C. H. Ray

[P.S.] Please make my respects to Mrs. Lincoln and Little Chin-Chopper.

Lincoln's reply has not been preserved, but it may be significant that Ray announced in his paper five days later that little Tad was seriously ill with scarlet fever.

During the summer the *Press and Tribune* stressed four political goals of the Republican Party: a homestead act, a home market for Western farmers, sound money, and freedom of the press. The Democrats could be censured consistently for their opposition to granting land to settlers on the public domain. Their land attitude accorded with their reputation as slave owners, fosterers of big plantations instead of the modest farmsteads favored by Republicans. Under a column captioned A WORD FOR VOTERS, Ray called readers' attention to the fact that:

Until the men in the West . . . get wise enough to see that they are kept in a state of commercial vassalage to the South . . . there is little hope that the growers of wheat and corn will receive adequate remuneration for their labor. . . . What the country wants is a home market, employment for all our labor, and a greater diversion of pursuits; and there is no way in which these may be obtained, except by clearing out the White House and the halls of Congress.

Ray believed that this vassalage to the South would be broken by the Republican tariff for the protection of industry. The South had opposed this, claiming that the tariff increased the price of the manufactured goods they bought. The *Press and Tribune* maintained that flourishing industry created general prosperity which would help the farmer in the West. Ray wrote:

> The development of the [coal and iron] mines . . . would be the means of employing large numbers of free men now tied to other and less profitable pursuits, of diversifying the national industry, and of adding largely to the national wealth. It would create a home market for the products of our Northern farms, and would at the same time, cut off our dependence upon the mines of the old world.

According to the *Press and Tribune*, the panic of 1857 was the result of the Democrats' fiscal policy, and a vote against the bunglers was the best assurance of good times in the future. As for freedom of the press, a recent ruling of the Democratic postmaster general declaring that his department should abide by a Virginia state law against antislavery literature spoke for itself.

These issues were all easy for the *Press and Tribune* to solve. The Know-Nothing situation was more complicated. Ray wanted both the foreign and antiforeign vote. Obviously he could not get all members of the two groups, but he worked out a plan by which he appealed to a large portion of both. The Know-Nothing Party had won converts by engendering hatred for Catholics and shouting "Popery." Many Americans took it for granted that all foreigners were Catholics, but Ray knew that most of the Germans who had come as revolutionary exiles were Protestants. With political shrewdness he appealed to anti-Catholic prejudices and at the same time exalted the Germans. The anti-Catholic theme served his purpose well. He belabored Douglas with it, using all the personal aspersions which had marked his long fight with the Little Giant. He accused Douglas of using Catholicism to win the vote of Tammany Hall. Ray wrote:

If Mr. Douglas, reared in the Protestant faith and permitting his friends to endorse him as a firm believer therein, has been seduced by his inordinate ambition into a profession of Catholicism, that he might gain political advantage thereby, it is right and proper, nay it is imperative, that the fact be exposed. If he is false in matters of eternal concern, he cannot be true in other and lesser things. If he is a Catholic, let him say so. It is his right to be what he pleases; but it is not his right to pretend to be one thing while he is another—to seem to be a Protestant while an earnest, if not a devout member of the mediaeval Church. If he is not a Catholic—if not yet divorced from the faith of his fathers—his case is not improved. Why is he able to command an almost unbroken Catholic support? All men know that in this country Catholicism does nothing without an object. . . . What has brought it about—what pledges, what guarantys, what assurances?

Always Ray drove home the principle which Lincoln had developed that the ultimate goal of the South was to impose slavery on the North. He made the most of the speech of Senator James H. Hammond of South Carolina, who compared free wage earners with slaves. Workmen, slave or free, this aristocrat said, were "the very mudsills of society." Ray called on all the millions of honest, self-respecting "mudsills" in the North to vote in the November election and turn out the rascals who dared debase them. What better example could be asked of the degrading influence of slavery on the masters? To strengthen his point, Ray clipped Southern newspapers for items which showed the South's contempt for labor.

At the time of the debates he had reprinted a heading from Virginia which began: GREASY MECHANICS, SMALL FISTED FARMERS AND FILTHY OPERATIVES. Now, with an election approaching, he asked workingmen if they would vote to keep Southerners with that attitude in office.

Ray also attacked Douglas' supporters who called the Republicans "Black," and made a campaign slogan out of the question, "Would your daughter marry a Negro?" Here again Ray had a good answer. He showed by statistics that miscegenation was widely practiced in the South under slavery—probably more so than it would be under freedom. Then he exposed the insincerity of Southern opposition to Mormon polygamy. What an inconsistency!

> The practical amalgamation, going on silently and steadily [in the South], and to such an extent that there is one mulatto, quadroon or octaroon for every Democratic voter in the Southern States, is called by another name. Perhaps properly enough; because it has advantages, in an economical sense, that do not belong to Mormon practice. . . . In the South, the amalgamationist may compel his slave to submit to his riotous embrace to-day, and be his workable, saleable, flagable chattel to-morrow; and the children of her bone and his bone, flesh of their flesh, instead of being responsible agents for contracting debts which the father must pay, are the copper-colored coin . . . by which the father's debt may be discharged. . . . The South is not in favor of Polygamy. She has a wickeder, a more convenient and more economical system by which, at the same time, lust may be sated and her open markets for the sale of children amply stocked.

When Southerners threatened secession if the election went against them, Ray replied that the United States should not be intimidated. A republic ceased to be a republic when expediency replaced the principle of popular balloting. Ray considered these threats all bluff anyway. Surely a one-crop country, such as the South, would not be insane enough to undertake an isolationist, self-sufficient economy.

On July 20 the *Press and Tribune* recapitulated the chances of victory and prophesied a majority of 20,000 for Lincoln. The Scripps biography was advertised as being available at five cents a copy on August 2, 1860. On August 9 Lincoln was serenaded by fifty Wide-Awake clubs—a procession ten miles long, which consumed three hours in passing his residence. Full particulars of the parade and of an enthusiastic meeting at the State Fair in Springfield were printed on August 10. "We are very sure that this gathering has never been surpassed in the West," the article said, "if, indeed, in any part of the Union." The editor considered it satisfying evidence "of a spirit which will insure us a glorious victory in November."

On August 13 the proslavery Breckinridge supporters held a rally in Chicago. Ray reported it with the same fidelity he showed Republican meetings. On September 7, the Douglas Democrats convened in the city for the 1860 equivalent of a pep talk. A militant political club in Milwaukee chartered a Lake Michigan steamboat, the *Lady Elgin*, to carry members and their families to the gathering. This club had recently been disarmed by Wisconsin's Republican governor, Alexander W. Randall, and was eager to uphold its rights.

In the evening, after the program was concluded, the members boarded the *Lady Elgin* for the return trip to Milwaukee —a hilarious crowd with bands and banners. The ship saloons were cleared for a grand ball. Dancers, smiling in one another's faces, swayed with the music and the waves, which were becoming rough on the lake. Now and again the merrymakers rocked into a laughing huddle against the wall. At about 2:00 A.M. the vessel—still blazing with lights—was rammed by a schooner loaded with lumber. The *Elgin's* timbers were badly sprung. Her engine toppled and fell through the hull, and the vessel sank with 393 people on board—a maritime disaster pronounced the worst in history. Lifeboats saved a few; others clung to the superstructure which floated free from the upper deck, but many of these perished as the wreckage broke under the force of the waves. Only about fifty of the passengers survived. All next day and for several days thereafter bodies were washed ashore near Evanston, Illinois. The whole nation was shocked.

The *Press and Tribune* printed harrowing details and feature stories about heroic rescues. Eastern newspapers reprinted the accounts. A composer, Henry Clay Work, later famous for his "Marching Through Georgia," wrote an immensely popular song entitled, "Lost on the Lady Elgin," destined to be sung for the next two decades by "little girls in pantalettes, big girls in bustles, fancy tenors in plaid vests, and quartettes in starched discomfort." Politically this catastrophe suffered by a prominent Douglasite club might or might not have imponderable repercussions in a campaign which was being conducted on an emotional plane.

On September 24, only six weeks before the election, Ray reported another straw ballot. This time Lincoln polled 176 electoral votes, 24 more than necessary to elect him. The tally showed that the Republican candidate carried all New England, New Jersey, Pennsylvania, Ohio, Michigan, Indiana, Illinois, Iowa, Wisconsin, and Minnesota. Oregon seemed doubtful. All others he conceded to the opposition. On October 3 with the election one month and three days away, the Republicans held a rally in the Wigwam. Seward came from New York to speak, and a Wide-Awake procession three miles long marched past the *Press and Tribune* office, saluting the paper which regularly featured the club's activities and had popularized their zig-zag "fence rail" drills.

The political program during the next four weeks was strenuous. On October 8 editor Ray listed among the prominent speakers at prospective rallies in Chicago the names of Frank Blair, Thomas Corwin, Richard Yates, Owen Lovejoy,

William L. Bross, Hermann Kreismann, Don Piatt, and E. B. Washburne. He made sport of Breckinridge, Douglas, and Bell, the three candidates opposing Lincoln. The first, he said, stood for slavery and all that the word implied. As for Douglas, Ray quoted Thomas Hart Benton's words that "the seat of Mr. Douglas' pants is too near the ground to admit of his climbing into the Presidential chair." Of Bell, whose Whig Party compromised every issue and stood only for the principles of the Declaration of Independence and the Constitution without daring to interpret either of them, Ray scoffed:

> If there is any man green enough to believe that the National Union Constitutional movement in Baltimore is anything more than a repetition of the Fillmore swindle of 1856, for the benefit of the mulatto-making Democracy, he surely ought not to be permitted to go abroad when the cows are at large, else he might be mistaken for some other verdant thing and be swallowed up. . . . This fight is for the rescue of free principles, for good, honest, economical government, and for perpetuity of the Union. . . . It is a fight of White men against Black Power. Men of Illinois, we must not lose it. There are the enemy. Up and at 'em!

Five days later Ray warned voters to discount opponents' accusations that Lincoln was an extremist on slavery and that the *Press and Tribune* was "Lincoln's abolition organ." Then, lest anyone still failed to comprehend Lincoln's position on slavery, the editor repeated it for the dozenth time.

As election day approached, the *Press and Tribune* continued to print extracts from Southern papers which contained threats of secession in case Lincoln won. Voters were urged to be unafraid and to "silence the disunion howls by electing Lincoln."

On October 25 the paper appeared with its old title of *Chicago Tribune*. Readers were told that all *Press* subscribers must know by this time that the two papers were the same. The editor wrote:

> Changed in nothing but in the omission of a part of its name, it will continue to be a live newspaper, fully up with the requirements of the city and country with which it is identified, a sleepless guardian of constitutional freedom, the zealous advocate of whatever is found in truth, justice and humanity, and the upholder of whatever will contribute to the renown and true glory of our country. . . .

On the eve of the election, a final rally was held in the Wigwam. Ray warned all Lincoln supporters to guard against trickery on the morrow. Don't let the Democrats, he cautioned, perpetrate the frauds that disgraced their party in Kansas. He uged all legitimate voters to watch for "invaders and repeaters"; to beware of "ticket peddlers" who posed as Republicans and handed out marked Democratic ballots. With a fair vote the Republicans were sure to win. The points of debate between the parties were summarized and reiterated:

> All the issues of the campaign have been merged into this, and it has come to be a question, not of Freedom or Slavery in the Territories merely, but whether there shall be freedom anywhere for anybody. Citizens of the free Northwest! Are you ready for the question?

November 6, 1860, dawned clear and beautiful in Chicago—a fine day to get out the vote. The morning issue of the *Tribune* told readers to vote. "The labor of the last six years . . . centers in this day." "BE SURE TO VOTE." Results of the election were to be received at the *Tribune* office, at the Wigwam, and at the Tremont House and Briggs House.

All day the voting progressed quietly. In the evening six or eight thousand people congregated in the great Wigwam to await the results of balloting. The first returns announced were from northern Illinois precincts—all for Lincoln—as expected—but when Alton, in the south-central zone of the state, was reported for the Rail Splitter, a flurry of excitement rippled through the crowd. Early returns from Missouri also favored Lincoln, but Democratic votes soon began to change the picture in that slave state. Indiana seemed safe enough for Honest Abe. The Republicans took the Hoosier State for granted.

Toward midnight Pennsylvania precincts began to report. The announcer called out: "Allegheny County, 10,000 majority for Lincoln. Philadelphia, 15,000 plurality." All right so far, but the politicians knew that pluralities could be deceptive. Then "5,000 majority over all," was reported. Finally a wire from Cameron announced that the City of Brotherly Love had given Lincoln a majority of 70,000 and that Pennsylvania looked safe. This, with Illinois, should almost assure Lincoln's election. Next, to cap Cameron's good news, returns began coming in from New York. Precinct after precinct voted for Lincoln.

Before dawn the result was known in Chicago. Two hundred guns boomed from the Randolph Street bridge, and Charles Ray went home to bed as newsboys announced the caption he had written for the *Tribune* of November 7: THE GREAT VICTORY. "Republicanism Triumphant over Fraud, Fusion, Cotton, Disunion and Treason. Honest Old Abe Elected." New York, Pennsylvania, Ohio, Indiana and Illinois had voted for Lincoln. "Rejoice and be Glad." The editor knew that the old friend whom he had groomed so assiduously for the last four years must be a happy man tonight.

Outside in the dark streets the Wide-Awakes, marching sixteen abreast with their torches, performed military evolutions before the *Tribune* office. Emotionally inspired, Ray wrote a new editorial:

The Republic renews its ancient glories. The great ideas which led the Revolution—which first found utterance in the Declaration of Independence, and which were afterward embodied in practical form in the Federal Constitution, still live in the hearts of the American people. The maxims of Jefferson, of Franklin, of Adams, of Madison, of Clay, and of Jackson survive. The patriotism which guided their every act has been transmitted to the present generation. There is hope yet for freedom, for honesty, for purity. Let distrust and apprehension be banished forever. Let the patriot fan the flame which ascends now fom the Altar of his country's freedom. Let the people shout. The battle has been fought and the victory won. Hail! all Hail!!

XV Stand Firm: The Tug Has to Come

After the election of Abraham Lincoln, Dr. Charles Ray had reason to consider himself a king-maker. In two short years, since the summer of 1858, he had risen from an unknown country editor to a Voice in the nation. With this rise the *Chicago Tribune* had also waxed important. The paper now claimed a distribution larger than all the other journals in Chicago combined. In the Midwest its out-of-town circulation was rivaled only by that of the old conservative Democratic sheet, the *St. Louis Republican.* The *Tribune's* present income amounted to more in a single week than Ray had paid for his share in the firm. The publishers decided to install permanent correspondents in the capitals of all the Midwestern states. Medill returned to Washington to report from there. Ray expected to divide his time between the Chicago office and Springfield, where he could keep in close touch with Lincoln.

With financial affluence Dr. Ray began to think of more comfortable living and better furnishings for Jane and the children, but he was much too sage to relax the political campaign at the moment of victory. A dozen self-appointed advisers were nudging the President-elect, suggesting compromises on the slavery issue to appease the South. The *Tribune* must see its plans for restriction of slavery consummated. The Southern states had threatened to secede if Lincoln won the election. Now that he had won it, did the South really intend to carry out its threats? If so, Charles Ray was sure that there must be but one response—uphold the Federal Union at any price, even at the cost of war. Buchanan compromises had led always to more concessions. This must end at once. Lincoln should be courteous but firm and give no ground in the nation's advance toward freedom for all men. During the first few days after the victory, Ray told his readers:

> Now while in the flush of triumph achieved after years of waiting and working, while the smoke of the conflict is in our garments, it will be wise and discreet of Republicans to avoid all causes of additional irritation and to convince the people of the South by our words and acts that we are not half so fierce and ravenous as we have been represented—that we are still their countrymen—bound to them by a thousand ties, which we would not rupture if we could!

Ray spent much of his time in Springfield watching Lincoln prepare to assume his exalted office. The little hamlet was more crowded than usual, its 9,000 inhabitants agog with excitement over the constant influx of the nation's most prominent statesmen. The hotels were packed. Guests unable to get accommodations slept in new-fangled "sleeping car" berths down on the railroad tracks. Lincoln had been given a room in the pillared capitol and had installed secretaries to read and arrange his mail. He insisted that the door stand open always for the crowds to come in and watch or interview him. Occasionally Lincoln retreated across the public square to his old legal office up the steep, dark stairs behind the swinging sign marked LINCOLN & HERNDON. He soon found it necessary to maintain another, more secluded, hiding place.

Charles Ray saw many old friends in the crowded Illinois capital. The Chicago and Eastern newspapers had correspondents on the lookout for news. Among them Ray spied Henry Villard, a Bavarian representing the *New York Herald*. Villard had been in the United States only seven years, but he already ranked high in the newspaper world. He knew Illinois politics and had reported the now famous Ottawa and Freeport debates, but he deferred to Charles Ray and his great paper. In the throng Ray also noticed many state legislators. They had come long ahead of the date for the next session and caucused constantly, arguing about the new national administration and the possibility of civil war. Slave-state Missouri was very close to the Illinois capital. Illinois and Missouri had a common border for over three hundred miles. Whatever happened in one state was sure to affect the other. If Missouri joined the Confederacy the whole Northwest would be in jeopardy. Fortunately Missouri had elected for governor a middle-of-the-road Douglas Democrat named Claibourne Jackson, rather than a simon-pure proslavery man. Evidently the slaveholders over there loved the Union more than they loved their chattels, or did they understand that a civil war would strip them not only of their slaves but also of all other property? The powerful and conservative *St. Louis Republican* deprecated secession. "We have no discretion but to yield obedience," Missouri readers were told.

The military commander of Missouri was an old army man, handsome, broad-shouldered General William S. Harney. At sixty he was flushed with health and pleasant memories of distinguished service in the Seminole and Mexican wars. A native of Louisiana, Harney was accustomed to slavery. He had married a wealthy St. Louis society woman and was intimate with the upper classes, who, according to the last vote, seemed to be loyal to the Union. Harney himself was said to be a man with good looks, little intellect, and a strong sense of honor—in short, an ideal dragoon. All in all, Missouri did not appear to be a trouble spot, and Illinois had little to fear from it when Lincoln's administration took up its duties. Charles Ray was further encouraged by a letter from Horace Greeley introducing the bearer, a Mr. F. Mrachek, according to Greeley's spelling. The traveler was bound for St. Louis to assume editorship of a Bohemian paper there. Greeley hoped that Mrachek might work in conjunction with Ray among Missouri's immigrant population.

When threats of war failed to materialize, Ray filled his columns with less portentous news. Readers must be kept interested until important events occurred. He devoted considerable space to a sensational divorce case during this period. However, while the presses thumped out various stories, editor Ray watched always for indications of the identity of the key men Lincoln might be considering for his cabinet. These officials would carry out or quash the administration's avowed determination to restrict slavery until it would eventually die. Not only did Ray feel a personal responsibility in this selection, but he knew that many liberals, East and West, looked to him and the *Tribune* to see that Lincoln made no mistakes. As soon as the election returns had been generally known, letters—some important, many trivial—started coming to Ray. Politicians across the nation realized the part he had played both in the nomination and in the election, and they appealed to him for Lincoln's attention. Among the first was a letter from John A. Andrew, who had been elected governor of Massachusetts on the Lincoln ticket. He was probably the most popular political figure in New England, much better known than Lincoln. He had endeared himself to the abolitionists by raising money to defend John Brown. Many people believed that the Rail Splitter had ridden to success in Massachusetts on Andrew's coattails. The governor-elect had headed the Massachusetts delegation at the Chicago convention, where he must have recognized Charles Ray's importance in the nomination, for he now wrote sending personal greetings to Lincoln through Ray and adding some political suggestions.

Another man in Massachusetts politics, Samuel Bowles, chose the same method of communicating with Lincoln. Ray received from Bowles a list of the men he wanted appointed to Lincoln's cabinet. Bowles was the founder of the Republican Party in Massachusetts and editor of the *Springfield Republican*, one of the most powerful newspapers in New England.

Still another Massachusetts Republican, Edward L. Pierce, wrote Ray "Privately." Pierce was a Quaker humanitarian—a member of the wealthy family of merchants whose cocoa cans displayed the profile of a Quaker lady carrying a steaming pot. This attractive and convenient tin box had been designed to woo the working classes from their devotion to ardent spirits. As a boy, Edward had been influenced by Sumner's oratory and, after being graduated from Harvard, had served as secretary for Salmon P. Chase. Pierce had been a delegate from Massachusetts to the Chicago convention. He had met Ray there and now sent him a list of possible cabinet appointees with the remark: "You are one of the few who have Mr. Lincoln's ear and I hope you will see to it that our cause, to use his own words, is 'intrusted to its own undoubted friends.' "

Pierce also said that he had been disturbed to learn that the flippant Tom Corwin and dilettante Don Piatt of Ohio had gone on a pilgrimage to Springfield to seek favors of Lincoln. Such reactionaries might color the President-elect's thinking while "true men" felt it immodest and unbecoming to thrust themselves forward. Pierce hoped that Ray would let Lincoln know that Piatt had become an admirer only since the election.

Pierce did not know that Piatt might still be classed as a questionable supporter of the Rail Splitter, since he had described a dinner at Lincoln's home as "an old-fashioned mess of indigestion, composed mainly of cakes, pies and chickens, the last evidently killed in the morning, to be eaten, as best they might, that evening." Piatt described Mrs. Lincoln as one who lacked "the quality necessary for a woman in her new position"—unkind reflections which may have come to him after Lincoln failed to grant the favor he desired.

Charles Ray put these letters down and consulted fellow correspondents in Springfield. He wanted to know about the nation's top statesmen who had visited Lincoln since the election. What had Lincoln promised them? The assembled correspondents laughed over the current gossip and told many amusing anecdotes concerning the multitude of political bigwigs who had come to advise Lincoln and suggest appointments. Ray learned that Salmon P. Chase had been in town urging Lincoln to adopt a strong antislavery policy. The sly and inscrutable Thurlow Weed had also offered counsel. No doubt the suave wire puller was laying plans to install Seward in the administration—but he was doing more than that, as it turned out. Ray learned that Weed had urged Lincoln to compromise the principles on which he had been elected. The South, Weed said, would cause no more trouble if the coming administration would only denounce the Republican Party's plank against extension of slavery. He argued that such a little concession might avert a civil war. Lincoln had stood firm against Weed's plan of appeasement but had been sympathetic to Chase's antislavery program.

When Charles Ray heard reports of these conversations, he applauded Lincoln's resolution. Had Buchanan shown as much determination in facing each crisis as it arose, the country might have been spared its present predicament. Ray published another editorial on December 5, 1860, reiterating the *Tribune's* advice to give not an inch.

This journal stands where it has always stood: it concedes nothing that weakens the worth of the great triumph over that infernally despotic institution which has debauched the national conscience and now strives to emasculate the national courage.

A week later he wrote again: "If war must come it ought to be waged in defense of the Constitution as our Fathers made it." This was followed next day with: "War is the last, the very last argument to be resorted to among children of a common parentage. Let it be avoided by every sacrifice short of the legacy left us in *the Constitution of the United States*."

South Carolina politicians, accustomed to a North that always appeased, voted on December 20, 1860, to secede from the Union. Charles Ray hurried home to Chicago and ordered a cut of the Charleston harbor to be printed in the *Tribune*. Let readers become familiar with the nest of secession and visualize the best way to eradicate it with military and naval forces. In Charleston the Federal commander, Robert Anderson, celebrated Christmas by evacuating Fort Moultrie, adjacent to the mainland. He moved his garrison to the less vulnerable Fort Sumter, out in Charleston harbor.

New Year's Day 1861 in Chicago dawned cold and bright. The river was frozen. After breakfast crowds began skating on a dozen ponds. Ray bundled up Jane and the three children and took them for a drive. He noticed that the lap robes had worn threadbare; he must buy new ones. He had worked so hard on his fight for better government and equality of opportunity for all men that he had overlooked personal matters. Now, with an ample bank account, he would rectify this negligence.

Chicago's prosperity, as well as Ray's own, seemed boundless. Last year the city's grain receipts had doubled those of the year before, and by all predictions next year's should double again. Immigrants arrived in great numbers, even in winter, and the mercantile business boomed. Never had commercial prospects been so bright. The rosy scheme was marred only by the continued insolence of the Southern states and their threats of war. Why did not Buchanan do something besides claim to be the great peacemaker, the compromiser who dared nothing and accomplished nothing—the "chinless one" offering wine to traitors who brought amendments to the Constitution to stave off secession?

Lincoln had said, "Let there be no compromise on the question of *extending* slavery. . . . Stand firm. The tug has to come, & better now, than any time hereafter." Charles Ray had written his New Year's editorial in this vein, and as he turned the horse's head toward home that morning, newsboys were selling the *Tribune* on the streets. It was good to know that people would read and ponder his words of resolution during the holiday. Let the irresolute strengthen their determination on his grisly tidings. The Constitution must not be amended to guarantee the rights of property in men. No!

He wrote: "The Constitution as it is and as the conservative men of the country would preserve it; or the Constitution just as its enemies would shape it. Which will the Northwest have?"

For Thursday's paper, Ray wrote:

> What a sight! The leading politicians of a great and once liberty loving and patriotic party, the chief executive officers of the government, and a full half of the people of one section of the Republic, all plotting and conspiring against the perpetuity of the fairest political fabric ever built by human hands, and provoking civil war between brothers—for what? That the representatives of a little oligarchy of 347,000 slaveholders may have the privilege, not authorized in the Constitution, of buying, selling, working without pay and whipping at will, men, women and children in the Territories which God made free. . . .
>
> But as we are not the advocates of a policy which will bring slavery to a sudden end at the point of the bayonet, we insist *that the Union and the supremacy of the Constitution be maintained.*

At the office next day Ray met Joe Medill, back from Washington for the holiday. The two men sat down together at one end of the long editorial conference table. The sky was dark, and sleet pecked at the frosted windows. Medill said things looked very bad in Washington. People prophesied that a mob would prevent Lincoln from being inaugurated. Perhaps he should take the oath of office in Springfield, then, as Chief Executive, move down to the capital. Already a palmetto flag had been raised over the Charleston customhouse. The rebel state was demanding the surrender of Major Anderson's little garrison at Fort Sumter out in the bay.

Ray determined to tell his readers about this latest act of treason. He demanded impeachment of the "hoary headed traitor in the White House" for violating his oath to uphold and defend the Constitution. The President's logic, Ray said,

> . . . which proves in one breath that States have no right to secede, but that the Federal government has no right to prevent them, deserves to be ranked, as an intellectual feat, with those which have made schoolmen famous.

Ray's name headed a list of patriots who called all liberty-loving citizens to meet in Bryan Hall on January 5. Then the editor boarded a train for the run to Springfield, southwest across the yellow prairies drifted deep with snow, to lay the latest danger before a dilatory legislature.

In Springfield he received a note from Horace White, a member of the *Tribune* staff who supervised the Chicago office in Ray's absence. White enclosed a letter from Joe Medill, who had gone back to Washington. "I send you the enclosed from Jo," White said. "It comes from a broken heart. Poor fellow, when I think how badly he must have felt I grieve down to my boot heels."

Ray unfolded the letter and read Medill's familiar handwriting. His partner had heard and believed that Lincoln had offered Cameron the Treasury post in the cabinet. Medill had written:

> We feared that Lincoln was too much indebted to certain factions and now it is proved. Lincoln is a failure. Perhaps it

is best to let disunionists take Washington and let Lincoln stay in Springfield.

Ray had been present when the deal was made to appoint Cameron—in fact had been party to it, with Medill's knowledge and consent, but the situation had changed since then. Ray's former confreres, Judge David Davis and Leonard Swett, were dealing directly with the Cameron group now, without consulting Ray. This seemed like a scheme to belittle the *Tribune* and grasp the Illinois patronage. Already Davis and Swett had enlisted John Wentworth's *Democrat* and Charlie Wilson's *Journal*—two rivals to the *Tribune* which exerted considerable power in Chicago. Wentworth's dislike for Ray had begun in the winter of 1855 when Long John's rival, Norman Judd, maneuvered Ray into the Senate clerkship. Dislike changed to hatred when the *Tribune* stood loyally by Judd and consistently opposed all of Wentworth's political aspirations. This rivalry within the party had become known in Chicago as the War of the Roses. With Cameron indebted to the Wentworth faction for the appointment, Ray, Medill, and Washburne might lose the whip hand in Illinois politics. The *Tribune* had promised voters to clean up government corruption as well as to restrict the extension of slavery, and Cameron's record held no promise of help for either. The Pennsylvania politician Thaddeus Stevens said of Cameron, "I don't think he would steal a red hot stove." Ray could not openly repudiate his agreement to get a cabinet seat for the spoilsman, but certainly his appointment now seemed to be against the best interests of the *Tribune*.

Ray read more of Medill's letter. The Washington correspondent quoted Thad Stevens of Pennsylvania as saying: "Yesterday all honest men in Pennsylvania called Cameron a thief: today he is the embodiment of honesty—the King can do no wrong, while you are exacting for his favors." Then

Medill added, "And to think we nominated, campaigned and elected Lincoln as Honest Abe and his first act is this."

Medill went on to say that some Republican senators were so incensed that they threatened not to confirm Cameron's appointment. "The long crooked fingers of Thurlow Weed are seen in all this. Weed, Geo. Low, John Wentworth and Charlie Wilson will be the powers behind the throne."

Charles Ray determined to sound out politicians in the Illinois capitol halls before writing to Medill. Two days later he received a letter from Washburne and another from Medill, addressed directly to him. Washburne seemed to be as worried as Medill had been. "If you can do anything," Washburne wrote, "if you have any influence for God's sake use it. Lincoln should make Cameron withdraw."

Medill's letter to Ray displayed as much excitement as the one he had written to Horace White:

> If the reports from Springfield are true, there will not be one *original Lincoln* man in the cabinet. It will be made up from many of his competitors, and enemies. The Cameron, Seward, Weed, George Low, Caleb B. Smith, Dr. Leib, Wilson, John Wentworth tribe of thieves, jobbers and peculators will control "honest Abe" body, soul and boots. . . . We made Abe and by G– we can *unmake* him . . . Excuse my under emphasis.

Then Medill added a little dialogue to express his feelings: "Boy:—'Gratitude is a sentiment of thankfulness for favors expected.'

" 'Right, Go up head,'—application *Honest* Abe."

Charles Ray put down the letter. These men were more excited than the situation warranted. Lincoln had come over to Ray's room at the hotel that very morning. He had obviously had something to say but had been interrupted by another of the roomers and had left to meet an engagement. Ray was sure that Lincoln had come to discuss this matter and that no rash appointment would be made. Ray knew too that a practical joke had been set on foot which might make Cameron change his mind about a place in the cabinet. Relieved of the troublesome fellow, the Rail Splitter could undoubtedly appoint department heads who could stand firm when the antislavery tug came.

The artifice which Ray had started was in the form of a sarcastically discrediting dispatch which he had persuaded Henry Villard to send east. This gem of satire depicted Cameron as an unwanted office-seeker whose suffering might be alleviated by "a plaster in the shape of a first class foreign mission." There was enough truth in this diagnosis of Cameron's malady to make the Pennsylvania politician ridiculous, and he would probably deny all cabinet ambitions. This dispatch was now in the mail, bound for release to the New York papers. Villard would get all the credit—or discredit—for it, but all the political repercussions would redound to the *Tribune's* benefit. Highly elated with the prospect, Charles Ray wrote Washburne the following reassuring letter:

Confidential Springfield, Jany 7th

My dear Washburne:

Keep your shirt on. Cameron has not a place in the Cabinet and will not get one—that's sure. The place that he is after was offered to Chase *as I know,* on Friday last; but the trouble is that he will not accept it without great urging. Now do you spend some of the energy which you write in denunciation of Cameron's appointment, in securing Chase's acceptance of the place that Cameron did not get, and all will be well.

Chase left here greatly pleased with Lincoln's plans, which latter comprehend, *I suppose,* the giving of the port-folio of State to Mr. Seward. That does not specially please Mr. C.; but I suspect that it would not be an insurmountable objection to his assisting at Cabinet councils. About Seward, I do not know positively; but because Lincoln is close-mouthed and cautious; and I do not like to ask him any questions direct. But the feeling here, shared by Judd and Koerner, is that that is a certainty if S. will accept. It does not please me; but I do not expect to be pleased with everything in this world. Up to today I had supposed that Dayton would be the man; and it may all result in that yet.

Lincoln was in my room this morning for a few minutes, apparently for a talk; but we were interrupted by a visitor and the chance went by. I shall see him again as soon as practicable and then I will write you again. He praised Chase very highly, saying among other things, that "take him all in all he is the foremost man in the party." This language would admit of no misconstruction even if I had not before been told by Mr. C. himself what was required of him. Beyond these two, S. & C., nothing is decided upon that I know of.

Now in conclusion let me say that you may trust Old Abe. He is rising every day in the estimation of all who know him best. He is wiser and more sagacious than I thought he would prove to be. Our cause is dearer to him than anything else; and he will make no mistakes. Depend on that.

Go to work and move heaven and earth (hell belongs to the Cameronians) to make Mr. Chase accept the place in which he can do the most good. Don't wait an hour; but begin!

Yours very Truly,
C. H. Ray

Ray sealed the letter and posted it. He was expecting the Cameron satire to break any day, almost any hour now. But he was not prepared for the next news that Medill wired from Washington.

XVI The Cameron Business Has Been Arrested

THE FIRST two months of 1861—from New Year's Day to Lincoln's inauguration—were trying ones for Dr. Charles Ray. The Republican Party, instead of uniting to support the platform on which the election had been won, seemed to be splitting over factional quarrels about jobs. Politicians who had ridden into office on the wave of promised reform now pleaded for moderation and a minimum of change. Ray, unlike these fellows, sought no office for himself. To him the victory was a clear mandate to restrict the extension of slavery and clean up the corruption in government. He was unwilling to deviate from these goals. The unexpected dispatch from Medill which diverted him from his plans to sidetrack the appointment of Cameron might be a godsend in disguise.

Medill had telegraphed on January 8, 1861, the anniversary of Jackson's victory at New Orleans, that South Carolina rebels had fired on the U.S.S. *Star of the West* as she steamed toward Anderson's Federal garrison at Fort Sumter in Charleston harbor. Medill followed his telegram with an angry letter. The South deserved to be taught a lesson, he said. The North should abandon any cautious plan for Lincoln to take the oath of office in Springfield. Loyal Americans must organize a suitably armed contingent and bring him in triumph to the national capital for the ceremonies:

The wind blows from the North this time. Any attempt to seize the capital, or the archives of government or to prevent the inauguration of the President-elect, will be resisted by a million men in arms.

Ray translated the spirit of this letter in his next editorial, but he was more cautious than his partner.

We have come upon a new era. We know our country is large, but will it hold together? Has it the elements of a stable government? Our flag is beautiful and striking, but are its colors fast? . . . Truly, the animal man is not ready for the millennium, nor the Congress of Nations. The present dark horizon may clear up, but it has aroused the military spirit.

To keep the North informed and fire the patriotic heart, Ray began a new column entitled ITEMS ON THE PROGRESS OF TREASON. Below this heading he continued his old practice of reprinting news from the Southern press. On January 9 Mississippi voted to secede; Florida and Alabama followed. The new governor of Missouri, Claibourne Jackson, abandoned the Douglas-Democratic platform on which he had been elected and announced that Missouri and Kentucky should "stand by the South." This declaration had been endorsed by prolonged applause in the Missouri legislature, and the governor recommended raising men and money for defense. A convention was called for February 15 to consider leaving the Union. Kentucky fire-eaters also clamored for secession, and Indiana, of all states, was reported to be on the verge of joining them. Violence in southern Illinois became more virulent than it had been prior to the election.

Ray hurried a petition to John A. Andrew in Massachusetts. Andrew had already raised a regiment to help preserve the Union, and Ray wanted him to use his great influence in Congress to get Federal aid for widening the canal connecting Lake Michigan and the Mississippi. Reasonable improvement, Ray said, would enable gunboats to pass through to the Western waters. Grain barges that now floated down to New Orleans could travel through the enlarged canal east through Chicago and on to the Atlantic seaboard, increasing commerce and friendly relations between East and West.

Before this letter could have reached Andrew, Ray received one from him. The editor tore it open and began to read. Evidently the Massachusetts politician did not know about the firing on the *Star of the West* when he wrote, because the letter was concerned only with Lincoln's appointments. The governor said that he considered either Seward or Cameron in the cabinet a disaster for the Republican Party in Massachusetts. "You may show this to Lincoln if you want to," the letter concluded.

Since the election Ray had divided his time between Chicago and Springfield. Lincoln had been difficult to approach recently. The cannonading at Charleston harbor, and in the Midwest a tense apprehension of impending war, an accumulation of urgent business, and ever-mounting piles of unanswered mail caused him to abandon his daily levees. He rented an additional office in town for some of his secretaries while he himself often disappeared to work on his inaugural address. Important visitors usually sought him at his residence, but Ray did not choose to wear out his welcome by such intrusion. He enclosed Andrew's letter with another of his own to Lincoln and instructed Lincoln's secretary, John G. Nicolay, to see that his chief received them personally. The day was unusually auspicious for delivering Andrew's diatribe against Cameron, because copies of the *New York Herald* containing the Villard-Ray dispatch had arrived in Springfield. Gossip said that Lincoln, when he read the satire about Cameron's futile effort to get a cabinet post, laughed until tears streamed down his sallow cheeks.

Ray needed this encouragement, for he had received two more disconcerting letters from the East, one from Medill and the other from Washburne. These men were still troubled about the prolonged uncertainty over the possibility of Cameron's appointment, even while cannon boomed at Charleston. Medill stated that Weed was backing the Wentworth-Davis gang by insisting on a seat in the cabinet for Cameron (a statement contradicted by Weed in his autobiography). Medill was sure that Chase would not serve in a cabinet with such tainted fellows as Seward, Cameron, and Caleb Smith. The last was alleged to have participated in a shady railroad deal. In any event, Medill was coming home, and Ray would have to take his place in Washington. Mrs. Medill, Joseph said, had her things packed, and a change in plans would make a family fuss. This shift meant that Ray would be in Washington during Lincoln's first year in office.

The letter Ray received from Washburne was a reply to one he had written saying that Cameron might do no harm in the cabinet provided he was not in the Treasury. After all, the Pennsylvanian had been promised a place, and the Republican Party might be hurt as much by a broken promise as by an unwise appointment. Washburne disagreed:

> It is universally conceded by all the best men in Pennsylvania that the appointment of Cameron would utterly demoralize and ruin the party in the State, and yet you seem to think it would hurt us there, if he should not go in!

Washburne added that everybody in Washington was in the dark concerning Lincoln's plans. Leonard Swett and Charles Wilson both claimed to be in Lincoln's confidence, and Washburne stated that if this were true the party was doomed. Washburne also lamented the fact that the Illinois legislature was not preparing the state for war. "We are in a revolution," he warned.

Ray did not have to be told about the revolution. It simmered all around him, and across the river in Missouri, it seemed to have boiled over. Abolitionists in Kansas were reported to be preparing for open warfare with the Missourians.

Firebrands in Missouri were taking advantage of the martial threats to urge the election of pro-secession delegates to the February 15 convention. To counteract this, Frank Blair was drilling Wide-Awake clubs to serve as Union soldiers if the convention voted to secede.

The Illinois legislature debated what it should do. Republicans urged the passage of a stringent militia bill. The Democrats replied by calling a party convention to decide on proper action in case of a civil war. Should Illinois remain neutral and deny assistance to the Federal government? Ray dashed off a note to Washburne. The present seemed no time to quibble about a seat in the cabinet for Cameron. He pointed out the immediate danger:

> We have got an enemy right here in Illinois whom we must down before we can approach the South. If a militia bill is passed, it must be by brute force and party drill. We are at it, but our men are poor cusses as politicians. Every man wants to be leader.

With the state Democrats leaning toward secession or neutrality and the Republicans splintering into factions Ray repeated his belief that Cameron was not sufficiently important to cause a party quarrel. Ray realized the danger of his appointment, saying that he did not approve the Pennsylvanian personally, but that Lincoln might feel that he needed the support of the crass wing of his party. Ray made no reference to his promise of a cabinet seat for Cameron, but he suggested that Washburne might keep him out by starting a flood of remonstrances to Lincoln's desk. "Now don't show this letter," Ray added. "If you do, I'll never write again, never."

The ink was hardly dry before Ray did write again. He had just talked with Lincoln and felt that outside pressure against Cameron might have its effect: The letter, a long one, read as follows:

My dear Washburne:

Do send in your remonstrances. Lincoln is open to conviction. He has been deceived, and knows it, and waits an opportunity to back out for a reason. So pitch in. The appointment is arrested at any rate; and a little effort will cause its entire abandonment. Hiram Ramsey, Geo Updyke and Judge Hogeboom of New York have been here today. They have had a three hour confab with Lincoln, and have told him a thousand truths which he ought to know. They say that if this work goes on and Thurlow Weed, Cameron and Cab. Smith get the reins, there is nothing but a disgraceful compromise with the South, and afterward a reconstruction of the Radical Democratic party in all the free States; that the Administration thus manned cannot command the confidence of the country and that if we die for Old Abe, we must die right here. They have talked very boldly and plainly. Coming, backed up by the *Tribune* and *Evening Post* influence, they could talk. Abe has got an eye-opener; and by the way, Swett and Charly Wilson got a lick back that they will feel. Updyke spoke in pointed terms of such representatives of the President-elect, in Washington—of their airs and graces &c so that Lincoln sees just what they are.

Letters keep pouring in from all quarters about Cameron; and now you have only to follow up the fire by sensational and other remonstrances, and all will be well.

These New Yorkers have gone back by Columbus to see Chase and persuade him to hold on to his refusal. He will go into the cabinet if Cameron is kept out. That, I take it, is sure. So bestir yourselves.

Ray signed and folded the letter. Next day, January 17, 1861, Ray wrote Governor Andrew, telling him, "the Cameron business has been arrested: and now if by such energetic remonstrances as yours, we can prevent its being reopened, a great victory will have been gained." He added that "Lincoln's original friends" must do what they could to get Chase into the cabinet to counterbalance Seward. He asked Andrew to write

Chase urging him to accept. Then Ray outlined the other possible appointees, adding:

I have told you all I know about what is in the line of Mr. Lincoln's intentions; but let me say that this little does not come directly from Mr. Lincoln himself. I have hardly changed a dozen words with him about his appointments; and I am sure that no friend in Illinois was consulted about the invitation to Cameron. Of late, he is most uncommunicative: and now that his eyes are opened to the fatal character of the mistake that he was about to make, I hope that he will more frequently call to his aid the men who have not his responsibilities and anxieties, etc.

Every day the man's purity of intention shines out with new lustre. He has only one desire; and that to so govern the country that its prosperity and happiness may be secure while our great cause is advancing. If he fails, his dislike to say *no* to friends upon whose judgment he would like to rely and of whose affection he feels sure will be chargeable with the misfortune. That he is patriotic and honest, and that he will bravely carry forward our flag, I cannot doubt, but more *iron* would do him no harm.

Yours very sincerely,
C. H. Ray.

In addition to getting at least one man in the cabinet, Charles Ray had two other objectives at this time. He wanted Lincoln to repay the Germans for their votes in his behalf, and he also sought the appointment of John Locke Scripps as postmaster of Chicago—a position which had commercial advantage for any newspaper. Country postmasters, courting favor from the metropolitan office would be sure to outdo themselves in promoting a journal owned by the Chicago postmaster. Ray pointed out to Lincoln the advantage of having the *Tribune* spread the best Republican doctrine throughout the state.

Noisy Charlie Wilson of the *Journal* also wanted the post

and promised a similar distribution of the best dogma in case he received the appointment. Charlie, a member of the dangerous Davis-Swett combination, must be squelched if possible. A third contender for the appointment was Lincoln's old friend and supporter Ebenezer Peck. A real schemer, Peck had induced George Schneider, editor of the *Staats-Zeitung*, to apply for the office also. Ray had always sought the friendship of the Germans. Would he dare oppose them on this issue? With three newspapers contending for the position, Lincoln might well decide against offending two to favor one and solve his dilemma by giving the post to his old friend Peck—which was obviously what Peck himself believed.

The situation, especially the prospect of offending Schneider's Germans, embarrassed Ray. He had favored one of them, Hermann Kreismann, by arranging to get him a pass to go east to talk with Governor Andrew and to visit in Washington. Kreismann had already visited Lincoln in Springfield and was furnishing Ray with political gossip for editorials—much of it too trivial for use. The German's letters included personal items ridiculing the gawky appearance of Lincoln's secretary, John G. Nicolay, stories about Mrs. Lincoln's bad temper and hasty speech, and rumors concerning a procurer for congressmen, named Darling, who sought the White House job of introducing guests to the incoming First Lady. Poor Mary Lincoln was making an unfavorable impression on newsmen even at this early day!

Kreismann had sent Ray accounts of the progress of treason in Maryland and Virginia. He reported hearing threats that Lincoln would never be allowed to take the oath of office in Washington in March. Ray had received similar warnings from Medill and he knew that there might be danger ahead. Furthermore, conditions in neighboring Missouri had worsened. An envoy from Mississippi had arrived in that doubtful state and was urging it to join the Confederacy. Medill wrote Ray that in case the Border Ruffians began expelling Republicans from Missouri, Illinois must join with Iowa and invade Missouri to maintain order.

Five days later Medill wrote again, enclosing a clipping from the *New York Tribune*. The printed account was enough to infuriate any patriotic citizen. The Maryland legislature, he read, contemplated a rump session to consider seceding from the Union.

Medill wrote Ray a third letter on January 18. In this one he deplored the fact that the Davis-Wentworth faction had won out with Lincoln. Medill did not intend to stand for much of this. "We are independent and are making money," he wrote. "We are not beholden to L. for anything." Medill suggested that Ray impress the President-elect with a formal letter instead of going around to his house for a call:

> Why don't you write L. remind him of our services and give him an ultimatum. If he makes this a Seward administration we will pursue our own course. The advantage of writing, is that you can get all you want to say in an enduring and impressive form and he can't stop the narrative or turn the conversation.

Medill, however, showed caution by adding, "It is yet too soon to take ground in the paper against him or in a relation to our future course." But Medill thought Lincoln understood the paper's position:

> Should his course be shaped at the last minute to admit Chase and exclude Cameron we should be [in] a position to back him up. But our ultimatum had better be placed before him in advance.

This was the fourth revengeful letter Ray had read from Medill—three direct to himself and one to Horace White—all condemning the President-elect as a failure before he had taken office. Ray decided to refrain from delivering the ultimatum at this time. He was very busy with newspaper work anyway, for he was writing a series of editorials on the progress of secession. He described the humiliating retreat of Major Anderson from Fort Moultrie to Sumter and the recent secessionist threat to shoot down the United States flag there. "If a million men are needed to thwart this," he said, "let the money be voted and the columns put in motion." He intimated that the people of the North might be united in a fight for the Union if South Carolina dared fire on Fort Sumter. "Then, perhaps, the North would arise in vindication of the Constitution and laws, and teach the South that this country and government were not made wholly for slaveholders." Let Lincoln read and ponder this when it was placed before him the next day.

The threat of open warfare made Governor Andrew's next communication seem strangely out of date. He was answering Ray's letter of January 17 and still seemed interested only in cabinet appointments. Andrew said that he had written Lincoln, as Ray had requested, regarding Cameron, Chase, etc., etc., and very much hoped that both Chase and Blair might get cabinet posts. Andrew stated further:

> I have urged Lincoln to act *himself*, not to permit himself to depart from his own judgment, out of deference to great names, or influences; the people voted for *him* not for *others*. I also urged that he . . . should still be seen to be *characteristically* as a *Western* man: that the enterprise, bravery, frankness and simplicity, supposed to belong to hardy volunteers in the great conquest over nature which are the supposed characteristics of pioneer life & manners among the best classes, are just the quality the people have bargained for.

Editor Ray's attention was drawn from Andrew's letter by a new and more urgent one from Medill which fairly smoked with vituperation. Medill, close to the government's cutting edge, worried about the fate of Major Anderson, isolated at Fort Sumter, and he wrote a furious denunciation of President Buchanan's unwillingness to do anything. The President, Medill fumed, had intimated that he would not resort to coercion.

If there is to be any fighting his successor will have to do it. He will give no other pledge than to preserve the peace of this district on the 4th of March. The imbecile old creature has completely shown the white feather since the *Star of the West* was cannonaded by the insurgents. . . . But the country has only to endure six weeks more of this miserable cowardice, incompetency and disloyalty.

Ray, writing many of his editorials on the train between Springfield and Chicago, delivered Medill's letter to the printer for publication in full. He had already branded the President with worse epithets when he wrote:

His Excellency, James Buchanan . . . is tottering through the sumptuous solitude of the White House, a chattering imbecile, a hopeless, helpless prisoner of vicious consellors, pandering to bad passions in others which age has extinguished in himself, alternately telling his beads and writing weak supplications for newspapers—an object of mingled compassion and contempt.

Oh, for the day when Lincoln and the Republican Party would take the ship of state's helm! Would the nation be a complete and unsalvageable wreck by then?

On February 11, 1861, the *Tribune* announced the election of Jefferson Davis as President of the Confederacy, and on the same day Lincoln left the Illinois capital for Washington. Ray gave up his Springfield room and hurried back to Chicago, where he could receive and publish daily accounts of Lincoln's progress through Cincinnati, Columbus, Pittsburgh, Cleveland, Buffalo, Albany, New York, and Philadelphia. Readers were assured that the President-elect would live up to every word of his campaign promises about the restriction of slavery and would give traitors their deserts even at the cost of war.

These were brave words. But the appeasing wing of the party, although it had shouted for slavery restriction to win the election, now offered compromises on the slavery issue to avert possible war. The defection seemed to Ray to be part of the Wentworth-Davis scheme to discredit the *Tribune* and encourage the South. The appeasers called a mass meeting which assembled at Bryan Hall in Chicago as Lincoln steamed toward the national capital. These dissenters, claiming to be Republicans, presented resolutions in favor of modifying the party's stand on slavery. Such boring from within might well undermine all that Ray had fought for, but the resolutions were still being argued when someone turned out the gaslights, an old trick. In 1861 the dissenters had no matches ready, as the Loco-focos had had in 1835, and the meeting adjourned in darkness with nothing accomplished.

Down in Washington other weak-willed Republicans tried to break down Lincoln's platform before the President-elect arrived. Congressman William Kellogg of Canton, Illinois, supposedly a Lincoln man, introduced an amendment to the Constitution which would protect slavery in the territories. This was the concession Lincoln had refused to make. Joe Medill, getting ready now to leave Washington, sent a scorching letter for publication in Chicago. Ray published the letter, and Kellogg, when he read it, determined to give Medill a farewell thrashing. He met the editor in the National Hotel and knocked him to the floor. Out in Illinois, the *Tribune* cried, "If he [Kellogg] thinks to commend his valor to any portion of Illinois by making a midnight assault upon an invalid

[Medill was crippled with rheumatism] we have only to say we believe he mistakes the temper of his constituents."

As Lincoln traveled leisurely to Washington speaking at all the large cities, Ray published in italics on the front page a statement which he said Lincoln had made personally to the *Tribune* before leaving. This was republished day after day as Lincoln moved toward Washington. The quotation said:

I will suffer death, before I will consent, or advise my friends to consent, to any concession or compromise which looks like buying the privilege of taking possession of the Government to which we have a Constitutional right; because, whatever I might think of the merit of various proposals before Congress, I should regard any concession in the face of menace as destructive of the Government itself.

Ray assured his readers:

Honest Old Abe will not be a wooden President. He is not a man of jelly to be moulded at will by the first man who seizes upon him. He promises to be a General Jackson. Squirt guns are suddenly at a discount.

On February 25, 1861, the *Tribune* announced that Lincoln had reached Washington safely, having traveled from Harrisburg to the capital in disguise. The President-elect was congratulated for his commendable caution. Ray and John Locke Scripps went down to Washington to report the inauguration, while the bruised Medill came back to Chicago. "Thank God, the country has at last got an honest brave and true MAN for President," Ray wrote his paper. "The people will stand by him to the end of the chapter, come what may. . . . Old Abe is now here. . . . All hail to the national regeneration!"

Washington was crowded for the inauguration. Rooms were at a premium—two men in a bed, three beds in a room, each occupant paying $20.00 in advance for three nights' lodging. Requests for one night's accommodations were not accepted. Fortunately Ray and Scripps could move into Medill's quarters.

The city trembled with rumors of revolution. Old Southern grandees in broad hats and trimmed goatees had vanished, and a new breed of Southerner swarmed in the streets. Rowdies had gathered thick as flies to pillage in case the government collapsed. They jostled crowds of Westerners in coarse boots who stood around the upper end of Pennsylvania Avenue gaping at the litter of cut stones and derricks surrounding the half-repaired Capitol. Ladies of the old order, which had been voted out of office, refrained from appearing—even in their carriages—among the questionable characters who filled the streets.

Ray and Scripps found the progress of treason in the capital almost incredible—worse than they had imagined. Peace-at-any-price conferences were still being held, but nothing acceptable was offered. Ray wrote his paper that the Peace Commission faced a hopeless task. Seven states, embracing six million people, half white and half black, had seceded from the Union, and nothing but military force would bring them back. The only business left the Commission was to patch up some compromise to hold the border states loyal to the central government. "The worst enemies of the Union in this perilous time," Ray wrote, "are Northern men who proclaim that the general government shall not be allowed to coerce obedience to its laws and authority."

On March 4, 1861, the two *Chicago Tribune* editors joined the crowd on the east lawn of the Capitol, beneath its unfinished dome. A squad of fifty riflemen stood under the platform where Lincoln was to be inaugurated. A newly constructed corridor connected the Senate Chamber with the outdoor stand. Boarded higher than a man's head, it would protect President-elect Lincoln from an assassin until he reached the platform. Overhead the portico's copings bristled with guns in the hands of alert guards.

President Buchanan and Lincoln rode down Pennsylvania Avenue. Mounted soldiers surrounded the carriage closely in order to protect the occupants from some sharpshooter's bullet. A line of armed men stood guard on the roofs of adjacent houses. General Scott marched troops in flanking formation down the back streets. Crowds displayed more curiosity than enthusiasm. The day was raw and blustery. Ray and Scripps stood on the cold damp ground below the speakers' stand, watching Lincoln take the oath of office and deliver his inaugural address. The unenthusiastic audience applauded politely and cannon boomed a salute. Then the crowd sauntered away, the men shivering in the raw air, the women, wrapped in their shawls, sweeping the crisp grass with their skirts.

Two days later the *Tribune* announced the new administration's cabinet appointments. Cameron had failed to get the Treasury, as Ray had prophesied, but Lincoln had named him Secretary of War. Caleb Smith, Indiana's questionable favorite son, was to be Secretary of the Interior. But Lincoln had rewarded the *Tribune* by appointing its man, Salmon P. Chase, Secretary of the Treasury. Since the President also appointed John Locke Scripps postmaster of Chicago, the paper felt doubly rewarded. The *Journal's* Charlie Wilson became Secretary of Legation in London. Edward Bates received the Attorney General's post and Montgomery Blair became Postmaster General. Charles Ray reported to his Chicago readers:

We believe that Lincoln has sought to make the Cabinet harmonious on all vital questions, and yet has sought to satisfy the largest number of those who gave him votes. In this he has done the right thing. The selection of Chase is eminently satisfactory. Let bygones be bygones and every honest and loyal citizen yield support to the administration in its patriotic effort to save the government from the perils threatening its destruction.

XVII The Sword of the Lord and of Gideon

SPRING comes suddenly in Chicago, the warm breath of the Gulf of Mexico blowing the winter clouds across the blue waters of Lake Michigan. Charles Ray returned from Lincoln's inauguration to find hollyhocks, dog fennel, and Jimson weed sprouting in the dirt around lumber piles and cellar excavations. Driving to work after his Eastern excursion, he experienced a touch of spring fever. The impending war and its worries seemed momentarily far away. Life had been very good to him these past five years.

He must begin at once to enjoy more home life, see more of his children, fix up the house, and buy the books he wanted to read—Macaulay's essays, Pepys' *Diary*, Disraeli's latest novel. He needed a new buggy too, or at least a fresh leather top for this old one.

He should also devote more attention to the Chicago Historical Society than he had been doing recently. Then he wanted to indulge his lifelong interest in art along with his friend Volk. Music too should be encouraged in the city. Charles Ray was particularly eager to have some fine paintings exhibited in Chicago and to attract enough musicians to start a symphony orchestra. Meditating these aesthetic matters, he proceeded toward the business district. His horse clumped across the wooden bridge over the Chicago River. At the livery stable a boy ran out to hold the animal's bridle. Ray put the whip in the dashboard socket, cramped the wheels until the step was clear, then swung to the ground and strode across to the *Tribune* office. He determined to write something different this morning from his usual aggressive demands for military action. On March 15, 1861, the following idyl was published:

> Spring is coming. The trees have caught a hint of it and are quietly busy with their buds. In little sunny nooks, patches of turf wax fresher and greener day by day. Yellow daffodils in the gardens are getting impatient in their imprisoned folds and the first kiss of sunshine will bring them out. The other day we heard a frog. . . . Nature goes right on, year after year, not in the least mindful of the fortunes of States and plots of statesmen. . . . Buds burst in their season, whether human governments burst or not. . . . Thank Providence this was all kept out of the hands of free and independent voters.

His morning stint finished, Ray walked around the office. Clerks were opening mail. A dozen papers from both North and South had been spread out on his worktable. They all screamed about the looming war. Injustice! *Treason!!* HUMAN SLAVERY!!! Lincoln, strange to his new duties, beset by compromisers and office-seekers, was doing as little as Buchanan had. Charles Ray forgot the fresh smell of spring air. A crisis faced the country. He had between sixty and ninety thousand readers, counting two or three individuals for each paper. These people were entitled to his best service as the hazards of war loomed. His personal relaxations with art, music, and literature would have to wait.

The *Tribune's* steady growth in circulation gave the editor great satisfaction. He and Medill checked the numbers in the counting room and decided that a new cylinder press must be purchased to anticipate the future demand. Ray had employed Villard to represent the *Tribune* in Washington while he came west, and he now took over Medill's writing while the press was being purchased and installed. On April 4, just a month after Lincoln's inauguration, Washington dispatches prompted the *Tribune* to announce that President Lincoln had the situation well in hand and was preparing to enforce Federal jurisdiction in the South. Medill and Ray arranged for special wire service from Washington, and on April 10 an editorial announced:

The country has a government. . . . Government vessels are off to Charleston harbor, with supplies for the gallant Anderson cooped up in Fort Sumter. . . . He who is not for the Administration is against it, and for our country's enemies. He who is not willing to do service under the old flag, is already a recruit under the rattlesnake banner. The echo of the first gun fired for the saving of the Union is the knell of faction. . . . The ball is opened. Now for a quick contest and a speedy peace.

Three days later the paper appeared with a bold heading:

WAR INAUGURATED. . . . The bombardment of Sumter is going on. . . . While we write, the issue of the conflict, which is yet going on, is doubtful. . . . Our fathers fought seven long years that the Constitution might be framed. We, their descendants, can afford any sacrifice, any exertion, that their labor may be preserved to the world for the blessing of mankind. Now, men of the North, for the struggle.

A little engraving of the American flag in the upper left corner of the paper's first page bore this caption:

Here is a flag like that which waves over beleagured Sumter, and the heads of the gallant and faithful ANDERSON and his little band! Let it be carried in triumph through this city. Will you assist in that good work, typical of its march through all the land?

A rally was called in Metropolitan Hall for all in favor of

maintaining the government. Next day, Sunday, April 14, 1861, no news came across the wires. Chicago was struck dumb with excitement. Church congregations, conscious of the bombardment raging in distant South Carolina, sang "America" with a new and determined cadence. Ray was desperate for copy concerning the battle which he knew might be the most significant in American history. In this crisis the *Tribune's* well-laid plan for news seemed to have broken down. It is easy to imagine the impatient Ray trying to keep his mind off the maddening void of intelligence from the East by striding through the office shaking his mane like a caged lion, eager for any morsel on which he could concentrate during the empty hours.

In the anxiety of this first moment in the nation's second revolution, his mind went back to the country's earlier war. His family on both sides had witnessed that struggle. As a youth in New York, Ray had read vigorous accounts of those heroic times. One forceful phrase still clung in his memory. At Sycamore Shoals the Reverend Thomas Doak had rallied patriots to seek vengeance against the redcoats at King's Mountain with the Old Testament battle cry: "The Sword of the Lord and of Gideon."

Now, in the awful period of waiting, Charles Ray eased his nervous tension by writing, and during the night, as he wrote, the wires began to click. Rebels had bombarded Fort Sumter for thirty-six hours. Then the commander, Major Anderson, had hauled the flag down into the ruins. In the morning, April 15, the headlines announced: ATTACK ON SUMTER–THE SURRENDER!

Down in the street grim crowds snatched papers faster than they could be distributed. Editor Ray's leader was headlined: EVERY MAN'S DUTY–READ.

Lenity and forbearance have only nursed the viper into life the *war has begun!* It may not be the present duty of each one of us to enlist and march to the sound of bugle and drum; but there is a duty, not less important, which is in the power of every man and woman in Chicago, and in the North, to perform—it is to be loyal in heart and word to the cause of the United States. From this hour, let no Northern man or woman tolerate in his or her presence the utterance of one word of treason. Let expressed rebuke and contempt rest on every man weak enough to be anywhere else in this crisis than on the side of the country against treason—of Lincoln and Scott against Davis and Twiggs—of God against Baal. We say to the Tories and lickspittles in this community, a patient and reluctant, but at last an outraged and maddened people, will no longer endure your hissing. You must keep your venom sealed or *go down!* There *is* a Republic! The gates of Janus are open: the storm is on us. Let the cry be, "The Sword of the Lord and of Gideon!"

This editorial became a battle cry copied and recopied in political publications. Lincoln called for 75,000 volunteers to put down the rebellion. Ray said that Illinois could furnish the entire national quota. Governor Yates ordered a special session of the legislature to meet the emergency. The *Tribune* printed his message jubilantly. The news that a battalion of regular soldiers was being transported to Washington from frontier posts in Minnesota attracted 10,000 spectators to the North Western station. The bronzed veterans were greeted with cheers as they marched through the streets.

To raise the six regiments allotted to Illinois, politicians opened recruiting offices. Orators spoke on boxes at street corners, from the top of lumber piles in vacant lots, and on the loading platforms of warehouses. Wide-Awake companies marched through the streets carrying fence rails in lieu of guns. German gymnastic societies mustered in their halls and marched with brass bands. A regiment of Irish carried a green banner embroidered with a golden harp. Scotsmen organized themselves as the Chicago Highlanders.

Charles Ray jogged around the city in his buggy and gloried in the free-flowing "Niagara of men and money" enlisted in the Union cause. He bought Zouave uniforms for his boys and drove the whole family out to Cottage Grove, where a city of tents covered sixty acres of open fields. The Rays visited the encampment, watched the soldiers performing their various duties, then drove on to a shady lane in the country where Jane and "little Minnie" unpacked the lunch baskets while Charles Ray showed his sons how to build a bivouac fire.

To keep Chicagoans posted on the war's developments, a bulletin board was erected on Clark Street, in front of the Tribune building. Dispatches were posted here as soon as editors had copied them. Virginia was reported to have seceded, and the trouble-making rump legislature in Maryland was said to be considering following her example. On April 22, 1861, the first Chicago companies, 700 men, left town. Most of them were Germans and Hungarians organized as infantry and artillery. Ray gave the departing troops the *Tribune's* blessing. The government must be maintained.

Compromisers still offered all kinds of assorted appeasements to prevent open war. It had even been recommended that two republics, one North and one South, be established. Ray ridiculed this plan. The South, he maintained, would be still more unhappy under it. In the Federal Union the South's great complaint was that Northern states refused to return fugitive slaves. Certainly slaves would be even harder to get back from a foreign country. No, the real test of the republican form of government could not be met by evasion and separation. The Constitution must be upheld. The true answer was this trainload of patriotic volunteers determined to enforce Federal law. Ray wrote:

> All hope of conciliation or compromise must now be abandoned. The battle must be fought out. Liberty or slavery must rule in this Republic. . . . The summons to battle is, thank Heavens, joyfully accepted. Now let the weakest go down!

The immediate war problem was to maintain order until commanding generals of the army organized their fast-swelling units in their respective geographical departments. The military contest would come in three fields: the areas east of the Alleghenies, along the Ohio River, and west of the Mississippi. The *Tribune* prepared to have correspondents in all three sections. Southern Illinois was reported to be belligerently pro-Confederacy. Ray received a note from Trumbull, in Belleville, begging for help and confirming the worst rumors that had filtered through to Chicago. Union people, Trumbull complained, lacked weapons to protect themselves from proslavery Missouri raiders. A supply of arms was known to be stored in the St. Louis arsenal. How could Illinoisans get them? The local commander in St. Louis, Captain Nathaniel Lyon, was a loyal Union man, but his superior, the comfort-loving General Harney, seemed indifferent. The desperate Union people dared not telegraph Washington for help lest the operators relay the message either to Harney or to the Confederacy. Trumbull said that one messenger had been sent across the river to Frank Blair in St. Louis and that another was on the train to Washington, where he planned to see Lincoln. Would Ray do his part to impress the President with the importance of the crisis in southern Illinois?

Ray was helpless. The war had progressed faster than anyone expected. All wires to Washington had been cut, and the railroads across Maryland were torn up. Neither messenger, mail, nor telegram could get through. People speculated wildly on the capital's fate. The *Tribune* correspondent, Henry Villard, was sending no dispatches whatever. Isolated from the Federal government, the governor of Missouri prepared to reassemble the legislature. Already he had pledged to co-operate with the Confederacy, and he was mobilizing the militia. Without doubt he planned to take the Federal arsenal in St. Louis himself and use the munitions against the government.

In that case Illinois would be bordered both south and west by rebellious states.

Then Ray received cheering news. Captain Lyon, without authority from his superior, had shipped a goodly number of the arsenal arms up the Illinois River. The *Tribune* would see to it that he was not censured for that insubordination. Next Senator Douglas, at the height of everyone's anxiety over the isolation of Washington and fear of a raid from Missouri, addressed the legislature in Springfield. Fearlessly he urged all Illinoisans to stand firm for the Union, to rally in defense of the nation's flag. The man with the split tongue had made a decision at last, no compromise now, and the *Tribune* applauded Douglas' patriotism.

On April 27, 1861, the Washington blockade was broken. Ray received a distracted message from Villard. No one, the correspondent said, who had not been through it could understand the anxiety of being surrounded by rebels and cut off from the outside world. Only one regiment, Governor Andrew's choice Massachusetts Sixth, had got through to the city's relief, and they had been roughly handled in Baltimore. For ten days, Villard said, he had been trying to send out dispatches and had at last succeeded in establishing a pony express of six-horse relays to cover a distance of ninety-eight miles. The collapse of the Federal government was still imminent, according to Villard. Lincoln had managed things badly.

Since the fall of Fort Sumter, the President had shrunk from striking direct blows at the enemy. Villard's report said:

> I know this from my conversation with him. Being without communication from the North he does not know the extent of the war feeling there. . . . I think the New York protest that reached him Friday morning opened his eyes. At least he showed much more promise at an interview I had with him that morning.

The reopening of telegraphic service was followed by exciting news from Missouri. Tough little Captain Lyon, still acting without authority from General Harney, had marched out and captured the assembled Missouri militia. Lincoln had recognized the captain's initiative by making him a brigadier and relieving Harney of command. Ray was delighted. Victory should come quickly now in the West. Command of the Department of the Ohio was given to George Brinton McClellan. Ray had known McClellan as chief engineer for the Illinois Central Railroad at the time of the Lincoln-Douglas debates. McClellan was then a retired army man, with a brilliant record as a youthful officer in the Mexican War. The *Tribune* endorsed him. At last Lincoln was getting started on the quick and sure victory of freedom over slavery.

By May 1, 1861, thirteen military companies were drilling in Chicago and twenty-five more were being organized. The *Tribune* cried:

> Let us advance. . . . Ten thousand men will soon be at Cairo [Illinois]. . . . The people burn with impatience to meet the enemies of the Republic, and open a way down their river to the sea.

Ray sent Horace White, one of the paper's best reporters, to follow the advance from Cairo. Ten days later Ray noticed a familiar name in the reports from the army in downstate Illinois. Captain U.S. Grant from Galena was listed as having received a colonel's commission.

On June 4, 1861, Charles Ray reported the sudden death of Stephen A. Douglas. Three columns of the *Tribune* were devoted to a eulogy of the dead senator. Ray was not one to retreat. From the beginning he had announced that he did not know the meaning of appeasement, but he could say of his old enemy:

It is well known that the *Chicago Tribune* had no sympathy with the political movements of the late Senator since 1853. He was content to go his way, and we ours. He had one line of policy, and we another. In all these years of difference, we have shared with others the animosity that our prejudice and his acts provided. . . . We draw a veil over that distracted period, and leave the historian to decide whether he and his friends, or his opposers, ourselves among the number, are right. We have nothing to apologize for . . . and he would have had nothing to unsay had he lived. . . . His last public speech is the standard by which his life is to be measured. We remember him by that, and lay down therefor this tribute of gratitude and praise.

The speech which Douglas had delivered before the Illinois legislature was reprinted in full on the *Tribune's* front page. The Little Giant's body lay in state at Bryan Hall. After his funeral the ceremonies were described in detail in the paper.

On June 12 General Nathaniel Lyon started up the Missouri with a flotilla of double-decked steamboats, their lofty decks blue with soldiers. In short order he captured the Missouri capital and began organizing to pursue the fleeing rebel governor and his legislature southward across their state. Victory seemed sure over there. At Cairo, the Ohio and Mississippi rivers were both in Federal hands. A great number of Union troops were concentrating on the river junction, but no immediate action seemed probable. In the East, old General Winfield Scott, top-ranking Union commander, was reported to have told Lincoln that an army of 65,000 men would soon be ready to march on Richmond.

"Give the soldiers something to do," the *Tribune* urged. But Scott seemed provokingly slow.

On June 29, 1861, the *Tribune* began an editorial with: THE NATION'S WAR CRY–FORWARD TO RICHMOND! Under this caption the editor said that the rebel congress must not be allowed to meet in Richmond on July 20. The city must be taken by Federal troops before that date. "Advance! Advance!" General Scott was pronounced a great military strategist but a child at politics. He should advance to the relief of the Union men of the South before it was too late. *Forward to Richmond* was repeated on June 30 with the reminder, "only twenty days left to take Richmond!" Charles Ray determined to go himself and report the impending battle in the East. He arranged for Jane's and the children's comfort in Chicago during his absence, packed a carpetbag, and boarded the train for Washington.

XVIII The Battle of Bull Run

Dr. Charles Ray stepped off the sleeping car in the Washington station and carried his carpetbag down the platform toward the waiting hacks. The city in July 1861 resembled a vast army cantonment. Long trains of commissary wagons with trembling canvas covers rumbled through the cobbled thoroughfares between lines of trees heavily leaved with midsummer foliage. Hundreds of idle soldiers in fantastic uniforms loafed along the shady streets. Against the hot summer sky the skeleton of the Capitol dome stood as discouragingly unfinished as it had appeared last March. People laughed about a distraught woman who had likened the dome to the disintegrating Union. She asked a soldier in Governor Andrew's newly arrived Sixth Massachusetts if he thought it would ever be repaired. "Yes, *ma'am*," the private replied with determined simplicity.

The soldier had spoken words which Charles Ray approved, for there was no question in his mind about the ultimate victory of American democracy if the soldiers knew the truth. He went directly to his hotel, registered, unpacked his bags and set off for the White House. The first floor was open to visitors. A doorman said the President's reception room was upstairs. Ray climbed to the second floor and walked into a waiting room. He was finally ushered into a small private chamber where Abraham Lincoln sat behind a table, his back to a window overlooking the lawn which sloped down toward a swamp north of the Potomac.

The President had barely learned his way around his new surroundings. Rebels were encamped within twenty-five or thirty miles of Washington, and the city was constantly disturbed by war alarms. Dozens of decisions, civil and military, had to be made daily in this little office. However Lincoln spared a few minutes to discuss Illinois affairs with his old friend. At the end of the conversation the President asked about Ray's children and gave him a note to General Winfield Scott, who in turn could furnish the latest news on the nation's war preparations. Ray walked next to the War Department, a little building on Seventeenth Street. General Scott was not in his office. Since he was probably driving in his shay among the encampments across the Potomac, Ray returned to the hotel.

In his room, he wrote a letter to Jane and the children, Minnie, Frank, and Paul. The eldest boy's name had not been changed in spite of its similarity to Frank Pierce's. The husband and father described Washington as he saw it—the companies of soldiers marching and countermarching in the streets, the German regiments with their inspiring bands, the kilted Highlanders, like the Chicago Scotsmen's regiment, marching with skirling bagpipes. Ray said also that he saw an Irish battalion with gold and green banners carried beside the Stars and Stripes and gay Zouaves marching in ranks, their white gaiters twinkling below baggy red culottes—uniforms exactly like the ones he had bought for his little boys. In the letter Ray told his children that tents dotted the south bank of the Potomac for ten miles. He concluded by saying that the President of the United States had asked about them all.

After sealing the letter and posting it, Ray stepped out in search of news that would interest readers of the *Tribune*. He went up the hill to the Capitol and called on Senator Trumbull and Orville H. Browning, who had been appointed to fill Douglas' empty chair. Ray talked also to members of the House—Isaac N. Arnold, Owen Lovejoy, Elihu B. Washburne—all old Illinois friends. He recognized other leaders in the abolition movement who now held top positions in the new Congress. Charles Sumner was chairman of the Senate Committee on Foreign Relations. Young William Pitt Fessenden of Maine headed Finance. Crippled Thaddeus Stevens headed the powerful Ways and Means Committee. Ben Wade and Zach Chandler stalked grimly through the Capitol's stone halls, determined to wreak vengeance on the South at last.

All agreed that Winfield Scott commanded the best army that had ever mustered on American soil. No time must be lost now in the administration's task of dispersing the rebels who were digging entrenchments along Bull Run, only a day's ride from Washington. General Pierre Beauregard, commander of the Southern army during the bombardment of Fort Sumter, was said to be in charge. Many senators and congressmen planned to go out with the soldiers and watch the fight. Ray accepted an invitation to go with some friends in a "four-wheeler."

Back at the hotel Ray watched from a window as regiment after regiment clumped south toward Long Bridge into Virginia. Surely there must be enough men over there now to open the offensive. As he waited for word of the impending battle, a strange man handed him an envelope. When Ray had broken the seal, he found a letter from Medill introducing the bearer in complimentary terms. Medill had already written Ray about this man—the inventor of a new process for casting cannon. In his previous letter Medill had said that he had warned the fellow to be prepared to sacrifice half, possibly two thirds, of his prospective profits to Cameron's henchmen before the War Department would consider his invention.

Ray gave the man a note to introduce him at the Department and went out on the street to watch for news from Virginia. Excited crowds in front of wineshops said that the fighting had started. On July 18 General Daniel Tyler with a division of Union troops had crossed Bull Run at Blackburn's Ford contrary to orders from the field commander, Irvin McDowell. Tyler was repulsed. Some said his men ran. Others maintained that they had retired in good order. In any event, Tyler deserved censure, but since he was a wealthy industrialist, he probably would not get it. He was nineteen years McDowell's senior, had enjoyed a brilliant military career, and had been known as the father of the United States Artillery before he resigned to enter business. Taking orders from anybody was a novel experience for such a man. Recognized as a mathematical genius, he had studied trajectory abroad and had introduced the best model guns into the army. One of his cherished cannons, a thirty-two pounder, was under his command down at the Bull Run front now.

Tyler's defeat was not considered important in Washington. In fact rebel prisoners had been brought in. Ray hurried to the War Department and obtained a letter of introduction from Scott to McDowell requesting the general to show him "all kindness." With this Ray went to McDowell's headquarters in Lee's deserted Arlington mansion. Next he hunted for the prisoners and interviewed a Mississippian who told him that Jeff Davis himself, on a white horse, was commanding the Confederates. He and Beauregard were prepared for a decisive battle. Ray dashed this scoop off to the *Tribune* and on July 20 started for the front with his Illinois friends in the four-wheeler.

The road to the village of Fairfax Courthouse was full of carriages bearing sight-seers and lunch hampers. A few brave women rode among them. At roadside cabins Negro children capered and waved. Satin high lights danced in their black eyes, and white teeth gleamed in their grinning mouths. At Fairfax Courthouse young Andrew Carnegie had established headquarters for his telegraph instruments. Couriers would bring the news here for transmittal to Washington.

Ray and his friends put their team in the livery stable and joined the crowd around the clicking machines to glean any available information. The road to Centreville, eight miles northwest, was said to be lined with bivouacking soldiers. West of Centreville three roads led to Bull Run. Beyond the stream Confederates were believed to be concentrated at the little town of Manassas. In all probability, the battle would be waged along this steep-banked creek.

In the lamp-lighted telegraph office Ray listened to the officers' conversations and talked with many of them. He estimated that the Union forces numbered approximately 40,000 men and that the battle line would be six to eight miles long.

The army was advancing tonight in three columns. Ray knew personally the commanders of two of them. At Centreville the right wing marched under David Hunter, a regular army man who had married Maria Kinzie, daughter of the famous Chicago fur trader. Hunter's aide was Illinois's newly elected Congressman Isaac N. Arnold. The center of the advancing Federals was commanded by Daniel Tyler, the industrialist who had suffered a setback when he had opened the conflict prematurely. Now, however, Tyler had his beloved artillery placed for a renewed assault. The Union left was commanded by Israel B. Richardson, a West Point veteran of the Mexican War known to his men as "Fighting Dick." He was the only one of these division commanders unknown to Ray.

The plan of battle became plain to Ray as the officers discussed their orders. Richardson was to open with a feint attack on the enemy's right, drawing as many Confederates as possible toward him. Meanwhile Hunter was to encircle the Confederates' left flank and roll back the rebel line, with Tyler and his artillery joining for the knockout blow.

An ugly rumor disconcerted a few officers. This questionable report said that the Confederates were being reinforced by Joseph E. Johnston's army from the Shenandoah Valley —all bosh, according to some of the war-hungry Union commanders. Hadn't old Scott sent General Robert Patterson with an army to prevent this very thing? Patterson, like Tyler, was elderly, but he was a veteran of the War of 1812 and had won a major-general's stars in Mexico. Since then he had resigned from the army and, like Tyler, had become a wealthy industrialist. Now, as newly appointed commander of the department which included Pennsylvania, Maryland, and the District of Columbia, this financial mogul could surely be depended upon.

Before morning General McDowell himself came into the telegraph office. He was a handsome six-footer who had studied abroad and had learned to trim his whiskers French fashion. McDowell had a reputation for being a ravenous eater and a teetotaler. Tonight he looked weary and careworn from the prolonged responsibility of moving a green army into its first battle. Ray saw him nod sleepily as he forced himself to dictate messages to the telegrapher.

Long before sunrise on Sunday, July 21, 1861, the Union army began to move forward. Charles Ray, carrying a telescope, drove with his friends up the Centreville road in the dark. Beyond the town deserted bivouac fires smoldered along all the fences. Many regiments had already passed across fields or along byroads toward Bull Run. Others stood waiting for their turn. At dawn firing started along the creek, where Richardson's left wing had deployed. Soon the sound of musketry rattled up Bull Run all the way to the Union right, beyond Centreville. Ray, on the road roughly parallel to the creek, found it difficult to observe such a long line intelligently. Union advances were impossible to detect with certainty when the regiments were moving forward out of sight across the rolling hill farms and wood lots.

Ray saw a few minor reverses—scattered battalions scampering back in panic, their guns thrown away. But he noticed that where one broke, ten were standing firm under a billow of white smoke along the battle line. From a side road an artilleryman galloped in with a caisson. He sought more ammunition but unwittingly stampeded a team of civilian teamsters who thought him retreating. At another lane Ray saw a party of frightened sight-seers racing to the rear. Their flight caused another civilian wagon train to break up. The drivers unhooked their mules and galloped away, deserting their wagons. But out on the firing line, beyond these minor panics, the Federal soldiers seemed to be holding firm, and messengers from the front reported many gains, although the Confederate left had not collapsed as expected. Perhaps Johnston had escaped Patterson and reinforced that line. However nobody could be sure. To observe the field independently Ray borrowed a saddle horse and rode toward Centreville.

Late in the day Ray noticed several regiments marching to the rear in good order. He talked the situation over with several correspondents, one of them William H. Russell of the *London Times*. Russell had reported the Crimean War from the field and should be a man who understood observing a battle. He and all the others agreed that the morning's advance had been checked, but that was all. Ray sent a dispatch to the *Tribune* stating that the Union army was regrouping to strike again tomorrow. After dark he jogged up the road to Washington.

In the morning Ray learned the truth and sent a special dispatch to Chicago which was printed under the bold caption: "A GREAT BATTLE! FIRST VICTORY—THEN DEFEAT. Disastrous Retreat of our Troops. *Panic among the Federal Troops*." Three days later his entire report, three thousand words long, was published. He began by accusing the high command of blundering. The first paragraph stated:

The battle is lost. The enemy have a substantial victory. The result, so unexpected, dangerous and mortifying, is due to causes that the country will by and bye [*sic*] discuss. Men who have been unattentive observers of the field of operations and of the tendency of the popular mind, will say that popular clamor has outrun military preparation; but this is not true. The well appointed and magnificent army that is now coming back broken and discouraged into the entrenchments on the opposite side of the river, ought never to have been beaten. It was known here, or at least so strongly suspected, that not to have been guided and controlled by the fact would have been madness—known that Paterson [*sic*], who shares with Pillow the honor of the Camargo ditch, had permitted the rebel general, Johnston, to outwit him and get away, carrying the greater part of his force to Manassas—leaving in his camp only men enough to maintain appearances and keep out the usual pickets. That, I say, was known. It was known also that Beauregard's position was very strong, and that his army, before Johnston's column came, was equal in number to our own, composed of the very flower of the Southern troops. . . .

Ray asked pointedly why 40,000 Union soldiers were driven into this trap between Beauregard and Johnston. Then he described the battle in detail as follows:

Centreville is a high point of land, mostly cleared and cultivated, three miles northeast of Manassas Junction. Midway between the two places is a rocky, shallow and narrow stream, known as "Bull Run." Infantry, and in places cavalry, can cross it; but the banks are so rough and precipitous that it is impassable for artillery. It is easy of transit in three places within the field of operations—at a ford, where, a few days since, the battery was first attacked, at another point four miles above, on a stone bridge, where we sent a column yesterday; and at a place about two miles still further up, where Col. Hunter's column debouched into the bottom on the opposite side. Between Centreville and the bridge which marked our centre, the ground is very broken and hilly, over which a rocky road is constructed, and prolonged into the country beyond. Opposite the bridge on the Manassas side, the face of the country is rolling and dry, and in places timbered, not by large but by little pines and cedars, which from the closeness of their growth, present almost impassable barriers to the progress of troops, who must in going from farm to farm, or position to position, make use of the roads. On the battle ground are many farms and open places, and many eminences that can be held by an inferior force. Back of the bridge of which I have spoken and which marked our centre, is Manassas, five or six miles distant, where the main part of the Confederate army is quartered. The attack being resolved upon, the troops in camp at and near Centreville started for the scene of action about half-past two in the morning—Col. Hunter having the right, Gen. Tyler the centre and Col. Richardson the left. The troops moved in capital order and in fine spirits. By some mismanagement or unlooked for delay, the rear of Tyler's column did not pass down the road to Bull Run bridge till half-past ten in the morning—the men meanwhile finishing their morning naps in the shade or under the fences, by which the way was lined. This was the first mishap. The men lost their morning freshness; they were without their customary coffee and warm breakfast, and remaining many hours idle, had time to get their apprehensions aroused that all was not right. Hunter's and Tyler's columns moved together down the road leading to the bridge, until within a mile and a half of the stream, when Hunter with 10,000 men took a direction nearly at right angles with the road along which they had passed and struck the stream a couple of miles above, where he was enabled to cross and deploy on the opposite bank about nine o'clock. Tyler's column kept down the road, and near the bridge, put his great gun in position, and at a quarter past six fired four rounds of shot into the supposed battery on the opposite side; but not a rebel could be persuaded to show his head. The bridge was understood to be mined, and crossing on it was not attempted. Richardson had gone to the old battery on the left, by another road, and about the time that Hunter deployed, his fire opened. This was the position of affairs at nine o'clock, when rapid battery firing from the line of Hunter's march, announced that the day's work had fairly begun. (I had forgotten to say, that, stationed on the highest points about Centreville were regiments composing the reserves—about ten thousand in all.) Thus, as will be seen, the lines of operations extended about six miles.

So much to give you an idea of the situation. What occurred at the fight must be told when the reports come in. I witnessed a part of it, and can at another time, add a chapter of personal experiences that will not be without value. Suffice it for the present, that from ten o'clock, with occasional intermissions, it raged with great violence all along the line—the brunt being borne by Col. Hunter's brave boys. I say "all along the line" but that is not correct—all along the line formed by Hunter's and [Samuel P.] Heintzelman's columns, which did the fighting of the day. I was not with them; but I know from those who bore a noble front in the fight that our boys did valiant deeds. More than once we, who could only judge of operations by the sound of the guns, the clouds of smoke, the chopping of axemen clearing their way and a way for the advancing column through the timber, supposed that the victory was ours. With a fine telescope (not field glass) which I carried with me, I could see a part of the operations of the enemy; but for the most part civilians were shut off by the timber that fringed the Run and covered the surface of the higher points of the position. My position was near the bridge where the road from Centreville debouches into the plain. There Tyler and his column were stationed, with, as I before said, the 32-pounder gun, and a little way to the right Capt. Ayer's battery. Almost half-past ten, when Richardson's fire had been heard for some time, and Col. Hunter's boys were hard at work, the 2d Ohio and a New York regiment, the name of which I have lost, stationed near to and at the left of the bridge, in a thicket, were ordered to advance, which they did in good order. They had just climbed a fence and were rushing gallantly on, when a fire from a masked battery before them and a second battery on their left flank, forced them to retire. Gen. [Robert C.] Schenck was at their head, and though the old error was committed of not throwing out skirmishers, to feel the position of the enemy, justice impels me to say that he displayed a great deal of personal heroism, leading his men gallantly and under a galling fire to which he, a conspicuous object in the field, was exposed. His men, demoralized by their distrust of his abilities as a commander, and by their recent experience in masked batteries, were forced to retire. They came back in good order but in haste to the road, and there remained all the remainder of the day, engaged in cursing the misfortune that had given them their commander. Capt. Ayer's battery went forward, and after about half an hour of brisk firing, silenced the rebel guns. While all this was going on, Hunter was progressing and Richardson's guns could be frequently heard. But the operations of the latter were merely a feint intended to call around him a force of the enemy; but as he made no attempt to storm the battery before him and cross over, and thus bring the left nearer the center and add to Hunter's and Heintzelman's strength, the rebels seemed to understand his orders, and paid little attention to his fire. Across the Run and in front of him to the left they attempted to form a column apparently to cross and take him in the flank; but a quick and rapid discharge of shell from his cannon soon made them scatter, and the remainder of the day he was quite unemployed. Hunter's fire was now brisk and unremitting. The cannonade was furious, and at intervals, as he came upon the rebel columns, the rattle of musketry was indicative of sharp work. About this time, say towards noon, a strong reinforcement went over to Hunter by the road along which he went, and and [*sic*] his first was followed by a second of nearly equal strength. Their arrival on the ground was the occasion of a great struggle in which the boys, facing towards Manassas, carried all before them and this fight went on until three o'clock. Then the centre of the rebel line had been forced and Heintzelman was far on their left flank. Thus pressed, they brought down on Manassas, a column which I should say was fully 10,000 strong, and directed it toward the bridge on Hunter's left. Our reserves were not ordered up. The demoralized and discouraged troops under Tyler, more than decimated by the stragglers who had gone for water or who I am sorry to say, skulked out of sight, were hastily formed to oppose them. But they could not be relied upon for the emergency. General McDowell, who had personally and bravely directed the operations of the forces across the

Run, seeing that if Tyler's column could not stand he would be broken, and his way of retreat cut off, was compelled to fall back. The day's work had convinced him that he had undertaken a job of too great magnitude for his force, and that, though his success might be flattering up to that point, he could not hope to overcome the numerous batteries in the way and force a passage to Manassas, though his last man was called to the field. The rebel reinforcement, letting McDowell retire, pushed on with their batteries towards the head of Tyler's column and commenced throwing shell into it with marked effect. I was at that time on the left of the line as it was formed, and the passage of shell and shot in the air over my head compelled me and all the civilians of the party to beat a quick retreat. Capt. Ayer brought up his battery and returned the fire; but by some means the fact of McDowell's retrograde movement becoming known, the troops left their position and fled. I was not there to see, as I will soon explain, but I did not hear that a retreat was ordered; but it is certain that when made, the officers were far in advance of the men. The panic was communicated to the crowd of civilians on the ground, and the scene that followed in which soldiers, officers, Congressmen, editors, distinguished citizens, camp followers, teamsters and baggage guard took part, beggars description. As I have explained, I had returned, going up the hill a mile. I then heard news which made it apparent that we had won a great victory—that Hunter's column had silenced all opponents on the right, that Richardson was triumphant on the left, and that the centre was in retreat. In a haste to communicate the news to your readers by telegraph, I exchanged my seat in the carriage, in which I went out, for a mount on Senator [James Alexander] McDougall's horse, took a lunch and started up the Centreville road. [McDougall was a former Illinoisan now representing California.] There I found just starting from their position, in column this side of Centreville, [Louis] Blenker's brigade of fresh troops with a fine battery going, as I then thought, to push the rebels in retreat. But at Centreville where on ground on which I could overlook the three roads by which the army went to attack, I saw clouds of dust rising from each, and on Tyler's road, a long line of baggage wagons in full retreat. We had during the day one or two minor stampedes of that sort, and supposed that this was one of them, caused by the firing at the bridge. Surveying the whole scene from the hill, and exultantly feeling that secession had met its great reverse, which would be at once followed up—wondering at the good fortune and bravery which had secured us a victory against such fearful odds, I turned my horse's head towards Washington, and struck a trot for home. I had not gone a mile, when the baggage wagons came flying past me, the horses on a round gallop. The road was full of them. Then came civilians in hot haste, bringing news of defeat. I did not believe the story, and halted until several officers came up and gave a confirmation of the news, when I again set out. I was soon overtaken by Col. Hunter's carriage in which he, wounded, was being taken in. It was attended by Hon. I. N. Arnold, mounted on the Colonel's horse, and he assured me that the fight was over and that our position gained would be maintained. But he was as greatly mistaken as myself. What ever the object of the retrograde movement, it was defeated when the panic was communicated to the troops. The roads behind me were full of them, hurrying away with all the speed they could make, throwing down their arms, their accoutrements and remaining rations to facilitate their flight. I met a few miles from Centreville, a New Jersey regiment going up as a support, and they began to arrest and turn the fugitives back, and better order on the road was restored. Jogging along leisurely, I reached Washington about eleven that night, and there found that the public, anxiously awaiting intelligence, had no other news than that which confirmed what I brought. Under that impression, I sent you the dispatch of Sunday night, in which a check was admitted and a victory for our arms promised for the next day.

This for what I saw and heard upon the field and the road home. It is but little of what occurred, and an imperfect and perhaps erroneous description of what I have attempted. To-day I have seen perhaps a hundred men who remained on the field to the last. They confirm what the telegraph has brought you concerning the scenes and incidents which attended the rout: and they are unanimous in the opinion that to the pressure and skillful disposition of Gen. Blenker who guarded the rear, the army owes its preservation. He continued his march down the road toward the bridge and formed near the hospital used by Tyler's column, and though the enemy showed himself over the hill, no pursuit was made. By squads, singly, in companies, the stragglers came in, protected by Blenker's line. Finally they nearly all reached Centreville, where an attempt to rally was made.

Of the conduct of our men, I have this to say—with the exception of two or three regiments, all that were engaged fought gallantly—as heroically as veterans. We had, opposed to that hornet's nest of batteries and full forty thousand men *in the field*, barely 24,000. [Ray had estimated the Union troops to be 40,000 before the battle.] In every encounter during the day, where their columns faced our's, they were compelled to retire. And more than once our boys, fighting in regiments or brigades, put double their number to hasty flight. When the panic commenced, the battle was concluded.

As for the enemy, let me not overrate them. Their's is the victory as it would have been had the battle raged until this hour; but they prefer entrenchments to the open field. If they have not learned a lesson that will cause them to respect Northern courage, a couple of thousand of their men have died in vain. The main question is—who ordered that fight without bringing Patterson's forces down? That the country must know. CHR

Immediately after the battle of Bull Run it was announced in Chicago that Wentworth's *Daily Democrat* had been discontinued. Its subscription list was taken over by the *Tribune*, and Ray's account of the battle was published in the largest edition yet to come from the *Tribune* press—36,000 copies. Ray returned to Chicago to assume his old position. The defeat, he told readers, had accomplished nothing except to instill in the North "a firmer resolution to conquer the traitors."

He approved the transfer of General Patterson from the army back to the big industrial negotiations which the magnate understood. The *Tribune* looked hopefully to the transfer of McClellan to the Eastern theater. Certainly new and younger men were needed to take the burden from commanders "weighed down with the fossil relics of the last century," Ray said.

The next bombshell which hit the nation was not military. William H. Russell's dispatch describing the battle had been sent to the *London Times*. Almost a month elapsed before it came back to America in printed form. The North was already irritated by a prevalent belief among the upper classes in Britain that the South would win the war. The Queen had recognized the Confederacy's belligerency, and might next recognize its independence. The State Department had been suspicious of Russell, but he had been given a pass, as Ray had been, to visit the front lines. The description of the panic which he sent the *Times* infuriated Americans and seemed to many a violation of the courtesy he had received. Russell's dispatch said:

> The scene on the road [between the battlefield and Washington] had now assumed an aspect which has not a parallel in any description I have ever read. Infantry soldiers on mules and draught horses, with the harness clinging to their heels, as much frightened as their riders; negro servants on their masters' chargers; ambulances crowded with unwounded soldiers; wagons swarming with men who threw out the contents in the road to make room, grinding through a shouting, screaming mass of men on foot, who were literally yelling with rage at every halt.

Russell described the battlefield as being "strewed with coats, blankets, firelocks, cooking tins, caps, belts, bayonets," but no dead soldiers. He said that the Americans had dishonored their Anglo-Saxon heritage. He reported seeing General

Hunter being driven to the rear in an ambulance escorted by a major who had deserted his battalion and was evidently using this means of escape. Stopping at Fairfax Courthouse to water his horse, Russell said he had been surrounded by country people beseeching him for news of the battle. They seemed delighted with reports of a Confederate victory. The innkeeper had assured him that the Virginia cavalry would soon come along and straighten out affairs.

The North, depending desperately on British sympathy to forestall the Queen's apparent tendency to favor the South, read Russell's dismal report and was at a loss for a reply. The retreat was bad enough when described by a loyal American, but for a Britisher to gloat over it added insult to injury. Then Charles Ray came to the rescue with some observations which were copied and commented on across the nation. He admitted that the battle had been a defeat and that some units broke and ran, but he maintained that there had been no such general panic as Russell had described. Furthermore the Britisher had not been where he could have seen what he reported. Ray happened to have met Russell two miles east of Centreville and had ridden with him to Fairfax Courthouse where they watered their horses together at the inn yard. Then they rode on another two miles, until Russell spurred off into the night for Washington, well ahead of the retreating army. If the Britisher saw any general panic, Ray said, it must have been on the other side of Centreville, where the main reverse occurred. Certainly there was none on the Centreville-Fairfax road when he and Russell rode along it. At that time both of them had agreed, Ray said, that the Union army had suffered a check but not a defeat.

To show the inaccuracy of Russell's report, Ray called attention to the major whom the Britisher had described as deserting his battalion in order to escape under the guise of assisting the wounded General Hunter to the rear. That major, said Ray, was none other than Isaac N. Arnold, congressman from Illinois, who had no line command and was accompanying the general as his aide. The conversation Russell had reported with the Fairfax innkeeper and the anxious inquiries from the Virginia crowd in the village simply had not occurred, Ray maintained. He had sat beside the Britisher at the water trough and knew exactly what had transpired. As for Russell's description of the panic among the soldiers on the road to Washington, Ray obtained statements from both Owen Lovejoy and E. B. Washburne, who were behind Russell, alleging that the road was deserted. The retreating army had not yet arrived. Ray concluded his article with these lines:

> The truth is probably this: The imaginative correspondent left the battle-ground before any confusion occurred, and when the retrograde movement was ordered, hearing the exaggerated stories of what came to be a flight, after he got into Washington, on Monday, while the excitement was at its height, he wove them into his letter as facts of his own observation. The rout was disgraceful enough to make any man's blood cold in his veins; but it was not what Mr. Russell describes. As we have asserted, he did not see it.

The disheartened North needed Ray's defense of its soldiers and copied his article eagerly. *Vanity Fair* pictured "Bull Run" Russell in a cover cartoon as a specimen in an insect collection being pinned down by Ray's newspaper dispatch. The caricature was entitled: "The great humbug of the *London Times*, nailed to the wall by C. H. Ray, of the *Chicago Tribune*."

William H. Russell read Ray's exposé and published a reply for private distribution among a few friends. He maintained that his statements were "exact to a letter." He admitted meeting Ray, "who was wringing his hands & in much distress of body & mind." Russell said further that Ray "begged of me to let him ride with me & I 'slowed' my pace to accommodate him for about 2 miles or so till fearing I shd. be prevented crossing the Bridge if I did not get on before midnight I pushed on & left him." This was a good enough excuse, but this confession proved that Russell must have led the race away from the battlefield.

Copies of Russell's reply were sent to Lord Lyon, British Minister to the United States, Senator Charles Sumner, chairman of the Foreign Relations Committee, "to a private friend," and to Henry J. Raymond, editor of the *New York Times*, whom Russell had met on the battlefield. Raymond was a friend of Ray's. The two men sometimes worked together on political matters. Raymond seems to have given Russell's letter to Dr. Ray, for it was found more than ninety years later in some Ray correspondence without any explanation. At the time it was written the "reply" failed to serve Russell's purpose. He had become *persona non grata* in America and soon returned to England where an indefatigable American lecturer, George Francis Train, taunted him with the plaguing Ray revelations. Train told an audience at Hanley, England:

Munchausen Russell was the first to get to Washington in order to give an eye-witness picture of a battle that he not only never saw, but was not within some miles of. Like the hound sent to clear the field of wolves, the latest report was, by the old farmer, who said they were going about forty miles an hour: but if anything the dog was a leetle ahead.

XIX Unconditional Surrender

THE WAR seemed to reach a stalemate in the East after Bull Run. Only in the West could Ray see signs of success. Lincoln had appointed John C. Frémont, Republican candidate for president four years ago, commander of the Western Department. Dispatches from William Bross, who was reporting from Frémont's headquarters in St. Louis, and from H. M. Smith, a new correspondent stationed at Cairo, Illinois, reported preparations for gigantic offensives. Smith, at the junction of the Ohio and Mississippi rivers, was an odd chap. Coached in the *Tribune* dogma of complete candor, he often let his opinions outrun his reports of facts, but he did have energy and imagination. Already he had visited the camp of Colonel John B. Turchin, a Russian-born Chicagoan whom Ray assisted in securing a commission. Smith was unenthusiastic about the appearance of Turchin's regiment and wrote:

> Their praise would fill only a small sheet. There is no discipline, nothing formal, and orderly about them. Perhaps they will fight well, but they certainly are a free and easy rabble now.

The immediate plan of military operation, Smith reported, was to push down the Mississippi, occupying the Kentucky and Missouri shores. A telegraph cable had been laid across the river in order to keep soldiers on both sides in quick communication.

Bross, in Missouri, reported that General Lyon had driven the rebels to the extreme southwest corner of the state where they were joined by Arkansas troops and had turned to fight. Lyon might be annihilated down there unless Frémont sent him proper reinforcements. As commander of the Western Department the Pathfinder might decide to send his reserves to Cairo instead. Certainly a reverse on the West's main waterway would be more disastrous than one down in the southwest corner of Missouri.

To give priority to the rivers seemed good policy for a careful commander, but stories about proslavery guerrillas raiding at will over northern Missouri indicated that Frémont was not even policing his department. Perhaps he was short of men and did not dare send his precious reinforcements on patrol duty there when two armies might need them elsewhere. Charles Ray understood Frémont's predicament and refrained from criticizing him, but he pleaded with *Tribune* readers to write their congressmen to vote for the improvement of the Illinois and Michigan Canal, his old love, in order that gunboats might pass to and fro in the Western waters. He also called readers' attention to a bill introduced by Senator Trumbull which provided for the confiscation of slaves belonging to rebels. In addition, Ray suggested that Frémont might solve his man shortage by policing northern Missouri with organizations of loyal farmers. Why not give such militia authority to hunt down rebels in their own neighborhoods and to confiscate slaves found on plantations where the owners were absent in the rebel forces? Surely such treatment would keep proslavery men at home where they belonged! "Slaves are the backbone of the rebellion," Ray wrote on August 22. "Let the government confiscate every slave of every rebel." He was delighted a week later when Frémont issued a proclamation authorizing just that in parts of his department.

The Northern press in city after city praised Frémont's emancipation proclamation. The *Tribune's* Washington correspondent wrote that people in the national capital had cheered this progressive act and hoped it might become an administration policy. Ray wrote a special article of commendation for publication on September 2, 1861.

> The expression of joyful satisfaction . . . in the city yesterday was quite unanimous. Men congratulated each other on the streets, that the bottom had been touched at last.

Slavery, readers were reminded, is "the *hardpan* of the rebellion." The horrid institution which caused the war must be abolished. "*This country shall continue to exist* though your rebel institution tumble about your ears and bury you forever [in] its ruins."

Shortly thereafter it was rumored that Lincoln had repudiated Frémont's proclamation. Ray could not believe it. He snatched his pen and scribbled:

> Frémont's proclamation is our platform henceforth to the end of the war. Attach no credit to the report . . . that the President disapproves of the proclamation of Maj. Gen. Frémont. Unless the President wishes to dampen the courage and crush the energies of millions of Union men, he will not compel Frémont to take a step backward.

Ray scorned the few inveterate compromisers "who cried out against emancipation because slaveholding unionists might resent it." Slavery had caused the war and abolition alone would end it.

Daily the *Tribune* praised Frémont's policy. On September 14 Ray wrote:

> It is impossible that Abraham Lincoln, Wm. H. Seward and Salmon P. Chase, whose words have so often and so deeply stirred the hearts of the people with the love of freedom—who have shown by such convincing logic that "this Government cannot endure permanently half slave and free" [*sic*]—should now take so definite a step backward.

But next day the truth was slapped on his desk. The President had countermanded the proclamation. Ray handed Lincoln's official letter to the pressmen to publish in full. Let the whole truth be printed. The *Tribune* would continue its fight for emancipation, the President's views to the contrary notwithstanding. Ray told his subscribers:

The people are a long way ahead of the Government, the Press and the Pulpit in a knowledge of the causes of the War. The march of human development sweeps grandly over the worst obstacles of venerable ignorance and wickedness. They who seek to oppose it, do but build sand hillocks on the sea shore, which the next wave shall level.

Immediately thereafter, news from the West reported the Union army defeated at Wilson's Creek in southwest Missouri and General Lyon killed in the biggest, hardest fought battle since Bull Run. Two such defeats were bitter pills for the North to swallow, and someone must pay. Frémont was criticized for withholding the reinforcements Lyon had requested. Then, to make things worse, the victorious rebels marched back into central Missouri and besieged the wealthy river town of Lexington. The defender, Colonel James Mulligan, was a Chicago Irishman. His volunteers stood their ground doggedly for almost a week. Then, half-starved and outnumbered, they surrendered. Chicagoans felt the defeat severely. Once more Frémont was blamed for failing to send reserve forces. Reports became current that he was indulging in dress parades and fancy drills in St. Louis while his fighting men on the front were neglected.

The editors of the *Tribune* disliked seeing the Republican Party's military idol maligned for incompetence. They could hardly believe him guilty. At least they refused to condemn him without further investigation. "Deacon" Bross, the St. Louis correspondent, was asked to make a careful study of the situation, and he reported Frémont to be fully as unfit for his job as the rumors intimated. Medill and Ray knew the deacon to be overly enthusiastic about everything, a man of extremes, of high praise or withering condemnation. Perhaps he did not see the general with understanding eyes. Medill decided that he himself would go to St. Louis and investigate. He came back thoroughly disillusioned concerning Frémont. Charles Ray still refused to repudiate the party's beau ideal, who had dared emancipate the slaves of rebels. There must be some valid excuse for the loss of two important battles—Wilson's Creek and Lexington. The *Tribune*, Ray insisted, must not kill the party it had created. Since the *Jeffersonian* days, Charles Ray had prided himself on the independence of his opinions. He had consistently asserted that there was no question he dared not examine, no man whom he dared not censure. By following this dogma he believed that he had made the *Tribune* a great paper. Now he refused to attack Frémont until satisfied in his own mind that the Pathfinder was unsuited for the job. He and John Locke Scripps must go independently to St. Louis and add their decisions to the reports on file.

Certainly Joseph Medill—as aggressive, impatient, and determined a man as Charles Ray—would not like this test of his own judgment, and henceforth the two powerful editors might find it more and more difficult to continue the crusade together. Charles Ray cared nothing about conciliation for harmony. The truth and nothing but the truth must be determined beyond a reasonable doubt. He and Scripps both went to St. Louis and both came back convinced that Frémont was culpable. Ray had been the guest of General Hunter, now recovered from his Bull Run wound and looking like himself again in freshly brushed wig and dyed mustache. The correspondent realized that the elderly Chicago soldier was probably prejudiced. No doubt Hunter, with his lifetime of service, resented being superseded by Frémont. He may have unduly colored everything he showed Charles Ray, but the fact remained that the Pathfinder had failed to support either Lyon or Mulligan, and both had been defeated by superior numbers after gallant fighting. True it may have seemed wiser at the time to hold Cairo rather than to reinforce Lyon, but no attack developed at the river junction. As a matter of fact, troops had been sent to Mulligan, but they failed to arrive—and a commander cannot be excused because his intentions are good.

The four editors agreed now that the *Tribune* should stop defending Frémont, but the argument leading to this decision had opened a rift which did not heal. Ray and Medill were the strong men on the staff. Neither of them was afraid to stand up and fight alone for his convictions. It was this independent courage which had made possible the nomination of Abraham Lincoln when a majority of the Illinois delegates had given up hope and wanted to back some other candidate. In the Frémont argument Scripps and Bross both tried to be conciliatory and to keep out of an office dispute. Compared to Ray and Medill, they both lacked leadership and color. Scripps's picture discloses flabby lips, a characteristic associated with men who usually probe for majority opinion before committing themselves. Talkative Bross was a fluent defender of decisions made by others. In an emergency Scripps was content to hide behind his whiskers. Medill owned the largest block of stock. No doubt he wanted the largest voice in the paper's affairs. All agreed on Frémont's incompetence, but the two top editors could not forget their bitter dispute, although they continued to pull together, albeit without good will. The *Tribune* began to print scalding criticisms of Frémont, demanding his removal—no halfway measures when the nation's existence was endangered.

A flurry of letters approving and disapproving his editorials came to Ray's desk. He thumbed through the sheets and espied the name of Schuyler Colfax, a man worthy of consideration. Congressman Colfax was one of the organizers of the Indiana Republican Party, and Indiana had been first to back Lincoln's nomination at the convention. The *Tribune* owed Colfax a debt of gratitude. It had endorsed him for Postmaster General, but Lincoln had selected Montgomery Blair instead. Colfax in his letter to Ray defended Frémont's record and said that the general was the victim of perennial bad luck. He explained that the Pathfinder had done his best to stamp out guerrillas in northern Missouri, but declared that the military commanders he sent there persisted in getting drunk. Charles Ray must have sniffed at such a specious apology.

Colfax's next excuses contained more substance. The congressman said that Frémont had completed elaborate plans for a down-river offensive to split the commands of General Gideon J. Pillow and Leonidas Polk and open the Mississippi, but the War Department had ordered the operation abandoned so that the armies to be engaged might strike on the upper Ohio. Certainly Frémont could not be blamed for that. Next, according to Colfax, the Pathfinder had worked out a detailed maneuver to push the rebels out of Missouri, but this operation had been halted by a sudden requisition from Washington for 5,000 men. Congressman Colfax blamed much of Frémont's misfortune on Frank Blair, a political rival who was trying to discredit the Pathfinder for personal reasons. Colfax omitted to say that Blair's brother had got the cabinet post he, Colfax, had sought. Mrs. Frémont had gone to Washington to see the President and plead her husband's cause in person, Colfax added, but found that Blair had been ahead of her and had already ruined her case.

Another letter in the pile on the *Tribune* editor's desk was from Scripps, who was reporting in the field. He had made an adverse report on Frémont, but now he feared that Ray's censure might hurt the paper's circulation. He wanted to know whether or not sales had fallen off since the criticism began. He suggested that it might be wiser for the paper to label hostile comments as opinions of Frémont's critics rather than as the *Tribune's* appraisals. Scripps owned enough *Tribune* stock to be entitled to a voice in the paper's policy, but Charles Ray, now positive that Frémont was incapable of directing the campaign in the West, could not be convinced that the paper should remain aloof. He continued to castigate the general, and Lincoln finally recalled him, giving the department to Ray's friend General Hunter. The removal of the popular officer caused a tremendous outcry. The Germans were particularly bitter, because Frémont had given their nationals high commands. German opinion was important to Charles Ray, but his editorials backed the President's decision to the limit, exposing Ray himself to the full blast of popular disfavor.

The attack on Ray was led by his old competitor, Charlie Wilson, editor of the *Chicago Journal.* Wilson begrudged the *Tribune's* success in getting the Chicago postmastership for Scripps. Wilson had been unhappy in the appointment which Lincoln gave him in the London consulate and had come back to his newspaper in the Windy City. He was now evidently trying to even the score with Ray by publishing a translation from a German paper which explained the *Tribune's* defense of Lincoln as a personal pique against Frémont. According to Wilson's translated "news note," Bross had been denied a colonel's commission by Frémont when he was investigating the general. Medill and Scripps, the article continued, had both asked and been denied lucrative contracts.

"Every allegation is false, without the shadow of excuse," Ray replied, "wantonly, maliciously and knowingly false, and the inventor is a liar." No one challenged this strong language, so the *Tribune* won the war of words. Charlie Wilson had to bide his time for another attack on the paper which opposed his faction.

During the furor Ray received a letter from Postmaster General Montgomery Blair, the man appointed to the position which the *Tribune* had requested for Colfax. Would he differ or agree with the Indianan on Frémont's removal? In all probability the cabinet had concurred in Lincoln's act against the popular general. Ray opened the envelope and read words of congratulation for the editorial he had written defending the President's action. Blair said that he had called Lincoln's attention to the editor's column and that, although he had not discussed it with him, he felt sure that the President would be pleased. Blair went on to say that he personally had believed Frémont to be a great man, but that his performance in Missouri proved his military judgment to be faulty. The Germans, Blair said, were causing the most serious trouble over the general's removal, but he thought it would soon subside. He acknowledged their weight in the Republican Party, but said that they were not "the people." In a democracy, though popular approval is important, he said, everyone cannot be satisfied. "We Blairs try to be honest and bold," he continued. "There is no doubt in my mind that the popular will is against Frémont."

Charles Ray believed so too and had no intention of reversing his decision. However, the petty quarrel with Medill about Frémont made Ray's position unpleasant. He thought seriously of quitting and joining some other newspaper to continue, in more congenial surroundings, his fight for Negro emancipation. Several of his staff tried to dissuade him, and Horace White wrote him a letter from the field, stressing the loss to the paper in case the editor-in-chief resigned. The entire editorial policy, he said, would devolve on Medill and Bross. Evidently the weaker men on the *Tribune* staff were beginning to take sides—a bad situation in any organization.

Ray forgot the feud for a time in a new excitement. Secretary of War Cameron took it on himself to decree that slaves who fled into the Federal lines should not be returned to their masters, but should instead be put to work building roads and fortifications. Ray applauded this as another step toward emancipation. He pronounced Cameron's attitude on slave confiscation a triumph and a vindication of the *Tribune's* policy. "The army regulars are too tender with slavery," he said. "The leaven must be worked out of them."

He claimed that many regular officers seemed more anxious to protect slavery than to win Union victories. Cameron's order, however, now rectified past dilatoriness and Ray wrote: "The clouds are rent and the sun of universal liberty is shining through."

In this assumption Ray was wrong. Lincoln revoked Cameron's decree, as he had Frémont's emancipation proclamation. The vacillating border slave states made him fear the risk of tampering with slavery. Ray, on the other hand, was sure that victory could not be accomplished without abolition. In a long editorial on November 15, 1861, he summed up the *Tribune's* consistent policy on this subject:

> When the war broke out, the *Chicago Tribune* took the ground that its end would be the destruction of slavery in the United States; and we, from the first, have been openly and warmly in favor of helping on that destruction, that the end might be more speedily reached. . . . Of course we have been bitterly denounced. . . . Men . . . wrote us saying that we were too fast and too radical. . . . Other men stopped their papers, and . . . a concerted effort was made to lessen our sales and coerce us into silence. But the *Tribune*, copying nobody, fearing nobody, asking nobody what to say and what to leave unsaid, acted upon its convictions, and persistently and unflinchingly followed the course that it had worked out; and while the other great journals of the country were timid or silent, we, all over the East and West, got the credit of *striking straight at the* CAUSE *of the rebellion*, and of being foremost if not alone, in this direct battle against the gigantic evil and wrong by which our country has been distracted and torn.

Charles Ray believed that the men in the ranks favored abolition and would bring the war to a speedy end when slavery was made the issue:

> In the answering throats of these brave soldiers, we hear the voice of God; and that hereafter this war is to be no longer a velvet-fingered dalliance with slavery; but a struggle honored by men and approved by Heaven. . . . Let the watchword be "LIBERTY" and six months will not elapse before peace will smile upon this land guiltless of the ownership of a slave.

The stalemate in the march toward emancipation and the stalemate on the battlefields increased the irritability of the *Tribune's* editors. None of them showed signs of giving up the fight, but they complained more and more about one another's opinions and argued more about the paper's policy. Scripps's factual, professorial background made him resent the chromatic dispatches from H. M. Smith which Ray sometimes published. Perhaps Smith had taken the editor's word a trifle too literally when told that the *Tribune* insisted on "complete candor." On a Washington assignment Smith had written that old General Scott was a traitor. "We cannot be ruled," Smith wrote, "by old fellows who have come down to us from a former generation." At another time, when Smith learned that a charming profligate with a degree from Yale, a slick tongue, and a knowledge of foreign courts had established himself in Mrs. Lincoln's good graces in the White House, he wrote: "Mrs. Lincoln is making herself both a fool and a nuisance. Chevalier Wykoff [*sic*] is her gallant. He is issuing invitations to her parties." Much of the confidential correspondence coming to Ray always belittled Mrs. Lincoln. Scripps, however, warned his chief to watch such a storyteller as Smith and to publish none of his reports without due consideration. He believed that the fellow was irresponsibly radical, apt to repeat every sensational bit of gossip.

Ray agreed with Scripps that Smith might be too outspoken

but preferred gossip to no report at all and believed that he had sufficient judgment to know what to put in the paper—especially as it was generally conceded that this fellow Henry Wikoff did have an entree to the White House.

Smith was equally critical of Lincoln himself and sent in a dispatch which read:

> Respect for government is wearing out under the most infamous imbecility and madness that ever cursed us at Washington. Buchanan seems to have been a granite pillar compared to the "good natured man" without any spinal column, who is drifting helplessly about among his rivals for the Presidency, all of them picking and grabbing for the best side of the dish of plums, (a mixed figure you can arrange to suit yourself).

Charles Ray could be counted on to arrange his own figures of speech, and there was always enough truth in the irrepressible Smith's dispatches for the editor to value his work in spite of Scripps's complaints.

The discouraging military deadlock in the winter of 1861-1862 inspired Smith to send another dispatch which happened to contain at least some hope for the frustrated *Tribune* editors. An effort to put the army into winter quarters and postpone the war until spring had been scotched, Smith said. "Several Senators and prominent men went at once to Lincoln and kindled a brush fire around his crazy and spavined old legs." The President, Smith continued, had submitted to the protests and had retired Scott and given the supreme command to George Brinton McClellan. "Little Mack," only thirty-five years old now, promised to retrieve the army's failing fortunes. The *Tribune* reported that things were beginning to happen at last. Certainly a winter campaign could be counted upon. In addition an expedition down the South Carolina coast was planned.

However, nothing of startling importance had occurred by December 1, 1861, and the *Tribune* shifted its searchlight back to the progress of abolition. The President was scheduled to deliver his annual message on the third day of the month. A few days before copies were released to the press, Cameron's report to the President reached Ray's desk. John Locke Scripps, in his capacity as postmaster, brought it to the office, admonishing Ray that it was not for publication until Lincoln delivered his message to Congress. Ray looked over Cameron's report curiously. It seemed odd for a member of the Cabinet to issue his report to the press before it had been received by the Chief Executive.

As Ray began to read the document, his face brightened. The Secretary of War had dared to repeat his former indiscretion and recommend that his officers liberate all slaves escaping into Federal lines. Hurray for the old placeman! Many people must have misjudged him, unless he was seeking radical sympathy to cover some new corruption.

Whether this was duplicity or not, the Negro reaped the benefits, and Ray reached for a pen to prepare a future leader proclaiming the good news. Then Scripps stamped excitedly in from the post office again. A wire had been received from Lincoln to call in all copies of the Cameron report. The President disapproved of the slavery emancipation paragraph, resented Cameron's insubordinate distribution of the report without executive clearance, and advised that an approved report would follow.

Ray shoved his half-finished editorial into a drawer. Next day the new printed report was delivered. Ray read it and on December 5, 1861, wrote:

My Dear Wash[burne]:

I have just got the news of the two reports of the Secty of War. What a *fiasco!* Old Abe is now unmasked, and we are sold out.

But do not give up. You have the power of making appropriations and imposing conditions. Do not give it up. The people, you know, are with you.

We want to keep the peace as long as there is hope of unity, but when the necessity for making things is upon us, we are ready to quarrel with Lincoln, the Cabinet, McClellan and anybody else. Be assured if worst comes to worst, we shall do our share. In God's name, stand for the right!

Yours Sincerely,
C. H. Ray

Then Ray wrote an editorial telling his readers that Lincoln was moving slowly but steadily toward emancipation. He said:

The cautious language which Mr. Lincoln employs, does not hide from us, who know the deep moral convictions of the man, the purpose that he has in view, nor the holy hate, which he must feel, of that giant iniquity that has at last brought war and desolation into this land. He has come, if not fully up to our advanced position at least within easy hail of those who have been looking anxiously back to see what progress he would make. . . .

And so we make progress. . . . We foresee the end, perhaps a long way off, to be reached only through toil and blood, and after a struggle that shall forever be a conspicuous landmark in the history of the world—a Republic without a traitor or a slave.

The *Tribune* was feeling its strength as it never had before. Demands for the paper made it necessary to print three editions. The presses thumped night and day. Trains going west and south carried a special morning edition. Next the one to be sold on the streets was printed. In the afternoon the third edition greeted workers going home from their offices. Special rates were given soldiers who subscribed for papers in camp.

Thus when Ray checked the paper's progress on the first New Year's Day since the beginning of the war, he had every reason to congratulate himself. But he was unhappy about the North's unexplainable delay in winning the war.

In January 1862, when Cameron was replaced by Edwin Stanton as Secretary of War, the *Tribune* rejoiced while many of the radical Republican papers complained bitterly that Lincoln had proscribed Cameron because he favored emancipation. Ray had always suspected the sincerity of Cameron's antislavery motives and was convinced of his corruption. When confronted with the good and the bad of Frémont's administration, Ray had approved the Pathfinder's emancipation proclamation but had also demanded his removal. So now, in the Cameron case, the *Tribune* backed the President and greeted the change with a hope for successful military action.

Under Stanton, the armies started to move again. In February, Bross wrote from Cairo, Illinois, that a vast flotilla was preparing to paddle up the Ohio, probably to capture the Confederate forts on the lower Cumberland and the Tennessee rivers and open a way into the deep South. U. S. Grant, a silent little man with a cigar in his mouth, seemed to be in charge. Ray had noticed other occasional reports about this Galenian, who apparently was doing a competent job. The editor, with a master-journalist's knowledge of reader interest, began to focus articles on Grant as he had previously on Lane and Lincoln. It was best to concentrate on one individual instead of a confused array of names. Assistant editors were ordered to prepare a biography of Grant to be printed if the new expedition succeeded. Newsworthy action seemed to be coming at last. On February 8 Ray demanded:

> Let the Western boys go in and win. We appeal to Washington to hurry up the reserves in arms, munitions and subsistence and to—keep hands off. Let us have no red-tape, no

hesitation, no more ill-times and costly timidity, no more distrust of the courage and endurance of our Western troops. They are ready and willing, nay, are burning with impatience to fight. . . . The road is open. Let the flag of the Union be advanced.

On February 11 the objective was plain. The *Tribune* published maps of Forts Henry and Donelson, and a new feature was started in the paper. Almost every family in Chicago had some member in the service or knew some boy who had gone to the front. Ray started publishing letters which the volunteers wrote home and was delighted to see the paper's circulation increase again.

At 10 A.M. on February 17 a final report of the battles for Forts Henry and Donelson came over the wires. A crowd had been congregating before the *Tribune* bulletin board. To keep warm, men swung their arms and stamped on the wooden blocks which now paved Clark Street. Traffic was stopped and the police made no effort to open it. When a dispatch beginning "Donelson is ours" was handed to Ray, he read only the first three words. That was enough. He handed the paper to a clerk, who announced the victory, the crowd standing outside in the cold. Watching from a window, Ray reported that the news:

. . . was followed by a pause whose hushed stillness might be felt, and then broke out such a cheer as men do not often hear in a lifetime. The scene that followed beggars description. Men went crazy with delight. Hats were thrown and crushed. . . .

Humanity will bless God for a great work accomplished, in Liberty avenged and triumphant, while Treason totters to its crumbling base.

During a lull in the tumult, Dr. Ray shouted from a window, "Friends, Deacon Bross has authorized me to say that any man who goes to bed sober tonight is a traitor to the government."

Charles Ray himself did not go to bed. Instead, he sat up writing happily and chuckling, no doubt, about the good deacon's dismay over his flippant remark. February 18, 1862, the *Tribune* appeared with the engraving of an American flag which Ray had published during the Fort Sumter bombardment. Henceforth this cut would be used preceding the announcement of all victories. The legend stated: "This is the glorious old banner that now waves in triumph over Fort Donelson." Below it Ray placed the secession Rattlesnake Flag—

. . . the emblem that slunk away before the resistless valor of our Illinois boys and will hurry to hide itself in the deepest fastnesses of Whippy Swamp.

Citizens, study these two emblems in the light of the stern conflict. . . . Did they die in vain and for a worthless prize, who lay down their lives at Donelson that the starry flag might float again over a re-united land?

Next day when Ray came to the office, a small cluster of watchers still lingered around the bulletin board. Ray passed them, stopped at the door to scrape the mud from his boots, and trudged up the stairs. Piecing together the dispatches and the maps spread out on his table, Ray worked on a five-column account of the heroic movements of "Gen. Grant's Grand Army," as he called it. He saw at once the strength in Grant's grim demand that he would consider no terms of the enemy except "unconditional and immediate surrender"—the kind of language Ray himself liked to use. He determined to begin a new feature in the paper headed FROM GEN. GRANT'S COLUMN. The editor was still working as darkness settled over Chicago and light after light appeared in the neighboring buildings.

Battle losses were reported to approximate 6,000. Ray promised to publish the names as soon as he received them. This he did, filling two closely set columns in the March 14 issue. He also posted the lists on the bulletin board outside the *Tribune* building. All day long men and women stood there, anxiously reading the names—a distressing sight. Now and again a man's face would blanch as he turned away with lips trembling. A woman's eyes suddenly brimmed with tears as she pulled down her veil and hurried off with a companion's consoling arm around her. Occasionally a shrill scream pierced the city's noises. In his next editorial, Ray asked:

> Who slew all these? They were murdered by Slavery. . . . that sanctified thing. Slavery which the "fanatics" who agree with the *Tribune* propose to throttle, and when dead, throw to the dogs of the Dark Ages.

Along with the casualty lists came the astounding news that Grant had been relieved of command. Relieved for gaining the first important victory of the war, Ray must have mused, although he did not commit himself in print. Charles Ray had not forgotten the conflicting opinions over the dismissal of Frémont, and he wanted to know more about the Grant episode before he opened fire with type. General Henry W. Halleck, department commander under whom Grant served, remained in his St. Louis headquarters, but claimed full credit for the victory at Forts Henry and Donelson.

General Don Carlos Buell, whose Department of the Ohio was partly in the scene of action, gave Grant slight mention in his report to the War Department. The top United States Army commander, George Brinton McClellan, also underrated Grant's achievement. Deacon Bross wrote Ray from the field that Grant, on a gunboat, had been drunk at the critical point of the siege. Many other letters, both censorious and laudatory, came to the editor's desk. Here was a puzzling situation. Ray published the letters without comment. Then Washburne wrote indignantly from Washington. He said that a great injustice was being done the "only real military fighting-man we now have in the army." Colonel J. D. Webster, from whom Ray had bought his interest in the *Tribune*, also wrote, saying that the derogatory letters did Grant a great injustice. Webster was on Grant's staff and should know—unless he was prejudiced.

Here was the Frémont case all over again, but with one great difference. Grant had won a victory. Charles Ray studied the conflicting correspondence in the light of this fact. Then he wrote the *Tribune's* opinion. He said:

> Gen. Grant is the only commanding officer in the army who has ever given us cause for personal dislike; but we forget that in the anxiety to do justice to his gallantry, daring and success. The charges against him are frivolous, such as they are and have no relation to his excesses. They are the product of red tape spirit and policy, and when they are known, will not affect his reputation as a soldier. . . . Gen. Grant planned well and fought well; and the success at Donelson is, after the bravery and endurance of our troops, due solely to the dispositions he made.

Ray had formed his opinion. Henceforth, in article after article, the *Tribune* would champion the little general to the end of the war.

XX "The Grandest Proclamation Ever Issued by Man"

CHICAGO was knee-deep in the feathery flakes of a March snow storm when news came that Grant had been reinstated in his old command. The limbs of trees were broken by the heavy weight of wet snow, and the roof of the *Times* building collapsed, preventing the issuance of the paper. Ray sympathized with his rivals' misfortune and encouraged them too. He knew that no energetic company could be held down long—even by three feet of wet snow.

The booming prosperity of Chicago had already exceeded the wildest hopes of even the fluent imagination of Deacon Bross. Ray had begun to invest in stocks, and the dividends were pyramiding his capital. Between his irregular newspaper hours, he found time to buy fine carved furniture, mahogany bookcases, and oil paintings for his home. He installed a marble mantle in the living room and purchased cut-glass decanters, goblets, and three dozen wine glasses, one dozen of them green. At last he was beginning to indulge his lifelong appreciation of fine *objets d'art* and gracious living.

Life was good to him, except for Jane's failing health. Doctors were unable to diagnose her malady. Ray began looking for a larger and more comfortable home, farther out of town where the air would be fresh and the children could romp without disturbing their mother. He considered a large house in Evanston. Four daily trains connected that suburb with Chicago. Closer to the city, he bought several lots—a good investment whether or not he built on them, for it was certain now that Chicago would be one of the great cities of America.

Its granaries bulged with five million bushels of wheat and corn. Its warehouses held a million barrels of flour, waiting for more railroad cars and more vessels—all being built in Chicago shops and shipyards. Chicago packing plants had outstripped those of both Cincinnati and St. Louis. The old river towns and the old river civilization had given way to the railroad era. In the heart of this throbbing industry the civil war seemed far away, and the idea that any men in America could still be held in slavery seemed preposterous.

Lincoln, in his message to Congress on March 6, 1862, suggested legislation for gradual compensated emancipation, to be completed before 1900. Ray considered this a step in the right direction, though a mincing one. He hoped that the armies, come spring, might stride toward victory with more assurance. In April news of the twin triumphs at Island No. 10 and Pittsburg Landing arrived simultaneously. Both the Mississippi and the Tennessee rivers were now open for Northern penetration into the deep South. Bross had sent details of the Island No. 10 engagement to the *Tribune* from his headquarters in Cairo. Dispatches from the Battle of Pittsburg Landing, or Shiloh, as it was soon called, were taken from the *Cincinnati Times*. The casualty lists which followed these conflicts seemed endless. Ray published an appeal for doctors and nurses and arranged their railway transportation to the front.

On May 11 the *Tribune* announced General B. F. Butler's victory at New Orleans. At last the tide seemed to have turned definitely in favor of the North. Next General David Hunter, newly assigned commander over South Carolina, Georgia, and Florida, proclaimed all slaves in his domain to be free. Then a strange thing happened. Charles Ray, though he had preached emancipation from the beginning of the war, did not defend his friend Hunter's proclamation as he had Frémont's and Cameron's the year before. Instead, Ray announced that generals must not usurp the Chief Executive's prerogative. Apparently Charles Ray had started on a new course to gain emancipation. The *Tribune* editorial on May 20 indicates that he knew about Lincoln's proposed Emancipation Proclamation. On that date readers were told:

> We have held and hold now that the day is ripe in which Mr. Lincoln's manifesto, made in his character as constitutional Commander-in-Chief of the Army and Navy, and in which the freedom of all slaves of rebels in arms against the Government is declared, should be given to the world. Anything short of that . . . is quackery—trifling with a matter which transcends all other matters of national concern.

Next day Ray wrote again: "We wait patiently the President's choice of a time when the trumpet which will startle the world, will sound. . . . Emancipation cannot be long deferred."

As was expected, Lincoln countermanded Hunter's decree. He deferred his own Emancipation Proclamation through the long hot summer of 1862, but he did call the senators and representatives of the border slave states to a meeting in the White House where he explained to them the growing popular insistence on emancipation and his own suggestion for compensation. In June, after McClellan had marched to within sight of the spires of Richmond and then withdrawn, Lincoln decided that he must have another commander. The most noteworthy victories had been won in the West, so Lincoln turned there for his next commanding general. General Halleck in the Western Department had taken—and received—credit for the victories won by Grant, and he seemed the logical man for the new appointment. Lincoln ordered him to come to Washington as commander of all the armies. Halleck was a serious student of military science who had translated books on Napoleon's campaigns from the original French. Indeed, his education and experience indicated eminence on a high military plane. But Charles Ray, not deceived about the general's character, commended his transfer and promotion as good riddance. He wrote:

> He is a closet general, who in his library will be able to give celerity and potency to military movements which in the field he would be powerless to direct. . . . He will be under the influence of the President, who by this time must be thoroughly tired of nigger catching and ditch digging.

With Halleck gone, Ray signed a manifesto, with other Chicagoans, demanding a more energetic prosecution of the war. "We believe that the condition of the country calls for greater sacrifice," the document said. In the *Tribune* Ray urged patriotic people to fill "our skeleton regiments." One company of soldiers was formed in the *Tribune* office.

At the height of this recruiting activity, a letter from John B. Turchin announced that he had been court-martialed and cashiered from the service. The presiding officer of the court was General James Garfield, an ambitious politician-soldier. The court found Turchin guilty of allowing his men to loot enemy property. He had been a troublemaker ever since Ray had helped him to get a commission. The Russian had even shunted the tailor's bill for his first uniform into the editor's mail. He had continually complained about the army and had called Sherman, under whom he had served, "that Seminary director." However, Ray knew that Turchin had a following among the foreign population of the city, and his ruffians did fight, so his dismissal seemed inopportune during the doldrums of 1862.

The question of chivalry, of Union soldiers' gentlemanly conduct in the field, became important as the war dragged on. People said that more ruthlessness, especially destruction of private property, more opportunity for the invaders to sack and burn, would cow the rebels into submission. A dozen regular recruiting officers cried futilely for enlistments while James H. Lane, a real senator from Kansas now, had rallied more men than he could arm, merely by promising the boys a great jayhawking expedition across enemy territory. Every footman was to ride back one "confiscated" horse and lead another; every horseman was to bring back an extra mount and a black squire to curry it. Ray published a statement of Lane's, scoffing at the regular army officers' policy of protecting the plantations belonging to members of the rebel army or its guerrilla bands. Lane boasted that as he marched he sent word to all absentee rebels: "I have left your families helpless and your presence is positively demanded or they will perish." A troop of riflemen traveling west to join Lane passed through Chicago. Under command of John Brown, Jr., they stopped in front of the *Tribune* office to sing "John Brown's Body." Perhaps it was better to permit more of this ruthless destruction of enemy property and save more human lives. Certainly the practice of destroying private property was becoming more common in spite of Turchin's court-martial.

Ray had received a letter from a Chicago soldier serving near Helena, Arkansas, criticizing the administration for not commissioning "live" generals who would destroy enemy plantations instead of protecting them while the owners were in the Confederate service. This Democratic correspondent wrote:

> You remember how widely different our politics were, and how I hated the *Tribune* and clamored loudly for the "*Times* policy" . . . Now I pray God to give renewed strength and power to your sheet in order that you may protest the milk and water policy . . . Give us Jim Lane, the Devil, or any other LIVE form of humanity that he may lead us through the Wilderness to victory or death.

Ray saw mobs marching through the streets of Chicago

shouting, "Give us Jennison the Jayhawker. We want our man of blood."

These soldiers all seemed to agree with Turchin's European policy of making the war terrible for civilians so that they would force it to end. Ray remembered a letter from the Russian which had stated: "West Pointers make good captains but not good Generals."

In any event Ray decided to call a mass meeting and invite the cashiered colonel to come and describe his battle experiences. Perhaps this might increase lagging enlistments. On the designated evening the hall was packed. There was no doubt about Turchin's popularity. Ray had prepared a special surprise for the audience. A brigadier general's commission for Turchin was announced amid wild applause. Evidently Ray and the *Tribune* still had plenty of authority in Washington when they cared to use it. A fund was also started and quickly subscribed for the purchase of a fine horse to be presented to Colonel J. D. Webster, former owner of the *Tribune*, now with the army near Corinth, Mississippi.

The new policy of destroying property and the old one of emancipating the slaves were part and parcel of the same problem. Ray believed in the confiscation of slave property, but the destruction of other property seemed different in spite of the soldiers' irrepressible desires. In July Congress passed a confiscation act which Lincoln neglected to enforce with vigor. The act included slaves and the *Tribune* chided the President good-naturedly. Certainly Ray did not object with his usual vehemence. He may have realized that the war would be ended by destructive "marches through Georgia," burning crops and farmsteads instead of killing Southern boys, but he seems to have preferred to let the President come to this conclusion in his own deliberate manner without being prodded by the *Tribune*. However, the question of the emancipation of slaves left no doubt in Ray's mind, and he never relaxed his constant insistence upon it. As has been said, he probably knew in May that Lincoln had prepared an Emancipation Proclamation, but the months dragged by without its promulgation. Then on August 20 Horace Greeley printed his "Prayer of Twenty Millions," demanding abolition or at least a clear statement of the President's position on this vexing subject. Lincoln released to the press a classic reply which Charles Ray published on the front page of the *Tribune* on August 24, 1862. The meat of Lincoln's letter was as follows:

> I would save the Union. I would save it the shortest way under the Constitution. The sooner the national authority can be restored; the nearer the Union will be "the Union as it was." If there be those who would not save the Union, unless they could at the same time *save* slavery, I do not agree with them. If there be those who would not have the Union unless they could at the same time *destroy* slavery, I do not agree with them. My paramount object in this struggle *is* to save the Union, and is *not* either to save or to destroy slavery. If I could save the Union without freeing *any* slave I would do it, and if I could save it by freeing *all* the slaves I would do it; and if I could save it by freeing some and leaving others alone I would also do that. What I do about slavery, and the colored race, I do because I believe it helps to save the Union; and what I forbear, I forbear because I do *not* believe it would help to save the Union. I shall do *less* whenever I shall believe what I am doing hurts the cause, and I shall do *more* whenever I shall believe doing more will help the cause. I shall try to correct errors when shown to be errors; and I shall adopt new views so fast as they shall appear to be true views.
>
> I have here stated my purpose according to my view of *official* duty; and I intend no modification of my oft-expressed *personal* wish that all men every where could be free.

The *Tribune* pointed out that this letter was a masterfully worded screen to cover the uncertainty of an executive who did not know exactly what to do at the moment. Finally, on

August 29, Ray announced that the much heralded Emancipation Proclamation would be issued after the next Union victory. With restraint the *Tribune* said:

President Lincoln possesses many qualifications and characteristics that attach to him the admiration and respect of our people. His unselfishness, his unambitious, unpretentious, undoubted patriotism, his logical ability and his pure character, give him a strong hold on the hearts of the people. Why can he not rise above the trammels of mere policy—always short sighted and time serving—to a clear comprehension of the requirements of this great exigency? He has it in his power to write his name alongside that of Washington, and all that is necessary is for him to prove himself, as Washington was, adequate to his place and position.

The victory for which Lincoln waited seemed to be impending on the old battlefield at Bull Run. A new general, John Pope, was sparring with Robert E. Lee there for position, but on August 30 Lee struck and sent Pope reeling back to the Washington defenses. Ray reported another defeat, with the capital city in danger. Dispatches said that another Confederate column was marching toward Cincinnati. Goodby to the Emancipation Proclamation! That radical document could be nothing but "a shriek in retreat" if issued now. Ray wrote in his column:

It is perfectly amazing that such a condition of things should exist with the great and unconquerable western army lying idle in Tennessee, Alabama, and Mississippi.

This is seemingly a dark day for the Union, but it is no time for discouragement or despair. The mighty North has hardly begun to put forth her energies.

To Charles Ray defeat was unthinkable. The Northwest was prospering as it never had before. A bumper wheat crop had been harvested by a new automatic reaper which permitted one man to do the work of ten, releasing nine to join the army and help uphold the government which had brought such prosperity for all men. Ray called Lincoln's attention to the war's progress in the Mississippi Valley. The President had already taken Halleck east, but victories continued in the West without him. Perhaps the wrong general had been given credit. Had the President overlooked the consistent success of that man Grant? The North, Ray said again and again, had the power to win but lacked only a prompt, bold, and strong hand to wield it.

Medill and Ray decided that the soldiers should have more voice in the conduct of the war. The *Tribune* started a campaign to allow soldiers to vote in the field, and the editors rejoiced when their demands were approved. They also hammered continually on emancipation, making the columns of the *Tribune* ring with paeans of freedom for all men. In September a convention of church members of all denominations assembled in Chicago. With *Tribune* prompting, it passed strong emancipation resolutions and sent them by special messenger to Lincoln. Joe Medill went along to remind the President that the *Tribune* was read now by a quarter of a million people who favored freedom of the slaves.

Lincoln met the delegation courteously and said that the subject was close to his heart and was under consideration, but the time was not opportune for action. The enemy across the Potomac yonder was at that moment grouping under Robert E. Lee for some great offensive. Lincoln did not say that the document was already written and waiting in a desk drawer, but Medill probably surmised as much. Certainly the *Tribune* had been telling readers about it all summer.

Medill had hardly got settled at his desk in Chicago again when news came that Lee had started to march north across Maryland. A glance at the map showed that he might encircle

Washington. Then good tidings arrived. The evening wire ticked the information that McClellan had stopped the Confederates at Antietam. Hallelujah! The editors hired a brass band to attract people to the bulletin board where news of the battle was posted. All the windows in the *Tribune* building glowed with light, while fireworks were exploded on the roof. Ray knew that the final battle report had not come in nor had Lincoln issued his promised emancipation, but he dared print in the morning:

> The demonstration was perhaps premature; but we cannot help it now! Our army has achieved decided advantages if not a decided victory; and the expense incurred in honor of the courage, patriotism and endurance of the brave men who are periling their lives in the field for our sake will not make us poor or cause a regret. The great victory is to come, and come it must.

For Charles Ray it came on September 22, 1862, immediately after Antietam. On that day Lincoln's cabinet met in the White House and the *Tribune* soon reported:

> President Lincoln has set his hand and affixed the great seal of the nation to the grandest proclamation ever issued by man. He has declared that after the first day of January next all the slaves in the then rebellious States *shall be free*. . . . So splendid a vision has hardly shone upon the world since the day of the Messiah. From the date of this proclamation begins the history of the republic as our fathers designed to have it—the home of freedom, the asylum of the oppressed, the seat of justice, the land of equal rights under the law, where each man, however humble, shall be entitled to life, liberty, and the pursuit of happiness. Let no one think to stay the glorious reformation. Every day's events are hastening its triumph, and whosoever shall place himself in its way it will grind him to powder.

XXI The Hundred Days

After the signing of the preliminary Emancipation Proclamation Charles Ray counted on the office calendar the time that would elapse—only three months and eight days—before all slaves in the rebellious South would be free. The editor determined to spend the intervening hundred days doing everything in his power to convince the President that the people's hearts and souls were behind freeing the slaves. The *Tribune* called a Liberty and Union mass meeting to rejoice in "the grandest event in modern history." On the morning after the meeting Ray devoted four columns of the paper to a description of its proceedings. "Let no one think to stay the glorious reformation," he crowed. Complete victory for the Union arms was all that remained to be achieved.

On September 30, with only three months now until emancipation, the *Tribune* called for military action in the West, less Washington red tape, and more authority for some aggressive commander. WANTED—A MAN, the caption read. Ray complained that an army of 200,000 men lay idle in the West.

Here are the conditions precedent for a great and successful campaign which shall carry our arms in triumph to the Gulf. . . . That army wants a leader.

Gen. Grant is to-day under the immediate command of Gen. Halleck [who, although in Washington, had not resigned his command of the Western Department]. Grant receives his orders from a Captain in St. Louis. . . .

We wait patiently for the march to begin.

Ray watched the paper containing this editorial being hawked in the streets as he wrote his next leader—with only two months and twenty-nine days before emancipation. He reaffirmed the *Tribune's* approval of the President's proclamation of September 22, insisting that the rebellion would be overthrown only by dealing sternly with its cause—slavery. "All men who have lately made the journey to Washington," he wrote, "return with the conviction that OLD ABE is master of the situation."

On October 7—two months and twenty-five days before emancipation—the *Tribune* reported the Battle of Corinth in Mississippi.

> There is a moral in this victory, following so closely the late triumph at Iuka. It is that the Western troops can drive the enemy on every field, when they have a fighting general at their head. The unbroken succession of victories of General Grant's department is not the result of an accident. All that is needed to drive the rebels into the Gulf is a commander who says "Go Forward" instead of "Go Back"—one who studies useful advances rather than brilliant retreats.

This from the West while McClellan stood stupefied as Lee retreated gracefully from Antietam! Always Ray kept Grant in the public eye. And the next mail brought a letter to Medill from O. M. Hatch, Lincoln's closest personal friend, one of the few who had stood boldly for his nomination at Chicago and had been a confidant ever since. Hatch wrote that the straggling of Union soldiers after Antietam had been unbelievable. It would have been suicide, he declared, for the army to follow Lee. Ray considered this report a reflection on McClellan and all the more reason for watching this man Grant. Hatch said also that he believed the officers of the opposing armies were negotiating secretly to uphold slavery, but that Lincoln could be depended on to abolish it at the first opportunity.

The consummation of the Proclamation and the advancement of U. S. Grant continued to be the two objectives of Charles Ray. On October 15, with two months and sixteen days before emancipation, the *Tribune* offered to pay $1000 in gold to any "Tory" who could put his finger on the section of the Constitution that forbids the President as commander in chief from issuing his proclamation. The editor continued:

It is with patriotic pride, with heartfelt satisfaction, that we can now, with deeper impressiveness than ever before, say to the public, that, whatever may be the faults and deficiencies of our President, in the sum and completeness of his character, his fitness for his position, his present stand before the bar of the civilized world, and the promise of the fame that he will leave behind him at the last, he is more nearly what a great and noble people desire to have in a chief magistrate than anyone who has filled the executive seat since the first President, or, that we have any hope or expectation could be found though the whole twenty millions of loyal people in our country had for that purpose been winnowed.

Ray's praise for Lincoln failed to bring success to the administration in the fall elections of 1862. Some political analysts attributed the reverse to the Emancipation Proclamation. Ray insisted that it was due to the failure of the war, but he pointed hopefully to Grant's latest aggressive maneuvers around Holly Springs, fifty miles below Memphis. The state of affairs was going to mend quickly now, he assured readers. A week later the *Tribune* announced Grant's capture of Holly Springs and asked pointedly what was happening back east. On November 25 Ray said, "We are glad to learn that General Grant is out of his leading strings, the hither end of which have been held by General Halleck in Washington." Ray was sure that Grant would use his new freedom with judgment and initiative. "He is looking for the enemy and when he finds him there will be bloodshed."

In spite of Ray's hopeful language, November ended gloomily in Chicago. Only monotonous news came from the South, while cold, raw winds from Lake Michigan whipped the city. The war had deadlocked once more, and with these discouraging events Jane's health became increasingly worse. The gay jingle of sleigh bells on spirited horses in the Chicago streets failed to bring happiness to the Ray home or a spirit of good will toward men in the war-weary city. The *Tribune* prepared an extract from the advance copy of Lincoln's annual message to Congress, and on the day of its delivery printed the paragraphs dealing with emancipation. In the message the President urged again, as he had in March, that compensated emancipation be adopted:

> In *giving* freedom to the *slave*, we *assure* freedom to the *free*—honorable alike in what we give, and what we preserve. We shall nobly save, or meanly lose, the last best, hope of earth. Other means may succeed; this could not fail. The way is plain, peaceful, generous, just—a way which, if followed, the world will forever applaud, and God must forever bless.

Ray was impressed with this sentiment and its wording. In the days that followed he printed it again and again and again. On December 8 the paper announced the purchase of a new type face to be initiated with the glorious announcement of the final proclamation. Four days later General Ambrose E. Burnside, McClellan's successor, was defeated at Fredericksburg, Virginia. Reports said that ten thousand men had been killed in one effort to take a single position. Powerful newspapers demanded a complete shake-up of the Cabinet. Others called for a dictator. Something, almost anything, must be done to stop this slaughter. From Washington, Horace White wrote the *Tribune* that Lincoln, almost beside himself, was becoming "weak kneed" on emancipation. Many of his advisers counseled against adding such a radical act to the already seething political scene.

If Lincoln backed down on the Emancipation Proclamation now, it meant the end of everything for which Charles Ray had struggled since he had invested his inheritance in the Galena *Jeffersonian* and his life in a crusade for freedom. Jane's life, too, had been dedicated to the cause, and her vitality was ebbing fast. Out in the gloomy streets the sleigh bells jingled derisively—maniac giggling at a man's defeat. Here was a crisis apparently as hopeless as that other one during the Chicago Convention when the majority of the Illinois delegation had wanted to desert Lincoln for a more popular man. Charles Ray acted now as he had then.

With the courage to fight for what he believed right, he redoubled his efforts to make the President stand firm. He filled space usually assigned to local news with accounts of religious meetings and petitions sent by them to the President begging him to free the slaves. Christians everywhere were exhorted to pray for the great day ahead. Ray published detailed accounts of the sinister political powers bearing down on the President, the sly lawyers pointing to loopholes in the preliminary Proclamation which would allow him to save face and still leave slavery alone. Charles Ray assured his readers that Lincoln would withstand the pressure, then he took pains to see that these words of trust reached the President in the White House. On December 29 the paper asked its readers to "Thank God and wait three days."

On January 1, with no news of Lincoln's final action, the *Tribune* reprinted the President's Proclamation of September 22 with the caption: WHAT THE PRESIDENT PROMISED. The many disappointments of the war were frankly stated and the editor continued:

> The new year is begun under brighter and better auspices, when the Proclamation shall call to the aid of the government four hundred thousand eager freedmen, to be henceforth men and no more slaves. Only in this promise can we wish our friends a HAPPY NEW YEAR.

All day, during the New Year's festivities, no report about Lincoln's action reached Chicago. Ray went to the office for the evening wire, but instead of announcing that Lincoln had signed the final Emancipation Proclamation, the telegraph ticked out a dismaying report of a terrible battle at Stone's River, down in Tennessee. The death lists promised to be worse than those from Fredericksburg. Would this second catastrophe deter the President from taking the risk of signing, or had he affixed his signature to the document before the fatal news came through? All next day, January 2, 1863, Ray waited for the final word. That night he sat up late under the yellow lamplight, preparing copy as the printers stamped in from the streets, kicking snow from their boots before they went down to the presses. Ray wrote orders for the make-up man to place mourning borders around the lists of dead.

Then a new dispatch caught his eye, words to flush the face of a dedicated man. He called for the old engraving of the flag which he used to announce victories on the battlefield. He ordered it to be printed on the front page above the heading: A NEW YEAR'S GIFT TO HUMANITY–A NATION BORN IN A DAY. Beside this, in the first column, he wrote:

> We have the Proclamation—a late but grateful recognition of the finger of God in the affairs of nations as of individual men. . . .
>
> There need be no fears as a result of what Mr. Lincoln has done. . . . From this day this nation is wedded to Freedom and a purer and better Democracy. . . .
>
> If we have never feared, it is because we had profound faith in the logic of events, and because with no mean prescience we knew that the day would surely come in which the wisdom and necessity of our course would be vindicated in a way to clear up and remove all questions of patriotism and right.

Charles Ray went home late that night feeling that his work was finished. Anything more would be anticlimax. As he looked back on the events of the last few years, it seemed that destiny had linked him in an inevitable chain of events. His purchase of the *Jeffersonian* had led to the *Tribune*, to the Bloomington Convention, to the Wigwam—all of which had enabled him to take a leading part in Lincoln's election campaign. His unremitting insistence, in editorial after editorial, must have had its effect on the final issuance of the Emancipation Proclamation.

True, the Proclamation did not disturb slavery in the loyal border states, but no one took this remnant of the institution seriously. To all intents and purposes slavery had been abolished in America. Little more could be done now except to terminate the war successfully, and Grant seemed to be the man for that. At Stone's River the Union forces under General William S. Rosecrans had failed to defeat the Confederates in a bloody battle. The *Tribune* lamented the losses but reminded readers that Grant was "going ahead again." The silent little cigar-smoking officer, thanks to the *Tribune's* help, had already become a national figure, and the general himself realized his debt to Ray. Five years later, on the eve of Grant's election to the presidency, the candidate invited Ray to spend the day with him at his Galena home—a gesture of friendship for a man he never knew well but who had seen and appreciated his merits while others were applauding more showy figures.

In January 1863, Dr. Ray purchased a brick house at 516 Wabash Avenue in Chicago. During the following summer Jane died. Charles Ray's grief over the loss of his wife and his worries about the three little children at home while he spent long hours at the office made him consider giving up his newspaper work. His own health showed signs of failing under the terrific strain of the last few years. He was extremely nervous, could not rest and found it difficult to concentrate. With emancipation granted, the chief purpose of his journalistic career had been accomplished. Why labor any more?

Before coming to any decision, however, Charles Ray sent

his children back to New York, where they were distributed among members of the family. This proved to be an unsatisfactory arrangement for the bereaved father. In addition, Ray's relations with Medill were becoming more difficult, so in the fall he resigned the editorship of the *Tribune* and sold his stock.

A free man now, with ample money, he began speculating in securities and Chicago real estate. A year later he married Julia Anna Clark, a young woman of twenty-three whose charming oval face smiled under silky hair parted demurely in the middle and knotted low on her neck. She was the daughter of Judge Lincoln Clark, who, like Charles Ray, had moved from New York state to Iowa and back to Chicago.

Charles and Julia Ray, after a wedding trip to their family homes in New York, settled in Chicago where Julia managed the household and reared the three children. Here two more daughters, Bertha and Julia, came to the family. Charles Ray, a man of leisure now though only forty-three years old, found time for business speculations and also for his various cultural interests. With his friend Leonard Volk he was influential in founding the Academy of Design and arranging for the first art exhibition in Chicago. In this new field Ray was as determined and as outspoken against bad art as he had been against compromising politicians.

Few men reach independence at such an early age. His complexion had retained its youthful freshness. His curly hair had not thinned with the years. His nervousness, however, had increased alarmingly, and within six years he was dead.

If during this rapid decline Charles Ray felt solemn pride in his contribution to the career of Abraham Lincoln and to the emancipation of the slaves, he kept it to himself. His character was a strange blend of modesty and self-assertive strength. So when Lincoln's law partner, William H. Herndon, wrote asking for personal data on the martyred President, Ray replied unpretentiously, "You knew Mr. L. far better than I did though I knew him well." The retired editor then summarized Lincoln's religion, not his political philosophy, as he remembered it from conversations with his old friend.

This letter of Ray's was one of his few lapses into retrospection. Seldom in his life did he let reminiscence overshadow his interest in future generations. A colleague qualified to know wrote in Ray's obituary:

> He was the best friend a young man commencing newspaper life could have, for the reason that he was chary of praise and never slow at pointing out faults and suggesting the remedy. Perhaps the most striking feature of his character was his hatred of cant and sham. He recognized a hypocrite instinctively, and he never stopped to select choice or elegant phrases in exposing him. We cannot remember a man so plain-spoken in denunciation of humbug or hypocrisy. He hit with all his might, and his might was immense.

NOTES, SOURCES, ACKNOWLEDGMENTS AND INDEX

NOTES

TEXT to which the following notes refer is indicated by page and paragraph. The number of the page is followed in parentheses by the *final word* of the paragraph. When a paragraph carries over from one page to another, the page notation cited may refer to text on the previous page.

Notes referring to passages longer than a single paragraph are located by the numbers of all pages involved and by the final words of all paragraphs covered. The correspondence cited but not specifically located was found in the Ray Papers.

PREFACE (pages vii-x)

x (emancipation): John William Tebbel, *American Dynasty*, p. 27.

CHAPTER I (pages 3-13)

5 (men): Letter, Levi Ray to Charles Ray, Dec. 19, 1847.
6 (Ocean): Certificates of appointment, medical diplomas, professional partnership agreements, etc., in Chicago Historical Society.
7 (location): Letter, Charles Ray, "On Board Bark Newton, Nineteen Days from New Bedford," July 8, 1841.
8 (State): Letter in Ray Papers dated June 15, 1844.
8 (playthings): Paul M. Angle, *Here I Have Lived*, p. 149.
9 (nothing): Letter dated Mar. 17, 1845.
10 (village): Letter, Jane Ray to Elsie Cuyler, Aug. 9, 1847.
10 (after): Letter dated Oct. 3, 1847.
10 (world): Letter, Charles Ray to Lincoln, July [?], 1858, Lincoln Papers.
11 (prescribing): Letter, Jane Ray to Elsie Cuyler, Aug. 9, 1847.
11 (reaction): Frederic Bancroft, *Slave-trading in the Old South*, p. 359; Emerson Fite, *Presidential Campaign of 1860*, p. 79.
12 (municipality): Lloyd Lewis, *Chicago*, p. 54.

CHAPTER II (pages 14-25)

14-15 (manipulations, man, stub): Letter, B. F. Wheeler to Ray, Aug. 24, 1852; Arthur C. Cole, *Era of the Civil War*, pp. 38, 42. The Breese railroad project is printed in Senate Doc. No. 466, 29th Cong., 1st Sess. The federal and state Illinois Central railroad acts passed in 1850 and 1851, respectively.

15 (it): Philip Kinsley, *Chicago Tribune*, p. 45.

16 (Mississippi): *Daily Evening Jeffersonian*, June 25, 1852.

16 (Ray): Letter, John Locke Scripps to Ray, Nov. 28, 1852.

16 (going): Letter, Elihu Washburne to Ray, Jan. 9, 1852.

17 (constituents): Susan Dixon, *History of Missouri Compromise*, p. 445.

17 (regularity): Francis Brown, *Raymond of the Times*, p. 147; John Bach McMaster, *History of the People of the United States*, VIII, 201.

18 *(Tribune):* The "Appeal" is printed in *Congressional Globe*, 33rd Cong., 1st Sess., pp. 281-282; Allan Nevins, *Ordeal of the Union: A House Dividing*, p. 146.

18 (progress): A. T. Andreas, *History of Cook County, Illinois*, pp. 370, 393.

19 (capitol): Letter, Ray to Jane, Feb. 18, 1854; Letter, Jane and Charles Ray to Elsie Cuyler, Feb. 14 and 15, 1847; Cole, *op. cit.*, p. 14.

20 (boss): Letter, Lincoln to Speed, Aug. 24, 1855, in Roy P. Basler (ed.), *Collected Works of Abraham Lincoln*, II, 322.

21 (Galena): Feb. 14, 1854.

21 (future): Lloyd Lewis, *Chicago*, p. 57.

22 (war): George Fort Milton, *Eve of Conflict*, p. 124.

22 (slavocracy): McMaster, *op. cit.*, p. 199.

23 (administration): Letter, Ray to Washburne, Feb. 14, 1854, Washburne Papers.

23 (slaves): F. I. Herriott, "James W. Grimes Versus the Southrons," p. 332.

24 (them): *Ibid.*, p. 336.

25 (royal): Letter, Washburne to Ray, Mar. 26, 1854.

CHAPTER III (pages 26-37)

27 (interests): E. L. Pierce, *Memoir and Letters of Charles Sumner*, III, 369-370.

28 (slavery): Jay Monaghan, *Diplomat in Carpet Slippers*, p. 165.

28 (election): Susan Dixon, *True History of the Missouri Compromise*, p. 444.

29 (again): Letter, Washburne to Ray, Mar. 26, 1854.

30 (development): J. G. Randall, *Lincoln the President*, I, 149.

31 (Union): Pierce, *op. cit.*, p. 469.

31 (Kansas, arrived): Badger's words have been paraphrased here. According to the *Congressional Globe*, 33rd Cong., 1st Sess., Appendix, pp. 149, 313, more than two weeks elapsed before Wade's comment on Badger's speech. The repartee is also recounted in George Fort Milton, *Eve of Conflict*, p. 131.

32 (speak): Lloyd Lewis, "He Hated Southern Gentlemen," pp. 474-481.

33 (editorial): *Congressional Globe*, 33rd Cong., 1st Sess., Appendix, pp. 326, 327, 328; Dixon, *op. cit.*, p. 438.

33 (voting): Carl Sandburg, *Abraham Lincoln: The Prairie Years*, II, 453.

34 (voted): *Congressional Globe*, 33rd Cong., 1st Sess., pt. 1, p. 532.

34 (re-elected): Charles F. Horner, *Life of James Redpath*, p. 74.

35 (killed): John Bach McMaster, *History of the People of the United States*, VIII, 205; Albert Richardson, *Garnered Sheaves*, p. 163.

36 (generation): St. Joseph *Gazette*, May 17, 1854; St. Joseph *Weekly Cycle*, Feb. 24, 1854; William Henry Smith, *Political History of Slavery*, I, 168.

37 (sir, Amen): James S. Pike, *First Blows of the Civil War*, pp. 220, 221.

37 (nation): *Congressional Globe*, 33rd Cong., 1st Sess., pt. 2, pp. 1254, 1321.

CHAPTER IV (pages 38-52)

38 (movement): Arthur C. Cole, *Era of the Civil War*, p. 126; Letter, F. P. Blair to Ray, Dec. 4, 1854.
39 (could): Cole, *op. cit.*, p. 128.
39 (considerations): Paul Selby, "Republican State Convention," p. 45; Paul M. Angle (ed.), *Herndon's Lincoln*, p. 299.
40 (ignoramuses): Letter, Ray to Washburne, Jan. 12, 1855, Washburne Papers.
40 (Senate): *Ibid.*, Dec. 16, 1854.
41 (Springfield): *Ibid.*, Dec. 24, 1854.
42 (hoped): Letter, Ray to Jane, Jan. 2, 1854 [5].
43 (view): John G. Nicolay and John Hay, *Abraham Lincoln: A History*, II, 27, give details of Bissell-Davis duel.
43 (failure): Illinois *Senate Journal*, Jan. 3, 1855; Letter, Lincoln to Washburne, Dec. [Jan.] 6, 1855, Roy P. Basler (ed.), *Collected Works of Abraham Lincoln*, II, 303.
44 (too): Letter, Jane and Charles Ray to Elsie Cuyler, Feb. 14 and 15, 1847.
45 (vote-getter): Letter, Ray to Washburne, Jan. 12, 1855, Washburne Papers.
45 (hence): Lincoln explains his reason for this concession in a letter dated Feb. 9, 1855, Basler, *op. cit.*, pp. 304, 306.
46 (location): William Bross, *History of Chicago*, p. 84.
46 (Pierce): Letter, Ray to Jane, Feb. 18, 1854 [5].
47 (imagined): *Ibid.*, Mar. 29, 1855.
48 (profits): *Ibid.*, Apr. 25, 1855.
49 (worry): Bross, *op. cit.*, p. 119; Lloyd Lewis, *Chicago*, pp. 65, 70.
49 (room): Letter, Ray to Jane, Apr. 27, 1855.
50 (eh): *Ibid.*, June 24, 1855.
50 (it): John Tebbel, *American Dynasty*, p. 17.
51 (hills): Philip Kinsley, *Chicago Tribune*, p. 44.
51 (sheet): H. I. Cleveland, "Booming the First Republican President," p. 84.
52 (4500): Letters, Ray to Jane, Sept. 10 and 29, 1855; Kinsley, *op. cit.*, p. 43.

CHAPTER V (pages 53-65)

53 (pockets): Leverett W. Spring, *Kansas*, p. 105.
54 (menace): *Report of the Special Committee*, p. 8. See also Spring, *op. cit.*, p. 41.
55 (nation): C. H. Ambler (ed.), *Correspondence of Robert M. T. Hunter*, p. 161.
56 (Atchison): Jay Monaghan, *Civil War on the Western Border*, p. 38. Atchison took pains to state that his senatorial term expired Mar. 3, 1855.
57 (determination): George W. Brown, *Reminiscences of Old John Brown*, p. 7.
57 (Kansas): Spring, *op. cit.*, p. 105.
58 (cease): *Chicago Tribune*, Jan. 8, 1856; Philip Kinsley, *Chicago Tribune*, p. 51.
58-59 (declare, Happiness, Union, dangerous, *do*): *Chicago Tribune*, Jan. 22, 1856.
59 (wrote): Kinsley, *op. cit.*, p. 50.
60 (serve): Feb. 19, 1856.
60 (attend): Paul Selby, "Editorial Convention," p. 34.
62 (party): *Ibid.*, pp. 36, 37; Charles A. Church, *History of Republican Party*, p. 30; Oliver P. Wharton, "Lincoln and the Beginning of the Republican Party," p. 4.
62 (existed): Selby, *op. cit.*, pp. 37, 38; *Sangamo Journal*, Feb. 27, 1856.
63 (saw): Otto R. Kyle, "Mr. Lincoln Steps Out," p. 36.
63 (home): Benjamin F. Shaw, "Owen Lovejoy," p. 68; Kyle, *op. cit.*, p. 35, records another of Lincoln's jokes at this meeting.
64 (Bissell): Frank M. Elliott, "Governor W. H. Bissell," p. 138.
64 (secretary): *Sangamo Journal*, May 1, 1856.
65 (Engelmann, Democrats): Letter, Ray to Washburne, May 4, 1856, Washburne Papers.

CHAPTER VI (pages 66-77)

66 (front): *New York Weekly Tribune*, Apr. 8, 1856; Jay Monaghan, *Civil War on the Western Border*, p. 23.

68 (Kansas): Harold E. Briggs, "Lawlessness in Cairo, Ill.," p. 72.
68 (issued): John Sherman, *Recollections*, I, 129.
69 (speak): Andrew H. Reeder, "Governor Reeder's Escape," p. 219.
70 (Kansas): Monaghan, *op. cit.*, pp. 52, 53.
70 (sight): Edward L. Pierce, *Memoir and Letters of Charles Sumner*, III, 446.
72 (floor): Ezra M. Prince (ed.), *Transactions of the McLean County Historical Society*, III, 168.
73 (Democrats): Paul Selby, "Editorial Convention," p. 42.
73 (steamboat): Theodore C. Pease and James G. Randall (eds.), *Diary of Orville Hickman Browning*, I, 239.
74 (Philadelphia): Prince, *op. cit.*, p. 170.
74 (behalf): "Official Record of Convention," p. 155.
75 (territories): Selby, *op. cit.*, p. 38; Otto Kyle, "Mr. Lincoln Steps Out," p. 33; "Official Record of Convention," p. 160. Kyle, *op. cit.*, p. 32, discusses these resolutions.
76 (it, reported, enthusiasm): George Schneider, "Address," p. 93; Thomas J. Henderson, "Remarks," p. 81.
76 (bounds): Prince, *op. cit.*, p. 178.
77 (States): John G. Nicolay and John Hay, *Abraham Lincoln; A History*, II, 29, state that Reeder spoke before the convention met. Contemporary newspapers do not substantiate this. See quotations from *Democratic Press* in Prince, *op. cit.*, pp. 168-177.

CHAPTER VII (pages 78-90)

79 (Missouri): *Chicago Daily Democratic Press*, June 2, 1856.
79 (slavery): Jay Monaghan, *Civil War on the Western Border*, p. 70.
80 (longer): *Ibid.*
81 (nation): *Ibid.*, p. 66.
82 (woman): L. W. Busbey, *Uncle Joe Cannon*, pp. 97-101.
83 (stand): July 9, 1856, Roy P. Basler (ed.), *Collected Works of Abraham Lincoln*, II, 347.
83 (yours): Aug. 27, 1856, *Ibid.*, p. 366.
84 (reinforcements): Monaghan, *op. cit.*, pp. 75-77.

84 (today): *Chicago Tribune*, Aug. 20, Sept. 19, 1856.
85 (politicians): Monaghan, *op. cit.*, p. 88.
86 (party): *Ibid.*, p. 89.
86 (horses): Arthur C. Cole, *Era of the Civil War*, pp. 147-148.
87 (here): Letter owned by Justin Turner, Los Angeles.
88 (abolitionist): *Chicago Tribune*, Aug. 7, 16, 21, Sept. 5, 13, 1856; Letter, Ray to Washburne, Oct. 9, 1856, Washburne Papers.
88 (Atchison): *Chicago Tribune*, Aug. 21, 1856.
88 (houses): *Chicago Tribune*, Sept. 16, 1856; Carl Sandburg, *Abraham Lincoln: The Prairie Years*, I, 466.
89 (Polk): Samuel J. Crawford, *Kansas in the Sixties*, p. 17.
89 (War): *Sangamo Journal*, Dec. 12, 1856.
90 (victory): *Ibid.*, Jan. 14, 1857.
90 (nomination): Ada M. Klett, "Belleville Germans Look at America," pp. 23-37.
90 (prizes): *Sangamo Journal*, Jan. 13, 23, 1857. See also four letters in Illinois and Michigan Canal Papers, dated Sept. 19, 1857, two on May 10, 1858, and one on Aug. 10, 1858.

CHAPTER VIII (pages 91-106)

91 (wish): *Chicago Tribune*, Jan. 8, 31, 1857.
92 (game): Allan Nevins, *Emergence of Lincoln*, I, 95; Albert J. Beveridge, *Abraham Lincoln*, II, 485.
94 (it, him): H. Donaldson Jordan, "A Politician of Expansion," pp. 377-378.
94 (change): Lloyd Lewis, *Chicago*, pp. 74, 77.
96 (Lawrence): This quotation was printed May 28, 1857.
96 (MEPHISTOPHELES): Arthur C. Cole, *Era of the Civil War*, p. 237.
96 (streets): Undated newspaper clippings in Ray Papers.
97 (pleader): *Chicago Tribune*, Jan. 21, 1859. The best study of the canal is James W. Putnam, *The Illinois and Michigan Canal: A study in Economic History*. Philip Kinsley, *Chicago Tribune*, p. 64; Oliver P. Wharton, "Lincoln and the Beginning of the Republican Party in Illinois," p. 3.
98 (readers): Leverett Spring, *Kansas*, pp. 218, 220.

99 (cause): Jay Monaghan, *Civil War on the Western Border*, p. 98.
99 (ballot): *Ibid.*, p. 99; *Chicago Tribune*, Jan. 1, 1858.
100 *(Tribune):* Spring, *op. cit.*, p. 229.
100 (them): *Herald of Freedom*, Dec. 12, 1857; Albert D. Richardson, *Beyond the Mississippi*, p. 87; *Illinois State Journal*, Feb. 19, 1858; Stephen A. Douglas, *Report*, p. 99.
101 (promised): Letter, Ray to Washburne [Apr. 15? 1858], Washburne Papers.
101 (Kansas): Letter, Ray to Trumbull, Dec. 18, 1857, Trumbull Papers.
102 (mercy): Culp MS, p. 37; John G. Nicolay and John Hay, *Abraham Lincoln: A History*, II, 140, quote a letter from Greeley to Medill censuring Medill for this stand against Douglas.
102 (editorial): Paul M. Angle, *Lincoln, 1854-1861*, p. 216. Douglas knew that he was beaten before Feb. 18, 1858.
103 (won): Culp MS, pp. 24-25.
103 (barometer): Letter, Ray to Washburne [Apr. 15? 1858], Washburne Papers.
104 (him): *Sangamo Journal*, June 17, 1858.
104 (LINCOLN): Albert J. Beveridge, *Abraham Lincoln, 1809-1858*, II, 571.
104 (couplet): *Ibid.*, p. 574; Horace White, *Lincoln and Douglas Debate*, p. 16.
106 (struck): Roy P. Basler (ed.), *Collected Works of Abraham Lincoln*, II, 465-466.

CHAPTER IX (pages 107-125)

107 (excitement): William Bross, *History of Chicago*, p. 86.
107 (predicament): John Tebbel, *American Dynasty*, pp. 18, 19.
108 (Europe): Lloyd Lewis, *Chicago*, p. 74; see also Bross, *op. cit.*, pp. 74-75.
108 (said): Bross, *op. cit.*, p. 77.
109 (1860): *Chicago Press and Tribune*, July 5, 1858.
110 (him): *Ibid.*, July 10, 1858.
111 (points): Philip Kinsley, *Chicago Tribune*, p. 80.

113 (challenger): *Chicago Press and Tribune*, July 26, 1858.
113 (it): Letter, Ray to Lincoln, July 27, 1858, Lincoln Papers.
114 (Ocean): Ida M. Tarbell, *Life of Abraham Lincoln*, I, 314; Horace White, *Lincoln-Douglas Debates*, p. 18; E. E. Sparks (ed.), "Lincoln-Douglas Debates of 1858," pp. 124-145.
115 (FRAUD): Charles A. Church, *History of the Republican Party*, p. 60; Henry Villard, *Memoirs*, p. 92; *Chicago Press and Tribune*, Aug. 23, 30, 1858.
115 (timed): *Chicago Press and Tribune*, Aug. 24, 1858.
116 (Ray): Undated letter in Washburne Papers.
116 (wouldn't): Tarbell, *op. cit.*, p. 315.
117 (qualification): Letter, Ray to Lincoln, n.d. [Aug. 1858], Lincoln Papers.
117 (themselves): James K. Magie, *Lecture on Lincoln*, p. [3].
119 (audience): Philip Kinsley, *Chicago Tribune*, pp. 86-87; note account in Sparks, *op. cit.*, p. 79.
119 (extension): Sparks, *op. cit.*, p. 161.
120 (gills): Culp MS, p. 48; *Chicago Press and Tribune*, Sept. 7, 1858.
120 (you): Kinsley, *op. cit.*, p. 87; *Chicago Press and Tribune*, Aug. 30, 1858.
121 (dead): Roy P. Basler (ed.), *Collected Works of Abraham Lincoln*, III, 228.
121 (premises): *Ibid.*, p. 231.
122 (announced): Arthur C. Cole, *Era of the Civil War*, p. 170.
122 (capital): *Chicago Press and Tribune*, Sept. 23, 1858.
123 (support): *Ibid.*, Nov. 5, 1858.
124 (well): Kinsley, *op. cit.*, p. 67.
124 (Lincoln): Letter, Lincoln to Ray, Nov. 20, 1858, Basler, *op. cit.*, pp. 341-342.
125 (mountains): *Chicago Press and Tribune*, Nov. 5, 1858.

CHAPTER X (pages 126-135)

127 (out): Letter, Ray to Washburne, Nov. 22, 1858, Washburne Papers.
128 (win): *Chicago Press and Tribune*, July 15, 1859.
129 (off): R. R. Hitt, *Report of the Trial of John Hossack*, p. 68.

129 (right): Jay Monaghan, "North Carolinians in Illinois History," p. 436.
130-131 (respected, run, possible, boy): *Ibid.*
131 (Lincoln): Roy P. Basler (ed.), *Collected Works of Abraham Lincoln*, III, 385.
132 (territories): Arthur C. Cole, *Era of the Civil War*, p. 184.
132 (slave-power): Stephen A. Douglas, "Popular Sovereignty in the Territories," pp. 519-537.
133 (wrote): *Chicago Press and Tribune*, Sept. 14, 1859.
133 (Congress): *Ibid.*, Aug. 13, 1859.
134 (applied): Basler, *op. cit.*, p. 405.
135 (clear): *Chicago Press and Tribune*, Oct. 19, 21, 1859.
135 (least): Oct. 31, 1859, Lincoln Papers.

CHAPTER XI (pages 136-145)

136 (country): *Chicago Press and Tribune*, Nov. 16, 1859.
137 (questions): Letters, Ray to Lincoln, Mar. 8, Apr. 14, May 10, 1858, Lincoln Papers.
138 (with): Roy P. Basler (ed.), *Collected Works of Abraham Lincoln*, III, 502.
138 (candidate): Thomas J. McCormack (ed.), *Memoirs of Gustave Koerner*, II, 80.
139 (wrote): *Chicago Press and Tribune*, Feb. 2, 25, 1860.
140 (occupied): Culp MS, p. 105.
141-142 (headings, government, day, success, inaugurate): *Chicago Press and Tribune*, Feb. 16, 1860.
142 (ago): *Ibid.*, Feb. 27, 1860.
143 (stairs): H. I. Cleveland, "Booming the First Republican President," p. 85; Carl Sandburg, *Abraham Lincoln: The Prairie Years*, II, 210.
144 (this): Basler, *op. cit.*, pp. 549-550.
145 (jokes): Cleveland, *op. cit.*, p. 85; Sandburg, *op. cit.*, p. 216.

CHAPTER XII (pages 146-157)

146 (audience): I. H. Bromley, "Historic Moments," p. 647.

147 (Act): Jay Monaghan, "North Carolinians in Illinois History," pp. 439-440; Arthur C. Cole, *Era of the Civil War*, p. 228.
148 (words): *Chicago Press and Tribune*, Feb. 29, Mar. 1, 1860.
148 (entitled): R. R. Hitt, *Report of the Trial of John Hossack*, pp. 171-172.
149 (molestation): *Ibid.*
150 (jury): *Chicago Press and Tribune*, Mar. 9, 1860.
150 (negro): Monaghan, *op. cit.*, p. 441.
151 (exist): Hitt, *op. cit.*, p. 202.
151 (law): *Ibid.*, pp. 202-203.
152 (spurn, source, follows, aforesaid, died): *Ibid.*
153 (excommunication, earth): *Ibid.*, pp. 218, 234.
153 (call): Monaghan, *op. cit.*, p. 443; *Chicago Press and Tribune*, Mar. 9, 1860.
154 (won): *Chicago Press and Tribune*, Mar. 2, 1860.
155 (properly): Paul M. Angle, *Lincoln, 1854-1861*, p. 325; Leonard Volk, "Lincoln Life-Mask," pp. 244-245.
155 (inscribed): Charles A. Church, *History of the Republican Party*, p. 79.
156 (Lincoln): Ida M. Tarbell, *Life of Abraham Lincoln*, I, 340.
157 (quarters): John Tebbel, *American Dynasty*, p. 18.

CHAPTER XIII (pages 158-175)

158 (copies): *Chicago Press and Tribune*, May 5, 1860.
158 (day): *Ibid.*, May 17, 1860.
159 (candidacy): Bessie L. Pierce, *History of Chicago*, II, 244.
159 (cheer): Lloyd Lewis, *Chicago*, p. 99.
160 (favorites): "The Nomination of Lincoln," p. 338.
161 (Seward): Ida M. Tarbell, *Life of Abraham Lincoln*, I, 345.
161 (side): Isaac H. Bromley, "Historic Moments," p. 646; Letter, Swett to Drummond, May 27, 1860, in O. H. Oldroyd, *Lincoln's Campaign*, pp. 70-73.
162 (rally): F. I. Herriott, "Germans of Davenport," p. 5.
162-163 (asked, said): Note that Dole, a former Indianan, sat in the Illinois delegation and that he got the appointment. The quotations are from John Tebbel, *American Dynasty*, p. 20.

This account from Medill's memory should be considered along with the fact that Lincoln wrote C. M. Allen, a delegate from Indiana, on May 1, 1860, to come early and confer with Davis and Dubois. Ida M. Tarbell, *op. cit.*, p. 347, states that Medill told her that half the Indiana delegation had been won for Lincoln before the convention met.

163 (Ray): This letter is dated May 14, 1860, in Lincoln Papers.

163 (spirits): Tarbell, *op. cit.*, p. 347.

164 (recognized): *Ibid.*, p. 348.

165 (ship, Republicans): *Chicago Press and Tribune*, June 8, 1860; Tarbell, *op. cit.*, p. 349; Murat Halstead, *Caucuses of 1860*, p. 130; Carl Sandburg, *Abraham Lincoln: The Prairie Years*, II, 342.

165 (slavery): Thomas J. McCormack (ed.), *Memoirs of Gustave Koerner*, II, 86.

166 (it): J. G. Randall, *Lincoln: The President*, I, 156.

166 (win): Bromley, *op. cit.*, p. 654; Halstead, *op. cit.*, p. 142.

167 (noncommittal): McCormack, *op. cit.*, p. 81; Tarbell, *op. cit.*, pp. 350, 351; John M. Palmer, *Personal Recollections*, p. 81.

168 (it): Henry C. Whitney, *Life of Lincoln*, I, 289.

168 (made): Sandburg, *op. cit.*, p. 342.

169 (it): *Ibid.* The secret deals for Lincoln's nomination, unquestioned by historians, have been accepted in this text. However, it should be pointed out that, as in any conspiracy, the details are hard to pin down. Since the account of Ray's deal with the Cameron forces is based on Joseph Medill's recollections after he had severed his partnership with Ray, there may be grounds for discounting Ray's part in the negotiation. On the other hand, the records show that Ray did ask Lincoln for permission to make deals. That Ray was party to an agreement which he later hoped to nullify seems to be confirmed by his letter to Washburne dated "Thursday P.M." in the Washburne Papers. In this Ray suggests a way to prevent the appointment of Cameron but adds, "Don't show this letter to anyone." These citations, however, are obviously inconclusive.

The facts are further obscured by statements of Thomas Dudley, a New Jersey delegate to the convention. In an article in *Century Magazine* on the Cameron deal, not published until July 1890, Dudley says that committees from the pivotal states met on the night before the nomination and agreed to do all they could to have their state delegations vote for Lincoln on the second ballot, not as a part of a political deal, but because Lincoln was more likely to carry the border states than Seward. The voting next day, however, didn't go that way. Pennsylvania did swing to Lincoln on the second ballot, but New Jersey switched four votes to Seward and none to Lincoln. Thus, New Jersey did not conform to the agreement which Dudley alleged had been made. It is possible, of course, that Ray may have influenced some of the Pennsylvania delegates by the offer of a cabinet post to Cameron. Other delegates may have been influenced by the Dudley agreement. It should be noted, too, that H. C. Whitney, in *Life on the Circuit with Lincoln*, p. 101, says that the deal with the Pennsylvania delegates was made by Davis, Swett, Logan, Judd and Dole. He does not mention Ray.

169 (House): Halstead, *op. cit.*, p. 144.

170 (failed): Tarbell, *op. cit.*, p. 353.

170 (Illinois): O. H. Oldroyd, *Lincoln's Campaign*, p. 43.

170 (ballot): *Ibid.*, p. 72.

171 (Lincoln): *Proceedings of the First Three Republican National Conventions*, p. 129.

171 (wants, promises, replied): H. I. Cleveland, "Booming the First Republican President," p. 85. Medill states that nineteen votes were switched. Contemporary records admit only four. However, these four gave Lincoln the nomination. It would be a mistake to believe that Lincoln would not have been nominated without them. Several other delegations were eager for the honor of clinching the nomination. Without doubt, unauthorized promises were made, but it is possible that the details of these deals may have grown in the minds of the makers after Lincoln appointed men to his cabinet whom he considered important in the party organization.

172 (Lincoln): Halstead, *op. cit.*, p. 149.

172 (child): Leonard Swett, *David Davis*, p. 18.

173 (Scripps): Wire dated May 18, 1860, in Lincoln Papers.

173 (importance): Gideon Welles, "Nomination and Election of Abraham Lincoln," p. 302.

174 (reverse): Tebbel, *op. cit.*, p. 21; Letter, Lincoln to C. M. Allen, May 1, 1860, in Roy P. Basler (ed.), *Collected Works of Abraham Lincoln*, IV, 46-47; William E. Baringer, *Lincoln's Rise to Power*, p. 335; Letter, Swett to Josiah Drummond, May 27, 1860, in Oldroyd, *op. cit.*, p. 73; Leonard Swett, *Remembrance of T. Lyle Dickey*, p. 9.

175 (deliverer, work, LINCOLN, government): *Chicago Press and Tribune*, May 19, 1860. The editorial has been paragraphed.

CHAPTER XIV (pages 176-193)

178 (Heaven): *Chicago Press and Tribune*, May 29, 1860.
178 (aristocracy): *Ibid.*, May 22, 1860.
179 (pledges): *Ibid.*, May 28-30, June 8, 1860.
179 (recounted): Tracy E. Strevey, "Joseph Medill and the Chicago Tribune," p. 62, lists *Tribune* publications.
181 (county): *Chicago Press and Tribune*, May 11, 1860.
181 (gray): *Ibid.*, June 8, 1860.
181 (Lincoln): Ida M. Tarbell, *Life of Abraham Lincoln*, I, 371.
182 (debt): *Chicago Press and Tribune*, June 5, 1860.
182 (feathers): Arthur C. Cole, *Era of the Civil War*, p. 201.
183 (Scripps): June 18, 1860, in Lincoln Papers.
184 (Chin-Chopper): June 27, 1860, in Lincoln Papers.
185 (Congress): *Chicago Press and Tribune*, Aug. 8, 1860.
185 (world): *Ibid.*, Sept. 6, 1860.
186 (assurances): *Ibid.*, Aug. 10, 1860.
187 (office): Culp MS, p. 113; *Chicago Press and Tribune*, Oct. 29, 1858.
187 (stocked): *Chicago Press and Tribune*, Mar. 28, 1860.
188 (economy): Culp MS, p. 117.
189 (plane): Dwight F. Clark, "Wreck of the Lady Elgin," p. 417.
190 (scoffed): *Chicago Press and Tribune*, May 2, 1860.
190 ('em): *Ibid.*, May 12, 1860; Culp MS, p. 120.
191 (question): *Chicago Tribune*, Nov. 5, 1860.
192 (Lincoln): Tarbell, *op. cit.*, p. 385.

193 (Hail): *Chicago Tribune*, Nov. 7, 1860.

CHAPTER XV (pages 194-206)

195 (could): Philip Kinsley, *Chicago Tribune*, p. 134.
195 (place): The exact wording of the Lincoln & Herndon sign is open to question.
196 (told): Robert J. Rombauer, *Union Cause in St. Louis*, p. 130.
197 (population): Thomas L. Snead, *Fight for Missouri*, p. 100; letter, Horace Greeley to Ray, Nov. 1 [?], 1860.
197 (suggestions): Letters, Andrew to Ray. This correspondence lasted until after Lincoln was inaugurated. See also letter, Kreismann to Ray, Nov. 25, 1860.
198 (friends): Letter dated Dec. 7, 1860.
198 (desired): Jay Monaghan, *Diplomat in Carpet Slippers*, p. 15.
199 (program): Letter, Ray to Washburne, Jan. 7, [1861], Washburne Papers.
200 *(States):* Dec. 12, 13, 1860.
200 (negligence): Payment receipts for new ones in Ray Papers.
201 (No): Roy P. Basler (ed.), *Collected Works of Abraham Lincoln*, IV, 149-150.
201 *(maintained): Chicago Tribune*, Jan. 3, 1861.
202 (bay): Letters, Medill to Ray, Jan. 4, 18, 1861.
203 (Springfield): Undated item in Ray Papers; Culp MS, p. 125.
203 *(Tribune):* Don E. Fehrenbacher, "Judd-Wentworth Feud," p. 197; Leonard Swett, *Remembrance of T. Lyle Dickey*, p. 9.
204 (throne): Letter, Medill to Horace White, Jan. 8, 1861, in Ray Papers.
204 (Abe): Letter, Medill to Ray, Jan. 6, 1861.
205 (came): Letter, Ray to Washburne, Jan. 7, 1861, Washburne Papers.
205 (letter): *New York Herald*, Jan. 17, 1861, and in *Weekly Herald*, Jan. 19, 1861. The unsigned dispatch gives no indication that Villard sent it. See fourth footnote on this in next chapter.
206 (Ray): Letter in Washburne Papers.

CHAPTER XVI (pages 207-221)

208 (spirit): Philip Kinsley, *Chicago Tribune*, p. 157.
208 (election): *Switzler's Illustrated History*, p. 303; James Peckham, *Gen. Nathaniel Lyon*, p. 22.
209 (concluded): Letter, Andrew to Ray, Jan. 8, 1861.
209 (cheeks): If the entry day of Jan. 16 in Villard's diary is correct, it is difficult to see much humor in his dispatch printed "last Saturday" [Jan. 12]. The quotation in the text is from his later dispatch of Sunday, Jan. 13, printed in the daily *Herald* on the seventeenth and in the weekly on Saturday, the nineteenth. Henry Villard, *Lincoln on the Eve of '61*, p. 48.
210 (office): Both dated Jan. 13, 1861.
210 (warned): Letter, Washburne to Ray, Jan. 13, 1861.
211 (leader): Letter, Ray to Washburne, n.d., Washburne Papers.
211 (never): *Ibid.*, "Thursday P.M.," n.d., Washburne Papers.
212 (yourselves): Letter, Jan. 16, 1861.
214 (believed): Bessie L. Pierce, *History of Chicago*, II, 253.
215 (order): Letter, Medill to Ray, Jan. 13, 1861.
216 (day): *Chicago Tribune*, Jan. 19, 1861.
216 (for): Letter dated Jan. 23, 1861.
217 (disloyalty): *Chicago Tribune*, Jan. 21, 1861.
217 (contempt): *Ibid.*, Dec. 21, 1860.
219 (constituents): John Tebbel, *American Dynasty*, p. 22; *Chicago Tribune*, Feb. 20, 1861.
219 (itself): *Chicago Tribune*, Feb. 9 to 21, 1861.
219 (discount): Kinsley, *op. cit.*, p. 174.
219 (regeneration): *Chicago Tribune*, Feb. 27, 1861.
220 (quarters): "Our Correspondent" to *Sydney* [Australia] *Morning Herald*, June 14, 1861.
220 (authority): *Chicago Tribune*, Feb. 8, 1861.
220 (guards): *Sydney* [Australia] *Morning Herald*, June 14, 1861.
221 (destruction): Kinsley, *op. cit.*, p. 177.

CHAPTER XVII (pages 222-232)

222 (one): Paid bills in Ray Papers.
224 (announced): Henry Villard, *Memoirs*, p. 153.

227 (fire): Letter, Ray to Minnie, Frank and Paul, July 10, 1861.
227 (down): *Chicago Tribune*, Apr. 23, 1861.
228 (Illinois): Trumbull note dated Apr. 19, 1861.
229 (states): Villard, *op. cit.*, p. 169.
229 (morning): Letter, Villard to Medill and Ray, Apr. 27, 1861.
230 (slavery): Jay Monaghan, *Civil War on the Western Border*, p. 134.
230 (sea): Dated May 8, 1861.
231 (Richmond): Lyon occupied Boonville, June 17, 1861.

CHAPTER XVIII (pages 233-250)

233 (simplicity): Margaret Leech, *Reveille in Washington*, p. 64.
234 (all): Letter dated July 10, 1861.
235 (invention): Letter dated July 6, 1861.
236 (four-wheeler): Letter dated July 19, 1861; *Chicago Tribune*, July 24, 1861.
237 (Ray): *Chicago Tribune*, Aug. 5, 1861.
238 (telegrapher): *Ibid.*, July 25, 1861.
239 (Centreville): *Ibid.*
239 (Washington): *Ibid.*, July 24, 1861.
239 (stated): *Ibid.*, July 23, 1861.
246 (CHR): Ray's report of Bull Run Battle, *Ibid.*, July 26, 1861.
247 (said): Jay Monaghan, *Diplomat in Carpet Slippers*, p. 95.
247 (halt): *Ibid.*, pp. 130-131.
249 (it): *Chicago Tribune*, Aug. 23, 1861.
249 *(Tribune):* Dated Sept. 14, 1861.
250 (England): Fragment of undated letter in Yates Correspondence owned by Mrs. J. L. Pickering; also letter, Russell to Raymond, Sept. 14, 1861.
250 (ahead): Monaghan, *op. cit.*, p. 131.

CHAPTER XIX (pages 251-269)

251 (wrote): *War of the Rebellion . . . Official Records*, Ser. I, Vol. III, 390.
251 (communication): Letter, Bross to Ray, Aug. 19, 1861.
252 (department): *Chicago Tribune*, Aug. 1, 1861.

254 (neglected): Jay Monaghan, *Civil War on the Western Border*, p. 193.
255 (file): *Chicago Tribune*, Nov. 6, 1861; William Bross, *History of Chicago*, p. 86.
256 (good): Note telegram from Ray to Lincoln, Sept. 6, 1861, in Lincoln Papers; Also Monaghan, *op. cit.*, p. 194.
257 (apology): Letter, Colfax to Ray, Sept. 19, 1861.
258 (faction): Philip Kinsley, *Chicago Tribune*, p. 217.
259 (Frémont): Letter, Montgomery Blair to Ray, Nov. 17, 1861.
259 (organization): White's letter is dated Oct. 10, 1861.
260 (through): *Chicago Tribune*, Oct. 29, 1861.
261 (slave): *Ibid.*, Nov. 15, 1861.
261 (gossip): Letter, Smith to "Bro. G." Oct. [?], 1861; Letter, Smith to "Editors of Tribune," Nov. 4 ? 1861; Henry Villard, *Memoirs*, p. 157.
262 (yourself): Letter, Smith to "Bro. G.," *op. cit.*
262 (planned): *Ibid.*
264 (slave): *Chicago Tribune*, Dec. 4, 1861.
267 (government): *Ibid.*, June 11, 1922.
268 (Ages): *Ibid.*, Mar. 1, 1862.
269 (prejudiced): Letter, Washburne to Ray, Apr. 25, 1862; Ray to Washburne, "H of R Tuesday" [1864], Washburne Papers.
269 (made): *Chicago Tribune*, Mar. 20, 1862.

CHAPTER XX (pages 270-279)

270 (living): Paid bills in Ray Papers.
271 (front): Philip Kinsley, *Chicago Tribune*, p. 234.
273 (wrote): The White House meeting is reported in the *Chicago Tribune*, July 22, 1862.
273 (digging): *Chicago Tribune*, July 19, 1862.
273 (1862): Letters, Turchin to Ray, Aug. 21, Sept. 8, Nov. 8, 1861.
274 (court-martial): Jay Monaghan, *Civil War on the Western Border*, pp. 182, 254; *Chicago Tribune*, Nov. 2, 1861.
274 (death): *Chicago Tribune*, Aug. 28, 1862.
275 (blood): *New York World*, June 9, 1863.
275 (Generals): Letter, Turchin to Ray, Dec. 21, 1861.

SOURCES

BOOKS AND ARTICLES

AMBLER, CHARLES HENRY (ed.). *Correspondence of Robert M. T. Hunter, 1826-1876. (Annual Report of the American Historical Association for the Year 1916*, II.) Washington, 1918.

ANDREAS, ALFRED THEODORE. *History of Cook County, Illinois*. Chicago: A. T. Andreas, 1884.

ANGLE, PAUL MCCLELLAND. *"Here I Have Lived"; A History of Lincoln's Springfield, 1821-1865*. New Brunswick, N.J.: Rutgers University Press, 1950.

——— (ed.). *Herndon's Life of Lincoln*. New York: A. & C. Boni, 1930.

———. *Lincoln, 1854-1861; Being the Day-By-Day Activities of Abraham Lincoln*. Springfield, Ill.: Abraham Lincoln Assn., c. 1933.

BANCROFT, FREDERIC. *Slave-trading in the Old South*. Baltimore: J. H. Furst Co., 1931.

BARINGER, WILLIAM E. *Lincoln's Rise to Power*. Boston: Little, Brown, 1937.

BASLER, ROY PRENTICE (ed.). *The Collected Works of Abraham Lincoln*. New Brunswick, N.J.: Rutgers University Press, 1953.

BEVERIDGE, ALBERT JEREMIAH. *Abraham Lincoln, 1809-1858*. Boston: Houghton, Mifflin, 1928.

BRIGGS, HAROLD E. "Lawlessness in Cairo, Illinois, 1848-1858," *Mid-America, An Historical Review*, XXXIII, No. 2 (April 1951), 67-88.

BROMLEY, ISAAC HILL. "Historic Moments: The Nomination of Lincoln," *Scribner's Magazine*, XIV, No. 5 (November 1893), 645-656.

BROSS, WILLIAM. *History of Chicago*. Chicago: Jansen, McClurg, 1876.

BROWN, ERNEST FRANCIS. *Raymond of the Times*. New York: Norton, c. 1951.

275 (Mississippi): Culp MS, p. 167; the account in *C*
une, Aug. 20, 1862, quotes Turchin as stating that
sion was in possession of his wife; *Chicago Tribu*
1862.

277 (energies): *Chicago Tribune*, Sept. 3, 1862.

279 (must): Sept. 19, 1862.

CHAPTER XXI (pages 280-288)

280 (achieved): *Chicago Tribune*, Sept. 26, 27, 1862.

281 (situation): *Ibid.*, Oct. 1, 1862; Philip Kinsley, *Ch*
une, p. 254.

281 (opportunity): Letter, Oct. 14, 1862.

282 (bloodshed): Letter, Hatch to Medill, Oct. 14, 18

283 (bless): Roy P. Basler (ed.), *Collected Works o*
Lincoln, V, 537.

283 (scene): *Chicago Tribune*, Dec. 13, 1861.

287 (stock): The contract for the house purchase is da
1863, in Ray Papers.

288 (friend): Letter, Feb. 11, 1866, in Weik Papers.

288 (immense): Obituary by George P. Upton in *Ch*
une, Sept. 25, 1870. Upton was the *Tribune* co
who reported the battle at Island No. 10.

BROWN, GEORGE WASHINGTON. *The Truth at Last. History Corrected. Reminiscences of Old John Brown.* Rockford, Ill.: Privately printed, 1880.

BUSBEY, L. WHITE. *Uncle Joe Cannon.* New York: Holt, c. 1927.

CHURCH, CHARLES A. *History of the Republican Party in Illinois 1854-1912.* Rockford, Ill.: Press of Wilson Brothers Co., c. 1912.

CLARK, DWIGHT F. "The Wreck of the *Lady Elgin*," *Journal of the Illinois State Historical Society*, XXXIX, No. 4 (December 1946), 407-418.

CLEVELAND, H. I. "Booming the First Republican President, A Talk with Abraham Lincoln's Friend . . . the Late Joseph Medill," *Saturday Evening Post*, CLXXII, No. 6 (August 5, 1899), 84-85.

COLE, ARTHUR CHARLES. *The Era of the Civil War, 1848-1870. (Centennial History of Illinois*, Vol. III.) Chicago: McClurg, 1922.

———. "President Lincoln and the Illinois Radical Republicans," *Mississippi Valley Historical Review*, IV, No. 4 (March 1918), 417-436.

Congressional Globe . . . Thirty-third Congress. Washington: 1854.

CRAWFORD, SAMUEL J. *Kansas in the Sixties.* Chicago: McClurg, 1911.

DEDMON, EMMETT. *Fabulous Chicago.* New York: Random House, 1953.

DIXON, SUSAN (MRS. ARCHIBALD). *History of Missouri Compromise and Slavery in American Politics*, 2 ed. Cincinnati: Robert Clarke Co., 1903 [c. 1898].

DODD, WILLIAM EDWARD. "The Rise of Abraham Lincoln," *Century Magazine*, CXIII (March 1927), 569-584.

DOUGLAS, STEPHEN ARNOLD. ". . . Popular Sovereignty in the Territories," *Harper's New Monthly Magazine*, XIX, No. 112 (September 1859), 519-537.

———. *Report of Senator Douglas, of Illinois, on the Kansas-Lecompton Constitution.* Washington, 1858.

DUDLEY, THOMAS H. "The Inside Facts of Lincoln's Nomination," *Century Magazine*, XL, No. 3 (July 1890), 477-479.

ELLIOTT, FRANK M. "Gov. William H. Bissell," *Transactions of the McLean County Historical Society*, III. Bloomington, Ill.: Pantagraph Printing and Stationery Co., 1900, 124-148.

FEHRENBACHER, DON E. "The Judd-Wentworth Feud," *Journal of the Illinois State Historical Society*, XLV, No. 3 (Autumn 1952), 197-211.

FITE, EMERSON DAVID. *The Presidential Campaign of 1860*. New York: Macmillan, 1911.

HALSTEAD, MURAT. *Caucuses of 1860: A History of the National Political Conventions of the Current Presidential Campaign*. Columbus: Follett, Foster and Co., 1860.

HENDERSON, THOMAS J. "Remarks," *Transactions of the McLean County Historical Society*, III. Bloomington, Ill.: Pantagraph Printing and Stationery Co., 1900, 78-86.

HERRIOTT, FRANK IRVING. "The Conference of German-Republicans in the Deutsches Haus, Chicago, May 14-15, 1860," *Transactions of the Illinois State Historical Society for the Year 1928*, Pub. No. 35, 101-191.

———. *The Germans of Davenport and the Chicago Convention of 1860*, reprinted from H. E. Downer's history of Davenport and Scott County, Iowa, pp. 3-10. Chicago: S. J. Clarke Pub. Co., n.d.

———. "James W. Grimes Versus the Southrons," *Annals of Iowa*, XV, No. 6, 3rd ser. (July and October 1926), 323-357, 403-432.

HITT, R. R. *Report on the Trial of John Hossack, Indicted for Rescuing a Fugitive Slave from the U.S. Deputy Marshal, at Ottawa, October 20th, 1859*. Chicago, 1860.

HORNER, CHARLES FRANCIS. *The Life of James Redpath and the Development of the Modern Lyceum*. New York: Barse & Hopkins, 1926.

Illinois Senate Journal, 1855. Springfield, Ill.

JORDAN, H. DONALDSON. "A Politician of Expansion: Robert J. Walker," *Mississippi Valley Historical Review*, XIX, No. 3 (December 1932), 362-381.

KINSLEY, PHILIP. *The Chicago Tribune: Its First Hundred Years, Volume I, 1847-1865*. New York: Knopf, 1943.

KIRKLAND, CAROLINE (ed.). *Chicago Yesterdays; A Sheaf of Reminiscences*. Chicago: Daughaday and Co., 1919.

KLETT, ADA M. "Belleville Germans Look at America (1833-1845)," *Journal of the Illinois State Historical Society*, XL, No. 1 (March 1947), 23-37.

KYLE, OTTO R. "Mr. Lincoln Steps Out: The Anti-Nebraska Editors' Convention," *Abraham Lincoln Quarterly*, V, No. 1 (March 1948), 25-37.

LEECH, MARGARET. *Reveille in Washington, 1860-1865*. New York: Harper, 1941.

LEWIS, LLOYD. "He Hated Southern Gentlemen," *American Mercury*, XVIII (December 1929), 474-481.

LEWIS, LLOYD, and SMITH, HENRY JUSTIN. *Chicago, the History of its Reputation*. New York: Harcourt, Brace, 1929.

LUTHIN, REINHARD HENRY. *The First Lincoln Campaign*. Cambridge: Harvard University Press, 1944.

MCCORMACK, THOMAS J. (ed.). *Memoirs of Gustave Koerner, 1809-1896*. Cedar Rapids: Torch Press, 1909.

MCMASTER, JOHN BACH. *A History of the People of the United States, from the Revolution to the Civil War*, Vol. VIII. New York: Appleton, 1926.

MAGIE, JAMES K. *Lecture on Lincoln before He Was President* (n.p., 1891).

MALIN, JAMES CLAUDE. "Colonel Harvey and His Forty Thieves," *Mississippi Valley Historical Review*, XIX, No. 1 (June 1932), 57-76.

MILTON, GEORGE FORT. *The Eve of Conflict: Stephen A. Douglas and the Needless War*. Boston: Houghton, Mifflin, 1934.

MONAGHAN, JAY. *Civil War on the Western Border, 1854-1865*. Boston: Little, Brown, c. 1955.

———. *Diplomat in Carpet Slippers: Abraham Lincoln Deals with Foreign Affairs*. Indianapolis: Bobbs-Merrill, c. 1945.

———. "North Carolinians in Illinois History," *North Carolina Historical Review*, XXII, No. 4 (October 1945), 418-459.

"Monthly Record of Current Events: United States," *Harper's New Monthly Magazine*, XXI, No. 122 (July 1860), 258-259.

NEVINS, ALLAN. *The Emergence of Lincoln*. New York: Scribner, 1950.

———. *Ordeal of the Union: A House Dividing*. New York: Scribner, 1947.

NICOLAY, JOHN G. "Abraham Lincoln," *Transactions of the McLean County Historical Society*, III. Bloomington, Ill.: Pantagraph Printing and Stationery Co., 1900, 95-101.

NICOLAY, JOHN G., and HAY, JOHN. *Abraham Lincoln; A History*. New York: Century Co., 1890.

"The Nomination of Lincoln," *Harper's Weekly*, IV (1860), 338.

"Official Record of Convention," *Transactions of the McLean County Historical Society*, III. Bloomington, Ill.: Pantagraph Printing and Stationery Co., 1900, 148-164.

OLDROYD, OSBORN HAMLINE. *Lincoln's Campaign; or, The Political Revolution of 1860*. Chicago: Laird & Lee, c. 1896.

PALMER, JOHN MCAULEY. "Address," *Transactions of the McLean County Historical Society*, III. Bloomington, Ill.: Pantagraph Printing and Stationery Co., 1900, 113-124.

———. *Personal Recollections; the Story of an Earnest Life*. Cincinnati: R. Clarke Co., 1901.

PEASE, THEODORE CALVIN, and RANDALL, JAMES G. (eds.). *The Diary of Orville Hickman Browning* ("Collections of the Illinois State Historical Library," Vol XX.) Springfield: Illinois State Historical Library, 1925.

PEASE, THEODORE C. *The Story of Illinois*. Chicago: McClurg, 1925.

PECKHAM, JAMES. *Gen. Nathaniel Lyon, and Missouri in 1861*. New York: American News Co., 1866.

PIERCE, BESSIE LOUISE. *A History of Chicago*, II. New York: Knopf, 1940.

PIERCE, EDWARD L. *Memoir and Letters of Charles Sumner*, III. Boston: Roberts Bros., 1893.

PIKE, JAMES SHEPHERD. *First Blows of the Civil War: The Ten Years of Preliminary Conflict in the United States. From 1850 to 1860*. New York: American News Co., c. 1879.

PRATT, HARRY EDWARD. "David Davis, 1815-1886," *Transactions of the Illinois State Historical Society for the Year 1930*, Pub. No. 37, 157-183.

———. "Simon Cameron's Fight for a Place in Lincoln's Cabinet," Abraham Lincoln Association *Bulletin*, No. 49 (September 1937), [3]-11.

PRINCE, EZRA M. (ed.). *Transactions of the McClean County Historical Society . . . Meeting of May 29, 1900 Commemorative of the Convention of May 29, 1856*, III. Bloomington, Ill.: Pantagraph Printing and Stationery Co., 1900.

Proceedings of the First Three Republican National Conventions of 1856, 1860 and 1864. Minneapolis: Charles W. Johnson, c. 1893.

PUTNAM, JAMES W. *The Illinois and Michigan Canal: A Study in Economic History* ("Chicago Historical Society's Collection," Vol. X), Chicago: University of Chicago Press, 1918.

RANDALL, JAMES GARFIELD. *Lincoln: The President. Springfield to Gettysburg*. New York: Dodd, Mead, 1945.

RAY, PERLEY ORMAN. *The Convention that Nominated Lincoln*. Chicago: University of Chicago Press, c. 1916.

———. *The Repeal of the Missouri Compromise: Its Origin and Authorship*. Cleveland: Arthur H. Clark Co., 1909.

REEDER, ANDREW H. "Governor Reeder's Escape from Kansas," *Transactions of the Kansas State Historical Society*, III, Pt. 2, 205-223.

Report of the Special Committee Appointed to Investigate the Troubles in Kansas. Washington: C. Wendell, printer, 1856.

RICHARDSON, ALBERT DEANE. *Beyond the Mississippi*. Hartford, Conn.: American Publishing Co., 1867.

———. *Garnered Sheaves from the Writings of Albert D. Richardson Collected and Arranged by his Wife*. Hartford, Conn.: Columbian Book Co., 1871.

ROMBAUER, ROBERT JULIUS. *The Union Cause in St. Louis in 1861*. St. Louis: Press of Nixon-Jones Printing Co., 1909.

SANDBURG, CARL. *Abraham Lincoln: The Prairie Years* and *The War Years*. New York: Harcourt, Brace, c. 1926, c. 1939.

SCHNEIDER, GEORGE. "Address," *Transactions of the McLean County Historical Society*, III. Bloomington, Ill.: Pantagraph Printing and Stationery Co., 1900, 87-94.

SELBY, PAUL. "The Editorial Convention, February 22, 1856," *Transactions of the McLean County Historical Society*, III. Bloomington, Ill.: Pantagraph Printing and Stationery Co., 1900, 30-43.

———. "Republican State Convention, Springfield, Ill., October 4-5, 1854," *Transactions of the McLean County Historical Society*, III. Bloomington, Ill.: Pantagraph Printing and Stationery Co., 1900, 43-47.

SHAW, BENJAMIN F. "Owen Lovejoy, Constitutional Abolitionists and the Republican Party," *Transactions of the McLean County Historical Society*, III. Bloomington, Ill.: Pantagraph Printing and Stationery Co., 1900, 59-73.

SHERMAN, JOHN. *John Sherman's Recollections of Forty Years in the House, Senate and Cabinet. An Autobiography*. Chicago: The Werner Co., 1895.

SMITH, WILLIAM HENRY. *A Political History of Slavery*. New York: Putnam, 1903.

SNEAD, THOMAS LOWNDES. *The Fight for Missouri, from the Election of Lincoln to the Death of Lyon.* New York: Scribner, 1886.

SPARKS, EDWIN ERLE (ed.). *The Lincoln-Douglas Debates of 1858*, ("Collections of the Illinois State Historical Library," Vol. III). Springfield: Illinois State Historical Library, 1908.

SPRING, LEVERETT WILSON. *Kansas; the Prelude to the War for the Union*, rev. ed. Boston: Houghton, Mifflin, c. 1907.

STREVEY, TRACY ELMER. "Joseph Medill and the Chicago Tribune in the Nomination and Election of Lincoln," *Papers in Illinois History for the Year 1938*. Springfield: Illinois State Historical Society, 1939, 39-63.

SWETT, LEONARD. *David Davis: Address before the Bar Association of the State of Illinois*. Chicago, n.d.

———. *Remembrance of T. Lyle Dickey*, n.p., n.d.

SWITZLER, WILLIAM F. *Switzler's Illustrated History of Missouri from 1541 to 1877*. St. Louis: C. R. Barns, 1879.

TARBELL, IDA MINERVA. *The Life of Abraham Lincoln*, new ed. 2 vols.; New York: Macmillan, 1917.

TEBBEL, JOHN WILLIAM. *... An American Dynasty*. Garden City, N.Y.: Doubleday, 1947.

VILLARD, HENRY. *Lincoln on the Eve of '61; a Journalist's Story*. Edited by Harold G. and Oswald Garrison Villard. New York: Knopf, 1941.

———. *Memoirs of Henry Villard, Journalist and Financier, 1835-1900*. Boston: Houghton, Mifflin, 1904.

VOLK, LEONARD W. "The Lincoln Life-Mask and How It Was Made," *Journal of the Illinois State Historical Society*, VIII, No. 1 (April 1915), 238-248.

War of the Rebellion: . . . Official Records of the Union and Confederate Armies. Washington: Government Printing Office, 1880-1901.

WELLES, GIDEON. "Nomination and Election of Abraham Lincoln," *Galaxy*, XXII (1876), 300-308, 437-446.

WHARTON, OLIVER P. "Lincoln and the Beginning of the Republican Party in Illinois," *Transactions of the Illinois State Historical Society for the Year 1911*, Pub. No. 16. Springfield, 1913, 62-64.

WHITE, HORACE. *The Lincoln and Douglas Debates.* Chicago: University of Chicago Press, c. 1914.

WHITNEY, HENRY C. *Lincoln the Citizen: Volume One of a Life of Lincoln.* New York: Baker & Taylor Co., 1908.

NEWSPAPERS

Chicago Daily Democratic Press
Chicago Daily Times
Chicago Tribune
Galena Daily Evening Jeffersonian
Lawrence, Kansas, *Herald of Freedom*
New York Herald
New York World
St. Joseph, Missouri, *Gazette*
St. Joseph, Missouri, *Weekly Cycle*
Springfield, Illinois, *Sangamo Journal*
Springfield, *Illinois State Journal*
Sydney [Australia] *Morning Herald*

MANUSCRIPTS

Culp, Dorothy, manuscript biography of Charles Ray. Huntington Library.

French, Augustus C., Papers. Illinois State Historical Library.

Illinois and Michigan Canal Papers. Archives Section, Illinois State Library.

Lincoln, Abraham, Papers. Library of Congress.

Ray, Dr. Charles H., Papers. Huntington Library.

Trumbull, Lyman, Papers. Huntington Library and Library of Congress.

Washburne, Elihu, Papers. Library of Congress.

Weik, Jesse, Papers. Illinois State Historical Library.

Yates, Richard, Papers. Illinois State Historical Library and also in possession of Mrs. J. L. Pickering, Springfield, Ill.

ACKNOWLEDGMENTS

For suggesting the writing of this book, I am indebted to Miss Norma Cuthbert, Head Cataloger at the Huntington Library. She was the first to see the importance of the Ray Papers and graciously called them to my attention. Mrs. James P. Andrews, donor of the Papers and a discerning critic, pointed out to me the errors of some historians who have attributed many of Charles Ray's articles in the *Chicago Tribune* to Joseph Medill. "I am sure," she told me, "that I know my own father's writing." Dr. Ray's grandson, Paul Ray, of Evanston, Illinois, kindly sent me revealing letters from his family collection.

Practically all of the printed material used collaterally in this book may be found in the Wyles Collection of Lincolniana at the University of California, Santa Barbara College, which, under the directorship of Dr. Donald C. Davidson, Librarian, has become one of the best Civil War libraries on the Pacific Coast. I am grateful to Dr. Davidson and members of his staff for their constant courtesy in assisting me with the Library's facilities. During the recent moving of the books to the new campus, Frazer G. Poole, Assistant Librarian, showed great skill in finding on the fast-moving assembly line any volume I needed and thus prevented an interruption of my labors on this work. Mrs. Violet Shue, Reference Librarian, has always been resourceful and untiring in her efforts to find the answers to perplexing questions. Mrs. Martha Peterson, Acquisitions Librarian, located the master film of the *Chicago Tribune* and arranged for purchase of a copy of it—an indispensable source for this study. Wendell Simons, in charge of the Library's audio-visual service center, generously provided me with photostats.

In the Library of Congress, David C. Mearns, Chief of the Manuscripts Division, and Roy Basler, Associate Director of Reference, have been indefatigable in answering questions and checking manuscripts. Dr. Harry E. Pratt, State Historian of Illinois, has skillfully unearthed rare Ray material in the Illinois State Historical Library. Miss Margaret A. Flint, Reference Librarian in the same institution, has always demonstrated the constructive imagination which must delight any researcher who consults her. Miss Margaret C. Norton, Head of the Archives Section of the Illinois State Library, generously sent me a photostat of a Ray letter. Mrs. Theodore C. Pease was good enough to peruse the Illinois Historical Survey's collection at the University of Illinois for pertinent data. Paul M. Angle sent me copies of Ray material in the library of the Chicago Historical Society. Herbert H. Hewitt, Chief of Reference at the Chicago Public Library, furnished me with microfilm unavailable elsewhere.

Philip Kinsley, author of *The Chicago Tribune*, helped me in my search for a file of the Galena *Jeffersonian*. Elmer E. Gertz has been generous in sharing information acquired in his own exhaustive study of the history of the *Chicago Tribune*. Justin G. Turner, collector of holographs extraordinary, called attention to Ray letters he found in his constant search for rare documents. King V. Hostick also supplied me with information concerning his discoveries in the field. Edouard Stackpole, Curator of Mystic Seaport in Connecticut, helped me to develop material on Ray's brief whaling career. Dr. Louis A. Warren generously sent me photostats of rare items in the library of the Lincoln National Life Foundation in Fort Wayne, Indiana. Miss Wilma Radford, Reference Librarian of the New South Wales State Library in Sydney, Australia, made available to me the files of Australian newspapers. Here, of all places, may be found an account of a foreign correspondent in Washington during Lincoln's administration—certainly a source heretofore unused by students of Lincolniana.

In this book, as in my earlier ones, my greatest debt is to Mildred, my wife, who has read the manuscript and proof with her usual judgment and care. She has converted the editorial drudgery necessary to any book into a happy game.

J. M.

INDEX